FRANCES BURNEY AND THE DOCTORS

Frances Burney is primarily known as a novelist and playwright, but in recent years there has been an increased interest in the medical writings found within her private letters and journals. John Wiltshire argues that Burney is the unconscious pioneer of the modern genre of pathography, or the illness narrative. Through her dramatic accounts of distinct medical events, such as her own infamous operation without anaesthetic, to those she witnessed, including the 'madness' of George III and the inoculation of her son against smallpox, Burney exposes the ethical issues and conflicts between patients and doctors. Her accounts are linked to a range of modern narratives in which similar events occur in the changed conditions of the public hospital. The genre that Burney initiated continues to make an important contribution to our understanding of medical practice in the modern world.

JOHN WILTSHIRE is an Emeritus Professor at La Trobe University, Melbourne. He specialises in later eighteenth-century literature and is the author of among other books *Samuel Johnson in the Medical World: The Doctor and the Patient* (Cambridge University Press, 1991), *Jane Austen and the Body: The Picture of Health* (Cambridge University Press, 1992) and *The Hidden Jane Austen* (Cambridge University Press, 2014).

FRANCES BURNEY AND THE DOCTORS

Patient Narratives Then and Now

JOHN WILTSHIRE

La Trobe University, Melbourne

CAMBRIDGE UNIVERSITY PRESS

CAMBRIDGE
UNIVERSITY PRESS

University Printing House, Cambridge CB2 8BS, United Kingdom

One Liberty Plaza, 20th Floor, New York, NY 10006, USA

477 Williamstown Road, Port Melbourne, VIC 3207, Australia

314–321, 3rd Floor, Plot 3, Splendor Forum, Jasola District Centre, New Delhi – 110025, India

79 Anson Road, #06–04/06, Singapore 079906

Cambridge University Press is part of the University of Cambridge.

It furthers the University's mission by disseminating knowledge in the pursuit of education, learning, and research at the highest international levels of excellence.

www.cambridge.org
Information on this title: www.cambridge.org/9781108476362
DOI: 10.1017/9781108629690

First published 2019

Printed and bound in Great Britain by Clays Ltd, Elcograf S.p.A.

A catalogue record for this publication is available from the British Library.

Library of Congress Cataloging-in-Publication Data
NAMES: Wiltshire, John, author.
TITLE: Frances Burney and the doctors : patient narratives then and now / John Wiltshire.
DESCRIPTION: Cambridge, United Kingdom ; New York, NY : Cambridge University Press, 2019. | Includes bibliographical references and index.
IDENTIFIERS: LCCN 2018060984 | ISBN 9781108476362 (hardback)
SUBJECTS: LCSH: Burney, Fanny, 1752–1840 – Health. | Physician and patient – Anecdotes.
CLASSIFICATION: LCC R727.3 .W554 2019 | DDC 610.69/6–dc23
LC record available at https://lccn.loc.gov/2018060984

ISBN 978-1-108-47636-2 Hardback

In memory of Denis Gibbs
and for
Paul Komesaroff

Contents

Acknowledgements

This book has been a long time in preparation. Three decades ago I worked for several years with a professor of nursing, Professor Judy Parker, then at La Trobe University, and with Dr Paul Komesaroff, at Monash University's Faculty of Medicine, Nursing and Health Sciences, on a range of research projects that concerned narrative aspects of medical and nursing practice. I am deeply grateful to both of them and to their colleagues for the re-education their professional wisdom and competence gave me. I also owe thanks to my colleague at La Trobe, Dr Kay Souter, with whom I taught a class on literature and 'the body' for many years. Dr Denis Gibbs, to whom this book is dedicated, and who was president of the Royal Society for the History of Medicine and later of the British Society for the History of Medicine, always gave my work the most generous encouragement.

The project of writing a book about Frances Burney and medical experience had to await the publication of her court journals, which commenced with Volume I of the *Court Journals and Letters* edited by the general editor of the series, Professor Peter Sabor, in 2011. It goes without saying that my book could not have been conceived, let alone written, without the previous labours of the team of Burney scholars in Montreal who have provided critics like me with a rich and fertile, not to mention voluminous, source through their extraordinarily thorough and meticulous work. Just how dependent on their editorial skills and scholarship this book is, will be obvious to its readers. Professor Sabor has been generous in allowing me access to two of the volumes before publication, which access has been vital to me in the writing of the first chapters of this book. Lorna J. Clark, editor of Volumes III and IV in the series, has always encouraged me to have confidence in my project.

Actual writing began as a joint undertaking with my friend and colleague Daniel Vuillermin, now a lecturer in the Institute for Medical Humanities at Peking University Health Science Centre. I'm very grateful for Daniel's support, encouragement and suggestions during its writing, and for his instant responses to questions sent to Beijing. Latterly, chapters of the book have benefitted from the attentions of my friends Hermi Burns, Robert Cole and Sue Le Rou, Bill Spence and David Mushin. I'm especially grateful to Dr Mushin for the suggestions he made to improve the book's last chapter and to Bill for conversations that cleared my mind and stimulated my thoughts. I also want to thank Dr Jocelyn Dunphy-Blomfield and Professor Richard Freadman, who both took trouble to answer specific queries arising from this project. I'm grateful too to Dr Ira Raja for a conversation on our journey from Udaipur to Chittorgarh which helped me to think anew about Simone de Beauvoir. The two anonymous readers for Cambridge University Press also deserve thanks for their heartening responses and stimulating suggestions.

I thank the staff of La Trobe University Library who assisted me during a period when normal services were disrupted: Karen Norden and her team at Document Delivery, Gillian Stacey and especially Sammy Bagdas, who so kindly kept the many volumes of Burney's *Journals and Letters* on his desk should I suddenly need to consult one of them. I'm also grateful to Louise Spence for her meticulous help with copy-editing. Dr Linda Bree, who has been my editor at Cambridge University Press for many years, commissioned this book. I take this opportunity to thank her for the generous support she has always given me. Her role has been taken by Bethany Thomas and Carrie Parkinson, and I thank them as well as Victoria Parrin for their help too.

Short Titles

The volumes of *The Journals and Letters of Fanny Burney* are cited in the form (JL VI, 610).

The volumes of *The Court Journals and Letters of Frances Burney* are cited in the form (CJL III, 61).

Austin Dobson, *Diary and Letters of Madame d'Arblay* (6 volumes) is cited in the form (D III, 61).

F. McKno Bladon, ed., *The Diaries of Robert Fulke Greville* is cited in the form (G 107).

B. R. Ward, ed., *A Week at Waterloo, Lady De Lancey's Narrative* is cited in the form (W 63).

Introduction

'Men have had every advantage of us in telling their own story . . . the pen has been in their hands.' In no field have Anne Elliot's famous words from *Persuasion* been more true than in medicine. Physicians and surgeons have for centuries been men, and the narratives of medicine and of medical history have been in their hands. Patients, male as well as female, have been feminised, in the possibly tendentious sense of subordinated, voiceless. In effect patients were for long the passive and unspeaking subjects on which medicine was practised and through whom discoveries and progress were made. After the introduction of teaching hospitals in the nineteenth century, attending to the patient's voice by consultants around the bed became more usual and often provided important and fruitful information, but this was the literal speaking voice, responding to questioning, not an independent testimony. Patients may have written accounts of their experiences of illness and their medical treatment, but these were fragmentary, informal or, at best, parts of works devoted to quite different ends. In the past half-century this has changed dramatically, and now patient narratives, and narratives by those who have cared for them, have been published in such great numbers so as to constitute more than a supplement to medical history, but indeed to form a new literary genre, sometimes called the 'pathography'.

This development might be compared to the direct revelation of the inner workings of the human body that Vesalius inaugurated with the first dissection of a human corpse in public in 1543. The publication of Vesalius's *De humani corporis fabrica*, with its many illustrations, brought about a break with more than 1,500 years of Galenic medical theory, education and practice.[1] Like Vesalius's opening of the previously sacrosanct space, the pathography, or patient narrative, discloses the formerly unknown, ignored or perhaps misunderstood: the inner and personal experience of patienthood. Paradoxically, though, it was Vesalius's procedure that inaugurated the view of the body as 'a carnal machine', the

I

scientific, 'objective' medicine which for the next centuries can be said to have depersonalised illness.[2] It is this very depersonalisation that the project of the patient narrative seeks now to remedy and to restore. Or, to put it another way, it again marshals the authority of experience against the authority of medical tradition. This has taken a gradual evolution over the past century and a half, but as Thomas Laqueur has put it, the present time is probably 'the golden age of pathography'.[3]

This book enlists Frances Burney's records of illness into this genre and argues that her letters and journals, which describe in detail and with a skilled novelist's intense focus several distinct medical crises, are not only substantive contributions to this history but also anticipate many of the features – and especially the powerful ethical and emotional issues – that circulate within modern illness narratives. She was a pioneer recorder of medical dramas from the patient's point of view. She was resident at the royal court in 1788–1789 when the most eminent doctors of the age struggled to understand and to treat those disturbing symptoms of King George III that were eventually called madness. Burney observed his behaviour and recorded his speeches with extraordinarily persuasive detail. The king's illness precipitated events within the court that led to the onset of Burney's own illness not long after. Seven years later she held her small son in her arms when an apothecary performed the risky procedure of inoculation against smallpox, and left the only detailed account of an operation which must have been performed thousands of times. Trapped in France during the Napoleonic wars, she wrote with similar attentiveness in 1811 a now famous account of her own mastectomy before anaesthesia, at a critical moment in the history of medicine, and in which conflicts with her doctors (as well as conflicts between her doctors) are recorded and her own physical sufferings are written up in almost unbearable detail. The tensions between patient and physicians that play such a significant role in these earlier accounts are present in heightened form in her self-titled 'Narrative of the Last Illness and Death of General d'Arblay' written in 1819, an extended account of her husband's last months, which presages many of the issues now current in contemporary carers' accounts of fatal illness.

Some outstanding modern books about illness experience are discussed in the book's final two chapters. They belong, however, to a very different medical world from the one in which Burney wrote her narratives. Though she lived at a time when public hospitals had already been instituted in London, these were charitable endeavours established to provide medical care for those who could not afford doctors' fees. If you could pay for it, your doctor or apothecary attended you in your home. The medical occasions that Burney describes all took place in private rooms, with doctors who were often known to the patient. These circumstances are very important because they fostered a key aspect of her accounts – that they describe not just a single patient's own experience, but that experience in and played out within a group. The home, family, intimacy, interplay between doctors and the patient, often with a third person or persons present, the medical occasion as an ensemble: these are the given, the natural circumstances of the occasions she wrote about.

This feature – broadly speaking, interplay between patient and doctor within a closed and private setting – carries over into the modern pathography, even though so much of contemporary medical and surgical experience takes place within the large public domain of the hospital. The familial setting, and Burney's practice as a novelist, led Burney to report her experience in detail and to evoke as part of that experience its accompanying psychological and emotional effects. Nervous tensions, fear, anger and hostility then came into play as frequent aspects of patienthood, as well as gratitude and respect. Thus the modern genre, which almost always presents the patient as a person within a family, has crucial affinities with Burney's. This is the case even though the representation of patienthood often carries an undercurrent of protest against the very circumstances (such as hospital bureaucracy) that divide the modern scene from hers. In this book I have extended the term 'patienthood' to encompass the carers of the nominated patient.

'Pathography', however, is a contested term, since its analogy with 'pathology' seems to suggest that the patient's narrative may be a record merely of disease and its treatment. Disease, as understood from the medical viewpoint, it is argued, is quite other than 'illness', the condition experienced by the sufferer or patient. This distinction was established by Arthur Kleinman MD in his book *The Illness Narratives* (1988), which opens with the declaration that illness is 'something fundamentally different from disease'. 'By invoking the term illness', he writes, 'I mean to conjure up the innately human experience of symptoms and suffering. Illness refers to how the sick person and the members of the family or wider social network perceive, live with, and respond to symptoms and disability.'[4] The distinction was maintained by Arthur W. Frank, himself the author of an important pathography, *At the Will of the Body: Reflections on Illness* (1991) in *The Wounded Storyteller* (1995), and has been developed and amplified more recently by the phenomenologist Havi Carel in her *Illness: The Cry of the Flesh* (2008): she too writes as a patient. Both 'pathography' and sometimes 'autopathography' are used, along with 'illness narrative' to distinguish these books from more mainstream memoirs and biographies.[5]

Disease is identifiable, a containable concept: illness is diffuse and pervasive and may seep into every aspect of the life of the sick person and their family or partners as well. Disease is usually thought of as transcultural. Illness is embedded within a particular culture and social world. The illness narrative, then, broadly speaking, as Carel shows, explores the phenomenon of illness as it is lived within that particular and distinctive setting. It must therefore dovetail with, and to a lesser or greater extent contest, the medical culture that is a crucial part of that setting. In fact some illness narratives have an adversarial relationship to medicine – medical practice, institutions, and medical discourse.

In this book the term 'pathography' is reserved for works that are wholly devoted to the course of a medical experience, such as Frances Burney's self-contained journal records of her mastectomy and of the months of her husband's final illness. The pathography, in this usage, is a genre of writing in which an illness (or sometimes an accident) is the instigating or key event: it is the matrix from which the narrative gets its organisation and purpose. The 'illness narrative' belongs in a broader field, where the boundary between memory and reflection, a specific case and general concerns, can be unclear. It may include pathographical material. The chapters in this book that deal with Burney's journals during the king's illness or 'madness' of 1788–1789 with its physical and psychological aftermath for Burney, and the chapter about her son's inoculation for smallpox are best considered under this more general and elastic rubric of the illness narrative. It must, however, be admitted that both 'pathography' and 'illness narrative' are flexible and imprecise terms, sometimes overlapping with each other. I have called Burney's account of inoculation an illness narrative because, existing merely as letters, it is not formally presented or shaped: but it could just as well be called a pathography since the letters focus, almost exclusively, on that experience.

Kate Chisholm, whose excellent biography *Fanny Burney: Her Life* came out in 1998, published four years later a short book called *Hungry Hell*, subtitled 'What It's Really Like to Be Anorexic: A Personal Story'.[6] This brief work nevertheless demonstrates the modern illness narrative's heterogeneric qualities. Its purpose is to give guidance and encouragement to others suffering the same condition (which links it with the self-help or advice manual); it includes research – references to and quotations from medical and psychiatric experts on anorexia – which gives it affinities with formal studies of the condition – and invented dialogues, aligning it with fiction. Fundamentally, though, it is an autobiography, but with personal testimony brought into a critical relationship with the subject's treatment by doctors and hospitals. Most, but not all, illness narratives share these elements. The 'personal story', whether by the patient or by their carer (most usually mother or child, close friend or partner) is certainly the key element, but with lots of other material brought in too.

Frances Burney was not, of course, the only author of her era to write about medicine, doctors, or being a patient. Her friend Samuel Johnson published in 1783 a poem on the death of his own friend and housemate Robert Levet that commemorates a man working as a doctor among the poor of London's slums, managing to imply at the same time the author's old age and his own fear of death.[7] Johnson also included passages in his *Lives of the Poets* (1779) which might be considered pre-pathographic, such as the page or so in his *Life of Pope* describing the poet's painful physical disabilities. When James Boswell in his turn came to write his first memoir of Johnson, *Journal of a Tour to the Hebrides*, in 1785, he included a similar 'character' of Johnson, uneasily mentioning his 'constitutional melancholy, the clouds of which darkened the brightness of his fancy'. More controversially he said that Johnson's body 'shook with a kind of motion like the effect of a palsy', which he diagnosed as 'that distemper called St Vitus's dance'.[8] An even earlier work, Robert Burton's *Anatomy of Melancholy* (1641), which is clearly prompted by its author's own propensity to depressive illness and was much valued by Johnson, might also be considered as an ur-illness narrative, especially as it is offered as a resource to fellow sufferers.

But these references are incidental; these texts have none of the impetus of a narrative, and none of them shares the dynamic charge of Burney's representations of medical occasions and conflicts. A text that is often cited as a pioneering illness narrative, the chapter in George Cheyne's *The English Malady* of 1733 entitled 'The Case of the Author', simply recites the story of his own 'nervous disorder', his melancholy symptoms, his own diagnosis of their cause, his diet, and his own eventual recovery. Cheyne finds it necessary to defend his 'Egotism' in writing so much about himself. He thought 'thus much was due to Truth, and necessary for my own Vindication; and perhaps it may not be quite useless to some low, desponding, valetudinary, over-grown Person, whose Case may have some resemblance to mine.'[9] Many fragmentary autobiographical records of suffering and medications exist, but there is a world of difference between a person's solipsistic account of their illness experience and the encounters between actors in a medical drama that constitute the pathography's important contribution to modern culture.

Certainly, other writings by Frances Burney's contemporaries contain elements of the illness narrative. William Godwin's *Memoir of the Author of A Vindication of the Rights of Woman* (1798) for example, includes a detailed and dreadful account of Mary Wollstonecraft's death following childbirth in its last chapter. William Cowper wrote a *Memoir* of his early life, which included an account of his suicide attempts and what he called his alienation from God: 'Satan plied me with horrible visions, and more horrible voices,' he wrote. 'My ears rang with the sound of torments, that seemed to await me. Then did the pains of hell get hold of me, and, before daybreak, the very sorrows of death encompassed me. A numbness seized the extremities of my body . . . My hands and feet became cold and stiff.' This led to his being taken to St Albans, where the 'mad doctor' Nathaniel Cotton took him in. Though Cowper writes of Cotton's 'well-known humanity and sweetness of temper', he also writes that '[i]t will be proper to draw a veil over the secrets of my prison-house,' so nothing can be known of his treatment.[10] Some striking passages were cut from this edition of 1816: they related occurrences which 'befell [him] indeed while in a state of insanity' in 1763. They describe the 'horrible visions' as well as hallucinatory states which convince Cowper that God is sending him personal messages (one of them is a thunderstorm in which a storm cloud appears to take the shape of a hand reaching out to him).[11] Cowper also wrote a memoir of his brother, known as *Adelphi*, which originally included 'An Account of his Last Illness' describing his own mental illness that led him to attempt suicide on at least three occasions. Neither of these memoirs was published until after Cowper's death in 1800. Both his seemingly psychotic symptoms and the 'veil' thrown over his treatment might be contrasted with George III's 'madness' twenty-five years later, over which a veil has certainly not been thrown.

Thomas De Quincey's *Confessions of an English Opium Eater*, first published in 1822, is much closer to an illness narrative of the modern type than these documents. 'I speak', he wrote, 'from the ground of a large and profound personal experience: whereas . . . even of those who have written expressly on the *materia medica*, make it evident, from the horror they express of it, that their experimental knowledge of [opium's] action is none at all.'[12] De Quincey seems to have been initially prompted to use the drug for pain relief by 'Dr Buchan'. William Buchan's *Domestic Medicine* (1769) was a highly successful handbook for the layperson and went into editions well into the nineteenth century. Buchan recommended 'not to take above five-and-twenty ounces of laudanum', and De Quincey managed to avoid addiction for eight years.[13] His book is written with a dual purpose: to advocate for the medicinal value of opium when taken moderately, but also to describe the horrors, both physical and mental, that beset him when he succumbed and became an addict. Like many a modern illness narrative author, he seeks to contribute to the understanding of illness (broadly described) 'illustratively', or from the alternative perspective of the patient, as well as to help to prevent others from succumbing to the addiction. He also includes a great deal of fascinating but not strictly relevant autobiographical detail.

Later in the nineteenth century Harriet Martineau published *Life in the Sickroom* in 1844, Bulwer Lytton's *Confessions of a Water Patient* went into four editions in the mid-century, and W. E. Henley's series of poems 'In Hospital', written about 1875, gave a vivid account of the grim conditions in a Victorian public hospital – 'half workhouse and half jail' – when he endured the amputation of his lower leg and of the nauseating effects of chloroform, by then introduced as an anaesthetic.[14] Earlier an anonymous patient had given James Young Simpson, the pioneer of anaesthesia, a description of his amputation without chloroform to publicise the virtues of the gas. 'Suffering so great as I underwent cannot be expressed in words', this man wrote, adding 'only the wish to save others makes me deliberately recall and confess the anguish and humiliation of such a personal experience.'[15] Fragments like this prompt us to read Burney's exquisitely exact and graphic account of her own amputation as a revelatory development in the pathographic form.

This document and the 'Narrative' written later were composed for Burney's family: addressed to her sisters, in one case, to her son in the other. It is interesting that the mastectomy account, which was written in the form of a letter, and presumably smuggled across the Channel, was copied out in full by her son and her husband. On the cover of a folder that contained this copy, Burney wrote, 'Respect this & beware not to injure it!!!'[16] Though these documents would certainly have been intended for posterity, the fact that they were written initially as private records as part of the family archive is important. The question of propriety, of what is allowable in public discourse (which De Quincey for instance had to negotiate in a preliminary note 'To the Reader' before he gave his personal account of addiction), would have entirely forbade a woman as conscious of propriety and reputation as Burney from publishing such works. Their candour, then, is a product of their privacy.

One facilitating condition for the appearance of illness narratives in the mid-twentieth century must certainly have been the lowering of these barriers of politeness: it was now becoming possible to reveal and to detail intense personal suffering without shaming oneself. Richard Hillary's *The Last Enemy*, the story of his being shot down in his plane during the Second World War and his subsequent plastic surgery and disfigurement, was published a year before his author's death in 1943. Betty Macdonald's *The Plague and I* was published in 1948; Denton Walsh's account of an accident, hospitalisation and subsequent disability, *A Voice through a Cloud*, came out in 1950. Grace Stuart's little-known but compelling account of her life with rheumatoid arthritis, *A Private World of Pain*, was published in 1953. These are only some examples. To them must be added Simone de Beauvoir's *Une Mort Très Douce*, translated into English as *A Very Easy Death* and published in 1966. This tells of her mother's last weeks in hospital, a work of extraordinary honesty and self-revelation which is discussed and compared with Burney's record of her husband's final illness in Chapter 7 of this book. If there is a classic of modern pathography, this is it.

What seems also to have happened is that gradually in the middle years of the twentieth century writers began to realise that illness – the experience of illness – was dramatic, meaning that like theatre or the novel the presence and actions, as well as the words, of other figures than the protagonist played a part, and could be represented in dialogues.[17] It also might be made into a compelling narrative because, like all dramas, it involved conflict. And the obvious site of conflict was between medicine and the patient. In a reversal of the classic stereotype of illness, incarcerated in the very term 'patient', in which a suffering, passive, certainly not responsible, figure is acted upon by an agent (patient and agent being antitheses), in the person of surgeon or doctor, writers began to see themselves as actively engaged, sometimes through the very act of composition itself, in an interaction with and intervention into the previously sacrosanct or sequestered medical domain. Drama involves conflict, but also heroes and villains, or at least figures representing some version of those attributes. A common feature of the illness narrative then became a contrast between the advice and often the personal style of one medical figure with another – 'the cool clipped manner and an air of restrained authority' of one physician as opposed to the 'vivid' personality, the 'optimism and enthusiasm' of his colleague, though in this example, from Sandra M. Gilbert's *Wrongful Death* (1997), the choice of consultant was probably mistaken.[18] Given the stress and fear in which patients and their relatives so often continuously live, it is not surprising that recalling narrators often slip into atavistic emotional states, dividing the world into good and bad, like the Kleinian child: the lovely caring nurse and the casual, careless witch.[19]

Death or mortality is a dark, hovering presence in many illness narratives. This confers on the genre another dramatic quality – suspense. More significantly, the apprehension of death is the occasion, the stimulus or condition for another pervasive feature of any drama – the ethical or moral issues that are inseparable from the course of a serious illness and medical practice. In a work that is referred to several times in this book, Robert A. Aronowitz, a physician, writes of the precarious balance that a consultant of a seriously or mortally ill person must somehow maintain between 'hope, trust, and truth';[20] a challenge that Paul Komesaroff, an ethicist as well as a physician, describes compellingly as 'riding a crocodile' – the everyday danger of making mistakes, being kind and attentive to one patient while at the same time being harassed by the needs of many others, the need to make quick decisions that one can rarely be sure are absolutely right.[21] Medical figures who act carelessly or unconscionably, accidental errors and unhelpful remarks are recorded relentlessly in some illness narratives. No one can blame their authors, though they sometimes reflect an unrealistic conception of medical institutional life.

But the moral issues presented by the imminence of death confront the patient, and especially perhaps their carers, more urgently and potently than their physicians. Is it right to soothe your dying mother with comforting lies? What is the cost of this to the carer's own integrity, their own sense of right? If a doctor takes the avenue of telling the blunt truth, because the patient asks to be told it or because he or she believes that preparing their patient for death is their duty, how does the patient or his wife manage this – especially if they or their husband refuses to believe it? What if a doctor's tones and gestures seem to the patient to intimate a more ominous future than her cheerful words imply? These are fundamental questions of right or wrong, dramatic aspects of the illness narrative that must be located within the consciousness of the narrating patient or their narrating carer. They are sometimes explored with great subtlety and harrowing honesty in modern pathographies. In the many lesser crises that a typical illness narrative confronts and navigates, the need to make possibly momentous decisions – such as the choice of doctor – is a recurrent theme. What also has to be stressed, though, is that excruciatingly difficult decisions regarding the choice of treatments – whether to order or to perform an operation or to prescribe a drug that may save the patient but that also might kill them, for example, have to be made by physicians riding the crocodile every day.

All of these dramatic aspects of the illness narrative are anticipated in Burney's work, as in none of her contemporaries, because they stage (and in this book, I also stage) each illness experience as an interplay, sometimes a confrontation, between two agencies – patienthood and medicine, the patient and the doctors. One feature is more transparently present in Burney's stories than in most modern narratives, and this is clashes between doctors themselves, their personalities, opinions and possible treatments. The doctors brought in to deal with George III's endless wild delirious speech, among other symptoms, could not agree either on treatment or on the likely prognosis. (Burney herself sided with the one doctor among them who believed that the king would neither die nor be condemned to permanent insanity, and later became friends with Dr Francis Willis, the 'mad doctor' brought in as a last resort to handle the patient.) Another intense conflict of medical opinion is revealed through Burney's acute observation of the faces and gestures, even the tones of voice, of the surgeons who arrived at her home in Paris to perform her mastectomy twenty-five years later. In this situation another conflict becomes very clear: Madame d'Arblay is engaged, as George III most certainly was, in a struggle to make her own authority felt, but like the king she does not succeed. Then six momentous years later when her husband was dying, Burney again found herself fighting against the treating medical men, in this case not eminent surgeons, but lower on the medical ladder, apothecaries in Bath, a provincial city. It seems that then she allowed her own fear of losing her husband to overwhelm any recognition of their honest concern and accurate opinions of his prognosis. If this is a judgement a reader might make, they would be themselves drawn into a dissenting ethical response to the fraught circumstances Burney relates.

Despite these uniquely dynamic tensions in Burney's reports of medical experience and the dearth of analogous or comparable accounts from her contemporaries, it has been possible to find interesting material to set alongside them in this book. In Chapter 2 her journal's accounts of the king's medical condition, and especially of its fallout on his family and the court, which she had to infer from conversations with other courtiers, with one of his doctors, or confidential sessions with the queen's vice-chancellor, are read alongside the diary kept by Robert Fulke Greville. Greville, one of the king's equerries, a reliable and devoted attendant upon His Majesty, kept a detailed daily record of the extraordinary events in the king's apartments, to which access was strictly controlled. Several courtiers (as well as the king's physicians, of course) have left records or reminiscences of those months, but Greville's are illuminating in their sober recounting of terrible crises that Miss Burney, as a lady, was almost certainly kept in ignorance of. This is followed by an account of the impact on Frances Burney of the confinement, fear and anxiety that distorted normal relations among the courtiers, and most crucially invaded the romantic, or presumptively romantic, relationship between Miss Burney and the aristocratic confidante of the queen, Stephen Digby, an affair that may have led to her tragic and almost fatal physical and psychological collapse. This chapter, 'Aftermath', treats Burney's record of these months as an informal or inadvertent illness narrative.

In Chapter 4 the inoculation of her small son against the deadly smallpox in 1787 is discussed in the context of late eighteenth-century practices of inoculation and Edward Jenner's ground-breaking discovery of the much greater efficacy of vaccination by cowpox that was discovered before, but only announced months later. In Chapter 5 the recent discovery of an account of a mastectomy without anaesthetic in the same decade as Burney's, but in the strikingly different circumstances of a Quaker family in New Jersey and with doctors well known to the patient, is discussed alongside hers, a lonely experience surrounded by French doctors in enemy Paris. In Chapter 6 her record of Alexandre d'Arblay's last illness, very possibly as a consequence of his war service against Napoleon, is counterpointed with a shorter but still remarkable document – harrowing but also uplifting – titled 'A Week at Waterloo in 1815', written by a much younger woman. Magdalene De Lancey, caught in the chaos that followed the battle, also tells a story of caring for a dying soldier husband, but to very different effect from Burney.

Out of the many hundreds of books in this genre published in recent decades the final two chapters focus on some which develop preoccupations outlined in the previous chapters on Burney. This may be the golden age of pathography, but it is also the age of brass and plastic. There are published accounts of medical experiences that seem obviously fictionalised (narratives in the present historic tense are usually to be avoided) and others that are amateurish and ill-informed. Nevertheless, there is now a library of seriously good books which, as I argue, have a significant contribution to make to the understanding, and perhaps also to the teaching, of modern medicine. Here one must mention a special category or sub-genre of the pathography – the book written by a doctor who finds themselves becoming, suddenly, unpredictably, dramatically, a patient. Oliver Sacks's *A Leg to Stand On* (1984) is a good example. Sacks powerfully recreates the sudden loss of caste that afflicts him when, from being a strong, fit, energetic physician he finds himself an injured, inert, solitary patient. Martha Weinman Lear's *Heartsounds* (1980) is written by the patient's wife, but since it draws extensively on Dr Lear's expertise, records and conversations, ranks in this category. In *Bleed* (2015) a general practitioner, travelling in the remote western desert of central Australia, is confronted by his wife's collapse with what he is sure is a cerebral aneurism, 1,000 miles from the nearest hospital equipped to deal with the case. Bill Williams tells the story from the point of view of a carer, simultaneously drawing on his knowledge and experience as a doctor. Three recent books by doctor-patients, Paul Kalanithi's *When Breath Becomes Air* (2016), and Rana Awdish's *In Shock* (2017), as well as the earlier *An Unquiet Mind* by Kay Redfield Jamison (first published in 1996 but reprinted with an introduction and afterword in 2016), are also remarkable additions to this sub-genre which raise, in their different ways, a number of arresting issues, and are discussed in Chapter 8. They constitute what might be called a premonitory fusion of medical expertise with personal illness experience, both realms contributing their knowledge in a mode that challenges the long-standing bifurcation of patient and doctor.

The choice of texts to discuss in these chapters, which focus on the 'now' of pathography ('now' being stretched to encompass books from the past fifty years), has been determined either because they offer contemporary parallels to the illnesses or treatments that Burney recorded or because they offer an opportunity to pursue further some of the ethical issues raised earlier. There are, for example, many accounts of various forms of mental illness which can be compared with George III's symptoms, from William Styron's *Darkness Visible: A Memoir of Madness* (1990) to Jay Griffith's *Tristimania* (2016) subtitled 'A Diary of Manic Depression'. There are also frightening accounts of misdiagnoses, as in Hilary Mantel's *Giving Up the Ghost* (2003), or more famously, in Janet Frame's *An Angel at My Table* (1984). So idiosyncratic is mental illness, so loosely deployed is the vocabulary surrounding it, so varied are the experiences described in this literature, that it would be presumptuous to claim any but slight affinity with the king's condition. But the differing approaches of the king's official doctors, who treated his 'madness' as originating in his body, and Willis, who addressed himself to the patient's psychology, is today still an aspect of the treatment of the mentally ill.

There are no modern accounts of breast surgery totally without anaesthesia, but in Chapter 8 I discuss some that do throw backwards light on Burney's document and that may also illuminate some aspects of its reception since publication. One of these is *My Breast* by Joyce Wadler (1992), whose excision of a cancer in the left breast took place under local anaesthetic and was cheerfully observed and amusingly described; another is Audre Lorde's more famous *The Cancer Journals* (1980), which resembles Burney's in its evocation of the fear induced by preparations for the operation. In the remarkable *Heartsounds* a urologist who has suffered two heart attacks undergoes an angiogram: somehow the anaesthetic is forgotten, so, fully conscious and informed, he is able to report step by step and in detail the bodily sensations caused by the operation.[22]

Frances Burney's account of her husband's dying months is the foundational example of a very common variant of the modern illness narrative – the story of a mortal illness witnessed and told by a close relative of the patient. The seventh chapter of this book is given over to some of the books subsequently written by 'carers'. The AIDS narratives published in great numbers during the 1980s and 1990s include many samples of this form, which often raises acute ethical, emotional, and even socio-political issues. Burney (to anticipate) acts less as her husband's carer than as his advocate. Completely unwilling or unable to accept that Alexandre d'Arblay is degenerating daily, she fights to the end, badgering his doctors for new medicine and challenging their opinions. Lear's *Heartsounds* exemplifies this stance in a modern setting. *A Very Easy Death* raises another issue that runs through Burney's account of her husband's demise – how much does the narrating carer understand of the patient subject's accommodation to their fate?

David Rieff's *Swimming in a Sea of Death* (2008) offers another treatment. This is about the moral quandary of a son who must support his mother, the fiercely determined intellectual Susan Sontag, dying of cancer, who utterly refuses to accept the fact that her condition is now incurable. In *The Spare Room* (2008) Helen Garner is caring for an old friend dying of bowel cancer, but finds herself becoming more and more exasperated by Nicola's stubborn, self-deceptive belief in various 'alternative' remedies, as well as more and more exhausted by the physical as well as emotional tasks of caring. *The Iceberg* by Marion Coutts (2014), without complaining, also brings out the important fact that a carer can suffer their own physical symptoms and psychological miseries. This chapter seeks to bring the moral issues or quandaries faced by carers into relation with the discipline of bioethics, a development within medicine or medical science that emerged at more or less the same time and rate as did formal narratives by patients. It also serves to underline the important fact that illness is not exclusively centred on one person, but seriously affects their family's emotional stability too.

Except for the brief chapter 'Aftermath' in which Burney's deterioration in her last eighteen months at the court is treated and an attempt is made to explain it, as well as, inevitably, the chapter 'A Mastectomy', this book does not focus on Frances Burney's own health. In other words, it does not aspire to become an illness narrative of her life in itself. However, though its focus is certainly on Burney's non-fictional journals, it is pertinent to glance here at medical matters in her novels – specifically *Cecilia* (1782) and *The Wanderer* (1814), even though these are not in any sense authentic pathographic narratives.[23] Both Dr Lyster in *Cecilia* and Mr Naird, the surgeon in *The Wanderer*, figure as benign and competent professionals: the rather hysterical drama is reserved, especially in the later novel, for the symptomatic behaviour of their patients.[24]

After a scene of violent family conflict in *Cecilia*, for example, Mrs Delvile, the hero's mother, cries, 'My brain is on fire!' and rushes from the room. Her son, Mortimer, tears after her, only to find her 'extended upon the floor, her face, hands and neck all covered with blood!'[25] Cecilia begs Mortimer to conciliate his mother: 'the violence of her agitation', she declares, 'has already almost destroyed her, and her frame is too weak for this struggle of contending passions'. 'The seat of his disorder was his mind,' Lyster, the family doctor, says of a previous illness of Mortimer; he has also attended Mr Delvile in 'a severe fit of the gout' in which 'agitation of spirits', he fears, 'will be thrown into his stomach'.[26] 'A frame too weak for the struggle of contending passions' was how Burney tried to understand her own collapse years later.

The Wanderer was probably conceived during Burney's years in France, but was only published in 1814, more than thirty years after *Cecilia*. But here too the heroine, overcome with anxiety and fear, collapses. 'She would have uttered a cry; but, shaken and dismayed, her voice refused to obey her; her eyes became dim; her tottering feet would no longer support her; her complexion wore the pallid hue of death, and she sunk motionless on the floor.'[27] In the same scene of high melodrama the anti-heroine (for some readers the heroine) Elinor Joddrell, who is deranged with frustrated passion, plunges a dagger into her breast, but a 'surgeon of eminence' who happens to be present manages to stem 'the effusion of blood'. This surgeon, who turns out to be Mr Naird, later tries by 'quietly fixing his eyes upon his patient', to calm her, but fails. When he takes her pulse she insults him, calling this a 'burlesque dumb show' filled with 'farcical forms' and 'professional mockeries'.[28] Naird responds with a comment that touches on a dilemma discussed in Chapter 8 of this book. 'A medical man, Madam', he says, 'lives in a constant round of perplexity; for either he must risk killing his patients by telling them unpleasant truths; or letting them kill themselves by nourishing false hopes.'[29] Elinor calls this 'hateful official cant'. It is clear that Naird, though a surgeon (and thus in this period lower in the medical hierarchy than a doctor), does think of himself as equal to a physician and that Burney respects this claim and his profession.

The Wanderer, however, raises acutely a technical question that has bearing on the study of non-fiction narratives. Originally published in five volumes, it is a long, strange, complex, and difficult novel that has been given widely different interpretations. Its editor, Margaret Anne Doody, for example, argues that '[i]n Elinor Burney examines her own sensibility, and her own capacities for both protest and self-destruction,' citing Burney's 'determinedly pining and being consumed away' during her court years, which as an account of Burney's illness then is certainly itself controversial.[30] Sara Salith – to take only one other example – focuses on Burney's interest in inter-gender issues and mentions too that queer theorists might find material in it. Much can be made of the frequent occurrence of disguise and cross-dressing, and a Freudian critic, as she also suggests, 'might argue that Elinor, cross-dressed as a foreigner, constitutes the return' of the heroine's "repressed"'.[31] And because the heroine is a dispossessed person, an interpretation could be mounted that draws on post-colonial theory or refugee studies. These are speculative post hoc readings, made 200 years after the novel was published: they belong to the realm of literary speculation, not historical fact. I mention them because the interpretation of journals and letters has to be conducted under quite different auspices.

One issue cannot be avoided in any account of Burney's narratives of medical experience, an issue frequently debated in literary discussions of autobiographical writings and that may be just as pertinent to modern pathographies. This is, briefly, whether these narratives are to be trusted. Burney's private journal letters, written to inform and to entertain her correspondents, or as documents for the family archive, and by a writer with practised skills, might well be unreliable as records of what exactly took place. The very process of writing may create an artefact out of the raw material, and in some instances this can be detected. Lorna J. Clark, the editor of Volumes III and IV of the *Court Journals*, for example, has offered a compelling reading of Burney's very extensive letters about her meetings with and feelings about Stephen Digby, in which she argues that Burney 'constructed' her accounts, and hence her self-presentation, on the model of the sentimental epistolary novel (making herself into a heroine and the gentleman into her suitor).[32] This article may be seen as a distinguished example of the critical practice that is often, after the French philosopher Paul Ricoeur, defined as the 'hermeneutics of suspicion'. Thus Clark's reading interprets the letters in which Burney retails her experiences very differently from the way their author would have intended, ultimately to her discredit.

Ricoeur defines two 'poles' of interpretation: 'According to the one pole, hermeneutics is understood as the manifestation and restoration of a meaning addressed to me in the manner of a message, a proclamation ... according to the other pole, it is understood as a demystification, a reduction of illusion.'[33] The first, which might be called 'the hermeneutics of trust', is my funda-mental strategy in this book: I accept Burney's and the non-fictional writings of others I discuss as trustworthy, and my readings are attempts to understand and to restore their meanings.[34] But, especially in that realm of memoir and autobiography inhabited by the pathography, suspicion cannot be absolutely banished. Trust, in this literary context, does not mean that one closes off the possibility of falsification or burnishing or enhancement, but that one recog-nises this as a natural feature of accomplished writing – writing that in various ways makes Burney's and many modern pathographies moving and compel-ling documents. Ricoeur, who speaks of 'faith' rather than trust, calls this the 'faith that has undergone criticism, postcritical faith'.[35] It's often the case that Burney provides material in her pathographic writings that allows or prompts one to give a different reading of events and judgements than hers. To do this is to exercise post-critical trust. If Burney is driven to conjure a romantic narrative out of the friendship of a cultivated and polished courtier, I want to understand this as at least in part a consequence of the particularly dire circumstances in which they were thrown together. My reading of Madame d'Arblay's account of her husband's last weeks seeks to understand her thoughts and actions sympathetically, but also offers, as I have mentioned, a dissenting and critical reading.

Frances Burney, then, this book argues, was not only an important novelist and a remarkable diarist. Without overt fictionalising, but with a novelist's skills, she produced writings that recreated dramas of patient-hood that anticipate by two centuries the emergence of the genres of pathography and the illness narrative. Although a small window honouring her name was installed in the Poets' Corner of Westminster Abbey in 2002, Burney, well known in literary circles, is much less familiar to the general public of today. Partly for this reason, the first chapter offers a short account of her long life. Not, one would think, a particularly resilient person; small in stature and short-sighted, she lived through many adventures and crises, dying in London at the age of eighty-seven. She had known many famous people, two of whom, Dr Johnson in London and Dominique-Jean Larrey in Paris, played significant roles in her life. This chapter also includes a brief survey of her reputation – her afterlife – and a further discussion of the fundamentally irresolvable issue of how much her journals are to be trusted, especially as they were worked over by herself and her first editor prior to publication.

The first chapter then helps the reader new to Burney to anchor each event described in the succeeding chapters in the appropriate context of her life, and the particular circumstances surrounding each one of them, widely separated in time and place. Her life spanned the high Augustan period of the later eighteenth century, the first regency crisis of 1788–1789, the French Revolution, the long Napoleonic wars that followed, and Waterloo, through to the early reign of Queen Victoria. It was a life not just lived against the background of cataclysmic political events in the wider world, but one interacting with – one might even say besieged by – them. And the medical events I discuss also occur at moments when, as I hope to show, medical practices were also undergoing radical changes. This book then aims to mount a literary argument and at the same time, and inevitably, to be an historical study of medicine and medical practice.

Notes

1. Galen's conclusions about the human body were based on dissections of animals. Leonardo Da Vinci, who in 1510 had received permission to dissect human corpses, did so in private. His famous anatomical drawings remained unpublished until the late nineteenth century. I am indebted to Daniel Vuillermin in this paragraph.
2. Tallis, R., *Hippocratic Oaths*, pp. 16–17.
3. Laqueur, T., 'Nothing Becomes Something: Pathography'.
4. Kleinman, A., *The Illness Narratives*, p. 3.
5. Couser, G. T., 'Autopathography'.
6. Chisholm, K., *Hungry Hell*; Macleod, S., *The Art of Starvation*, is a fuller, but similar narrative incorporating professional views of anorexia with personal experiences and critique.
7. "'On the Death of Dr Robert Levet' by Dr Johnson"', *The Gentleman's Magazine*, Vol. LIII, 1783, pp. 695–696. Subsequent printings of this poem stripped Levet of his title, with which Johnson certainly meant to honour his officially unqualified friend.

8. Boswell, *Life of Johnson*, V, pp. 17, 18. St Vitus's Dance was also known as Sydenham's chorea. William Osler began his study of movement disorders in 1894 by writing that 'chorea has served as a sort of nosological pot into which authors have cast indiscriminately affections characterised by irregular, purposeless movements.' *On Chorea and Choreiform Affections*, London: H. K. Lewis & Company, 1894, p. 3. Joshua Reynolds, the painter, who knew Johnson much better than Boswell and had painted several portraits of him, vigorously contested this description and diagnosis.

9. Porter, R., ed., *George Cheyne*, p. 362.

10. Cowper, W., *Memoir of the Early Life of William Cowper*. This short book was published as a religious tract against suicide.

11. King, J., 'Cowper's *Adelphi* Restored', pp. 303–304.

12. Elwin, M., ed., De Quincey, T., *Confessions of an Opium Eater*, p. 391.

13. Ibid., p. 402.

14. Henley, W. E., *A Book of Verses*.

15. Robinson, V., *Victory over Pain*, 'An Anonymous Letter', p. 211.

16. *Journals and Letters*, VI, p. 597.

17. In the section 'The Emergence of the Illness Narrative in the Twentieth Century', in her *Illness As Narrative*, Ann Jurecic discusses this matter and gives a range of other reasons for the genre's genesis (pp. 4–10).

18. Gilbert, S. M., *Wrongful Death*, p. 47.

19. On Klein, see, for instance, Michell, J., ed., *The Selected Melanie Klein*, introduction, p. 20, and pp. 50–51, etc.

20. Aronowitz, R. A., *Unnatural History*, p. 17.

21. Komesaroff, P., *Riding a Crocodile*.

22. Weinman Lear, M., *Heartsounds*, chapter 14, pp. 12–17. This chapter was evidently written from information given to the author by her husband.

23. See McCrea, B., 'Frances Burney and Professional Men'. I am indebted to Professor McCrae's article in this discussion.

24. The Delvile family in *Cecilia*, apparently of ancient lineage, is riven by conflict. Mortimer, the son and heir, has fallen in love with Cecilia Beverley, an heiress, and she with him. This is unfortunate because the instigating plot device of *Cecilia* is that it is a condition of the heroine's inheriting her fortune that her husband must take her surname for his own. Mr Delvile absolutely forbids his son taking another name and betraying his heritage. Mortimer is torn between loyalty to his father (who refuses to see him) and his wish to marry Cecilia; his mother, who is very fond of Cecilia, is also torn by conflicting emotions as she watches her family fall apart.

25. Doody, M. A. and Sabor, P., eds, Burney, F., *Cecilia*, p. 680.

26. Ibid., p. 690.

27. Doody, M. A., Mack, R. L., and Sabor, P., eds, Burney, F., *The Wanderer*, pp. 358–359.

28. Ibid., p. 377.

29. Ibid., p. 380.

30. Doody, M. A., *Frances Burney*, p. 342.

31. Sabor, P., ed., *The Cambridge Companion to Frances Burney*; Salith, S., '*Camilla* and *The Wanderer*', p. 49.
32. Clark, L., 'Epistolarity in Frances Burney'.
33. Ricoeur, P., *Freud and Philosophy*, p. 27. I am indebted to Dr Jocelyn Dunphy-Blomfield for help with Ricoeur.
34. 'Ricoeur distinguishes between a hermeneutics of suspicion and a hermeneutics of trust, between a reading that demystifies and a reading that restores' (Felski, R., *The Limits of Critique*, p. 107).
35. Ricoeur, *Freud and Philosophy*, p. 28.

CHAPTER I

Frances Burney's Long and Extraordinary Life:
1752–1840

Frances Burney was born in June 1752 into a family of precarious gentility. The Burneys had just moved to King's Lynn in Norfolk, where Frances's father, who was to become a signally important figure in her life, had secured a post as organist at St Margaret's Church. Charles Burney, a musician and composer and a man of ambition, later became the author of the pioneering *A General History of Music*, published in four volumes from 1776 to 1789. While still a girl Frances acted as his amanuensis, and at ten, in her own words, 'began scribbling ... little works of invention'.[1] There were five children in the family, who all remained close: Susanna, Frances's younger sister, was especially dear to her, and it was to Susanna that many of the enormous number of letters that Frances was eventually to write were addressed. In 1759 the family moved to London, where three years later their mother died. Frances's father was awarded the degrees of Mus.B and Mus.D at Oxford and, though he could never stop working, began to enjoy the status of a confirmed professional gentleman.[2]

Frances, or 'Fanny', as she was affectionately known in the family and to many generations of later readers, began to keep a journal when she was fourteen, and continued throughout her extraordinary, long, and varied life until old age. These records, often supplemented by letters written to her sisters, her father, and female friends, were often detailed and dramatic, and there are indications that she meant them also to be something more than confidential or personal, especially when she became involved in or witness to dramatic events, sometimes of historical importance, such as the Battle of Waterloo of 1815. Lengthy and detailed, sometimes overwhelming, these journals and letters have been collected in the scholarly Oxford editions which make up *The Early Journals and Letters of Fanny Burney* (in five volumes), *The Journals and Letters of Fanny Burney 1791–1840* (in twelve volumes) and *The Court Journals of Frances Burney* (six volumes, in progress), which are supplemented by *The Additional Journals and*

Letters of Frances Burney (recently published in two volumes): twenty-five solid volumes in all, with perhaps more to come. From this voluminous output this book takes account only of Burney's experiences of four widely separated episodes.

It was not her journals, though, but her novels that made Frances famous among her contemporaries and enjoyed by a smaller but devoted readership today. The first, *Evelina* (1778), was published surreptitiously and anonymously lest her father should discover that his daughter had done such an unladylike thing as to publish for profit. When *Evelina*, which is subtitled *The History of a Young Lady's Entrance into the World*, became the talk of the town, she owned up to him, and he seems then to have been delighted. It was through her father that, as a successful authoress, she was introduced to the leading minds and celebrities of the time including David Garrick, Edmund Burke, Dr Samuel Johnson, and Sir Joshua Reynolds. This was at the Streatham home of Hester Thrale, the witty and gregarious high-born wife of a rich brewer who, though she at first thought the book 'flimsy', if 'pretty enough', adopted Johnson's very high view of it, and became Frances's champion and friend.[3] Frances accompanied the Thrales to the resorts of Tunbridge Wells and Brighton in October of that year. Burney was to stay at Streatham quite often, and sometimes when Johnson too was a guest. Like James Boswell, her contemporary, but probably with more fidelity, Burney recorded Johnson's conversation (and the ladies' responses) when he entertained her and their hostess over dinner, just as she recorded in detail everything else of interest she witnessed or experienced.[4] She delighted in capturing the dramatic interplay of talk. When Johnson offered and began to teach Fanny Latin and Greek, her father quickly put an end to such an improper pursuit.

Hester and Frances became good friends. The Thrales took Frances on holiday again with them in October 1779. On one occasion, though, in December 1779 Mrs Thrale, who could be acerbic, wrote in her own journal, *Thraliana*:

> Fanny Burney has kept her Room here in my house seven Days with a Fever, or something that She called a Fever: I gave her every Medcine, and every Slop with own hand; took away her dirty Cups, Spoons &c. moved her Tables, in short was Doctor & Nurse & Maid – for I did not like the Servants should have additional Trouble lest they should hate her for't – and now – with the true Gratitude of a Wit, She tells me, that the *World thinks the better of me* for my Civilities to her.
> It does! does it?[5]

Allowing for Hester Thrale's crossness – and her private views of her friends were rarely flattering – this still throws a useful light on Frances Burney's character. She was certainly very prone to exaggeration and, as her diaries suggest, sometimes exceedingly self-absorbed. But these were, one might say, the coefficients of her particular genius.

Evelina deserved its success. It brings off the feat of combining a female-oriented romantic love story with the male-oriented picaresque and comic novel, sometimes knock-about, even raucous, that eighteenth-century novelists like Henry Fielding and Tobias Smollett had made popular. Evelina's 'adventures' occur not on a journey, but on excursions to various public venues in London, so the novel still offers readers an amusing tour of late eighteenth-century city entertainments, like the opera and the pleasure gardens of Ranelagh and Vauxhall. What also made the novel successful is the acute (and Burneyesque) observation of vulgar, would-be-genteel manners and social embarrassments, topics cutting-edge in a city burgeoning with new arrivals and where the gentry were nervously patrolling class borders. Another, more ambitious novel, *Cecilia* (1782), followed, possibly written under Johnson's influence, since, as has been suggested, it raises the plot of a young lady's entrance into the world from mere romantic story to the status of serious morality.[6] A rich orphan heiress, the heroine has to think carefully before choosing which of her guardians she will live with. *Cecilia* was another great success, went into three editions, and was translated into French and German. (Burney's novels being known in France was to prove important later in her life.) About this time she also wrote a stage comedy, *The Witlings*, which her father forbade her to get produced – the theatre not being a suitable place for a lady.

After their mutual friend Hester Thrale, now widowed, married the musician Gabriel Piozzi in June 1784, a marriage they both deplored, Frances Burney became still closer to Samuel Johnson, and recorded several occasions when in his last weeks he confided intimate thoughts to her. One of these conversations occurred about three weeks before his death, and her account of it demonstrates both their intimacy and her delicate responsiveness to the tragi-comedy of the situation. Johnson has been very ill in London, but tells her he is 'going to try what sleeping out of town might do for him':

> 'I remember', said he, 'that my wife, when she was near her end, poor woman, was also advised to sleep out of town; and when she was carried to the lodgings that had been prepared for her, she complained that the staircase was in very bad condition – for the plaster was beaten off the walls in many places. "Oh," said the man of the house, "that's nothing but

by the knocks against it of the coffins of the poor souls that have died in the lodgings!'"

He laughed, though not without apparent secret anguish, in telling me this. I felt extremely shocked, but, willing to confine my words at least to the literal story, I only exclaimed against the unfeeling absurdity of such a confession. (DL II, 270)

She tried to see him when he was manifestly dying on 8 December, but was told Johnson was too ill. Charles Burney managed to see him on 11 December, when Johnson asked '*How Fanny did*' and on parting said, 'I think I shall throw the Ball at Fanny yet' – in other words, he would still enjoy the to-and-fro of their conversational exchanges.[7] Taking this as a request to see her, Fanny tried again, despite her father's objections, on 12 December, but after waiting round for hours, was told it was too late. 'This you may be sure over-set our poor Fan terribly,' her father wrote to her sister, an indication that the family knew Fanny could be a little unstable and prone to excesses of feeling.[8] It had been an important friendship: Johnson died the next day.

In December 1782 Frances had met George Owen Cambridge, a clergyman three years younger than herself from a family of higher social status, and eminently acceptable as a husband. He made his enjoyment of her company apparent, and Frances, it seems, fell in love with him. He was '*both* elegant and sensible', she wrote, and for some time he seemed to be courting her. Mrs Thrale thought he had serious intentions. But as Burney's journals and letters of the time demonstrate, it was never quite clear what his intentions were. She recorded every meeting in great detail, with 'the detail increasing as she tries to bring in every bit of evidence that could make for reassurance'.[9] In the words of Joyce Hemlow, Burney's first scholarly biographer, Cambridge was a 'young clergyman who seemed by his manner and actions to intimate thoughts of love, but who did not come forth with the offer of his hand, who did not, and did not, and did not *speak*'.[10] Their acquaintance continued three years, but it became clear by 1786 that he would never propose.

The failure of this affair with Cambridge was a crucial event in Frances Burney's life, and presaged circumstances covered in the next chapter. Particularly pertinent to these is a passage from a long letter to Susanna in January 1785 when Burney, made momentarily happy by Cambridge's behaviour, makes a comment on the nature of their intercourse:

How different this parting from the meeting! ... nothing explanatory, apologising, or *utterable* passing on either side, – the whole effected by Voice and Countenance, yet so effected as to seem already conclusive! I felt almost sure I was Dreaming though afraid, not desirous, to wake.[11]

'The whole effected by Voice and Countenance', not directly spoken, having to be inferred, but inferred as confirmation of her wishes – her construction of the gentleman's meaning – anticipates the salient feature of her reporting of her later conversations with another apparent suitor, Stephen Digby. As this brief passage exemplifies, Frances Burney's personal style often anticipates the lady in Henry James who 'felt in italics and thought in capitals'.[12]

She was thirty-two in 1786, well past the conventionally marriageable age, when she was invited to stay with Mrs Delany, who lived in a small house very close to Windsor Castle, the home of the royal court. Mary Delany was elderly, a distinguished artist and a favourite with the king and queen, who had given her the house and a pension. Frances met the royals there, and evidently made a good impression. Soon Miss Burney was invited to accept the post of Keeper of the Robes to Queen Charlotte, the consort of King George III. It was a prestigious and sought-after appointment. Her father was thrilled at the prospect, probably because this would certainly lift the family's social standing. Though very reluctant, and foreseeing that she would have to abandon her plans for new novels, Frances was persuaded that the job was a great honour, would secure her for life, and was very likely, as acquaintances encouraged her to think, to bring bonuses to the family. Arriving there, she wrote to her sister: 'I am *married*, my dearest Susan – I look upon it in that light – I was averse to forming the union, & I endeavoured to escape it; but my friends interfered, – they prevailed – & the knot is tied. What, then, now remains, but to make the best Wife in my power?'[13] It would be a strange marriage: permanent establishment, but permanent celibacy.

As will become clear in what follows, this suppression of her feelings and her sexuality proved impossible. And her appointment was not, at least within the court, prestigious. This woman who had earned the respect and admiration of some of the greatest English intellects of her time was looked down upon by the aristocratic courtiers. One of the Maids of Honour, for example, was to Frances often 'haughty, silent, & supercilious' (though the lady in question had her reasons).[14] The queen was 'condescending', an adjective, meant as praise, that Frances uses continually in her letters to her sister, but it soon became clear that Miss Burney was little more than a servant. When the court visited the great house, Stanton Harcourt, no provision at all was made for her reception; when her French visitors Madame la Fite and Madame la Roche hinted that they would like to be invited to tea (especially as it began to rain outside), Burney dreaded to take the hint, knowing that court protocol forbade her having anyone to dine with her without the prior permission of the queen. This and many other humiliating and embarrassing occasions she reports in detail to her sister. In addition, she had to spend many hours in the company of Mrs Schwellenberg, the other Keeper of the Robes.

Mrs Schwellenberg, who had been brought over to England with her mistress, Queen Charlotte, in 1761, became the curse of Frances Burney's court life. Apparently jealous of her younger colleague, who seemed to be liked by the queen, and popular with the gentlemen (as well as better paid, though she may not have known this), she insisted that Burney entertain her in the long evenings they both spent waiting around until they were called to assist at their royal mistress's disrobing. Burney was required to be her partner at piquet, a not-very-demanding card game for two which she found insufferably tedious, night after night. Worse than this, Mrs Schwellenberg (the 'Mrs' was a courtesy title for an elderly spinster), who had never mastered English and was often unwell, disliked and lonely, took out her misery on Frances, and was carping, angry, insulting, and vicious. Burney's private name for her became 'Cerbera', meaning the bitch that guards the gates of the underworld and prevents its dead from escaping, a bitterly comic reference to her own imprisonment.

Despite Frances's soon prevailing misery, she employed her memory and her novelistic skills during these first months in amusing her correspondents with comic vignettes of characters around the court, as when she hits off the equerry Colonel Goldsworthy's 'style of rattle' when he has been out late hunting with the king:

'after all the labours, cried he, of the Chace, – all the riding, the trotting, the galloping, the leaping, the – with your favour, ladies! I beg pardon, – I was going to say a strange word, but the – the *perspiration*, &, – & all that, – after being wet through over Head, and soused through underfeet, & popt into Diches, & jerked over Gates, – Lord help us! what lives we do lead! – well it's all *honour*! That's my only comfort! – well after all this, fagging away like mad from 8 in the morning to 5 or 6 in the afternoon, – Home we come, looking like so many drowned Rats, – with not a dry thread about us, nor a morsel within us, sore to the very bone, & forced to smile all the time! & then – after all this what do you think follows? – "Here Goldsworthy!" cries his Majesty, – so up I comes to him, Bowing profoundly, & my Hair dripping down to my Shoes – "Goldsworthy!" cries His Majesty, – "Sir!" says I, smiling agreeably, with the Rheumatism just creeping all over me! – but expecting something a little comfortable, I waited patiently to know his gracious pleasure, & then – "Here, Goldsworthy, I say!" – he cries, – "*will you have a little Barley Water?*"'[15]

This is 'truly comic' as Burney herself says, and quite possibly heightened by her own invention. The Colonel also teases her about the privations she too will have to endure in the name of '*honour*' when winter comes: 'Running along in those cold passages; then bursting into rooms fit to bake you . . . there's wind enough in those passages to carry off a man of war! And there you'll have your share, ma'am, I promise you that! You'll get knocked up in three days, take my word for that.'[16] Most of which came, in the course of the next few years, dreadfully true. Burney found herself compelled to stand for hours attending her royal mistress, forced to play cards for hours with Mrs Schwellenberg, and even to suffer cruelty at the old woman's hands, as on a November carriage journey from Windsor to London in 1787 when, as Burney wrote bitterly, she found it 'expedient to have the Glass down on my side, whence there blew in a sharp wind, which so painfully attacked my Eyes, that they were inflamed even before we arrived in Town'.[17] Everyone who saw her, including her father, who met her the next day, she reports, was distressed at the 'piteous' state of her eyes. An old housemaid, who ministered to her eyes with warm milk and butter, told her that her predecessor in the job, Madam Haggerdorn, 'grew nearly blind' from being forced by Mrs Schwellenberg to sit in cold winds for journey after journey, which as Frances writes, was hardly a comfort.

Her first two years at court were alleviated a little, however, by her friendship with Mary Delany, whose house just outside the castle walls became a refuge she visited whenever she could. But Delany died at the age of eighty-eight in April 1788, 'leaving Frances alone to bear the worst period of her captivity'.[18] For it was not long after this that the king's severe so-called bilious symptoms led to the court travelling to Cheltenham Spa so that the supposedly curative waters might help him. Burney, as the queen's attendant, travelled too, as did her personal assistant, the vice-chancellor, Colonel Stephen Digby, and in this diminished group and under these more confined circumstances, the two became friends. Digby, who was suffering severely from gout, and still grieving over the death of his wife the previous year, evidently found Miss Burney a very congenial companion, and visited her room and talked with her as often as he could. The queen, when she heard of this, made her disapproval felt. After all, Digby was an aristocrat, related to the Earl of Illchester, and Miss Burney a mere commoner.

The waters did nothing to cure His Majesty's symptoms. His behaviour was making everyone around him uneasy. Frances shared her anxieties by writing every morning to her sisters about the events of the previous day, capturing the unnerving quality of the king's utterances as well as communicating her own half-hysterical distress. Her journals for the half year from October 1788 became an invaluable source of information, not only about the king but because, as one might say, his illness metastasised, causing dysfunctional behaviour not only in his family but throughout the court. These events and their consequences are the subject of the next chapter.

During this time, delayed at Kew by the king's illness, Burney, 'to while away the tediousness', began to write or sketch out 'a *Tragedy*'. This would have probably been *Edwy and Elgiva*, a blank-verse drama set in AD 956, which she eventually returned to and completed in 1790. It was followed by two other tragic plays. They have been called therapeutic, and Burney obviously found writing them a help in periods of otherwise unbearable boredom and sadness. They may also read as psycho-dramas, as a way in which Burney could play out, in disguised and perhaps even pathological form, some of the tensions of her personal circumstances. As Claire Harman writes in her biography, '[t]he repeated themes of constraint, monasticism and forced marriage' in these plays 'are fairly obvious metaphors for court life'.[19]

Soon came the full-blown onset of the famous, or notorious, 'madness' of King George. The king's illness and 'his punitive treatment, or mistreatment, by state-appointed physicians'[20] placed intolerable strains not only on the royal family but also on everyone at court. There were also immense political consequences, which are outlined in the next chapter. But until the full publication of Volumes III, IV, V, and VI in the Oxford edition of Frances Burney's *Court Journals and Letters* almost nothing has been known about another consequence of the king's condition and the confinement of the courtiers to a virtual prison together, first at Windsor and then at Kew. That is the problematic, intimate, and tantalisingly ambiguous relationship (according to Burney's accounts) that developed, in the shadow of tension and terror, between Miss Burney and Colonel Digby. The many pages of her diaries which recount exhaustively, in a style hedged about with uninterpretable nuance, their meetings in her room were completely censored by her early editors, and hence remained undiscussed in biographies.[21] The consequences of this relationship played a part in a decline which eventually brought Frances Burney, as she thought, to the brink of madness or death.

For following the king's recovery in the early months of 1789, Burney's own health began to fail inexorably, as seen in Chapter 3. Her friend Mrs Ord, a fervent royalist, spent a week at Windsor in October 1790 and was dismayed at the toll Fanny's duties had taken, and left her, so Frances reported, 'in great & visible uneasiness'.[22] Frances had pains in her side, a cough, and difficulty breathing, but above all, exhaustion. She had composed a 'Memorial', or rather a petition to the queen asking to be released from her duties, which even her father was urging her to present. But she could not summon up the courage to present it. Frances's struggles and the attempts of many people – her family, her friends both inside and outside the court, her many acquaintances in intellectual and literary circles – to bring about her release before she finally collapsed make distressing reading. Even after Frances had finally presented her memorial, the queen could not seem to understand how desperate her condition was. It seems incredible that Her Majesty asked Frances to attend and to report on the trial of Warren Hastings in Westminster Hall when it was reopened in May 1791, and showed displeasure when Burney stood up to her and declined. Ultimately, when Miss Burney was exhausted from constant attendance, obviously ill, terribly thin, and haggard, the queen condescended to allow her to resign from her position in July 1791. Frances Burney went on a recuperative tour of the west country with Mrs Ord, and recovered her strength soon enough.

In January 1793, Frances went to stay with friends at Norbury Park in Surrey, which was not far from a community of French exiles, distinguished figures who had managed to lease Juniper Hall at the foot of Box Hill. Among them were ex-Minister of War Louis de Narbonne and his friend the career soldier Alexandre d'Arblay, who had escaped after the capture of his commander the Marquis de Lafayette by Austrian troops, and made his way to London. Frances became acquainted with them not long before the execution of Louis XVI in Paris on 21 January that year, which would have made their return to France impossible. Fanny's sister Susan with her husband, Major Molesworth Phillips, and her family were also living close by. Susan was very taken with d'Arblay, and soon Fanny was too. She described him as 'one of the most delightful Characters I have ever met, for openness, probity, intellectual knowledge, and unhackned manners'.[23] After a fortnight's acquaintance, d'Arblay offered to teach Frances French, though she already, it seems, knew it well enough. They conducted a courtship under cover of the exchange of *thèmes* or exercises in French (rather like Levin and Kitty's courtship in *Anna Karenina*), and soon d'Arblay proposed. Despite the stubborn disapproval of Frances's father, Burney and d'Arblay were married in July 1793. The Protestant marriage was followed a few days later by a Catholic ceremony. Money was certainly going to be a problem, but Frances was confident that she would be able to earn enough to support them by her pen.

Madame d'Arblay, as she was now to be styled by the first editors of her journals among others, gave birth to a son, Alexander, in December 1794. She was forty-two. She published another substantial novel, *Camilla, or A Picture of Youth*, 'by subscription' in March 1797. (One of the subscribers was 'Miss J. Austen, Steventon'.[24]) Since she was very well known by now, and had formed illustrious acquaintances at the court, the subscription raised enough money for the d'Arblays to start building a home in a Surrey village called West Humble. They were to call the house 'Camilla Cottage'. (Many late eighteenth-century women writers, such as Charlotte Lennox and Charlotte Smith, as well as Fanny's half-sister Sarah Harriet Burney, were more or less driven to publish to support themselves or their families, but Burney is probably alone in intending to make a sum of money sufficient to keep a family and to build a house.) Fearing that the construction would bring all sorts of characters in contact with their son, the d'Arblays decided that Alexander must be inoculated against the widespread, very contagious, and greatly dreaded disease of small-pox. This was early in 1797, when Alex was just three. Frances's letters describing his inoculation, a common event, but a taxing experience for his mother, form the focus of Chapter 4.

There was a good chance of another comedy, called *Love and Fashion*, being performed at Covent Garden in 1799 until the manager changed his mind, which was a pity since a successful play could make a lot of money and the d'Arblays needed it. The general set to and worked a vegetable patch, which after a while provided well for the family. But these years of happy rustic seclusion in Surrey were tragically broken into by the death of Fanny's beloved sister Susanna on 6 January 1800, and still more by the circumstances of her death. Four years before, Susan had reluctantly consented to Phillips's wish to settle in County Lough on the east coast of Ireland, where her life in a desolate unfinished farmhouse with her irascible, tyrannical husband has some resemblance to her sister's isolated sojourn in the very different setting of the court ten years before. Like her sister, Susan became seriously ill, but Phillips refused to let her return to her family, where she would be cared for. Frances became frantically concerned. When the major finally relented, it was too late, and his wife, having endured the rigours of the journey to England, died four days after arriving. When the news reached West Humble, 'Fanny's grief was con-vulsive and uncontrollable.'[25] This meant that no more of the detailed records of her daily life addressed to and confiding in her beloved sister could be written, and only occasional letters, or more formalised narratives of specific occasions addressed to other members of her family or other people, would tell the story of her life henceforth.

Joyce Hemlow speaks of the d'Arblays for the next few years as 'pawns of fate and politics'.[26] The war declared on England by Revolutionary France in 1793 was still continuing, now under the dynamic, charismatic, and relentlessly ambitious Napoleon Bonaparte. Though they lived quietly in West Humble with their growing boy, Madame and General d'Arblay were certainly disturbed at intervals by ominous news from abroad. When in March 1802 the Treaty of Amiens was signed between Britain and France, promising – so it was thought – a lasting peace, General d'Arblay immediately returned to France with the aim of recovering some of his estate. His wife and son followed him on 14 April. But when after little more than a year Britain ended the peace by declaring war on France in May 1803, the family were trapped in a hostile Paris, with few possibilities of communication with the Burneys at home. Bonaparte issued a decree on 22 May that all English men and women in France between the ages of sixteen and sixty were to be considered prisoners of war.[27] Since Burney was unable to access her pension or to publish, and d'Arblay had failed in his attempt to retrieve his estate, they would have been in a penniless and perilous state but for help from d'Arblay's family (and possibly from their connections). The general eventually took a menial job as a clerk in the Ministry of the Interior in 1805. The d'Arblays were marooned in Paris for ten years while Napoleon's armies went from victory to victory.

Since she could not send letters home, Frances more or less stopped keeping daily records of her life and adventures, and only worked sporadically on a new novel. There is evidence, however, that though the family were living in a quiet and humble way, they were able to make friends with several, perhaps many, affluent and influential French people. This is an important factor in the circumstances surrounding the episode which she did write up and which is the focus of Chapter 5 in this book, her now famous account of her operation for the removal of the right breast, at their home in the rue Miroménil in September 1811. Frances was able, through friends, to consult and ultimately be attended to by two of the most eminent medical men in Paris, the most important of them briefly back home, Napoleon's chief army surgeon Dominique-Jean Larrey.

Larrey's name is not well known in the Anglo-Saxon world, though he was a key figure in the history of surgery. Since 2011, he has been honoured by the Committee of Chiefs of Medical Services in NATO by an annual award, largely in recognition of his invention of triage. This was the principle that on the battlefield men who most urgently needed surgery and whose lives would be saved by it should be attended to first, regardless of nationality or rank, a procedure now followed universally in hospitals and emergency services. He also invented the field ambulance, a vehicle with suspension which spared the injured, who had been carried across battlefields in carts, even more pain. Larrey's commitment to drastic surgery, if it meant saving a life, can be seen in his readiness to operate on Frances Burney.

When she had presumably recovered from this ordeal, Madame d'Arblay and her son undertook the dangerous clandestine journey across the Channel to England in August 1812. There was a brief interval in the war following an armistice a year later, but it only lasted two months. Communication with her stranded husband was difficult, so back in England Burney followed newspaper accounts of the war obsessively. It looked increasingly, after the defeat of Napoleon by the Russian winter in 1812, as if the long period of warfare might soon be over. On 30 March 1814 the allied forces of England, Russia and Prussia entered Paris, and on 11 April Napoleon renounced his titles and was sent into exile on the island of Elba, off the Italian coast. General d'Arblay could at last come home, but in June, back in France, he was offered a place in the Garde du Corps of the new king, Louis XVIII, which seemed an honour that might actually lead to the old soldier (he was sixty at this time) retrieving his fortunes. Leaving their son, who was twenty, in England, his wife joined him in France for what looked like a bright future together. *The Wanderer, or, Female Difficulties*, the fruit of many years of gestation, was published in England in 1814, but was not well received.

Then Napoleon famously escaped from Elba in February the next year and, gathering an ever-increasing army of followers, made his way from Italy and through France towards Paris. D'Arblay was ordered to join his corps and march south to join the Duc de Berry and do battle with Napoleon's advancing troops. But in the fog of war the duc's army had disintegrated, and d'Arblay was left to follow his king, who had fled northwards. He managed to get a note to his wife begging her to leave Paris 'as soon as possible'. Taking with her very few possessions (among them her favourite medicine, Dr James's Fever Powders), she made a terrifying journey by coach through enemy territory towards Belgium, where she and her companions arrived on 24 March. She was to remain in Brussels for four months. The city was about ten miles away from the village of Waterloo, and Burney went through all the anxiety of conflicting reports as the battle raged in June, including terror when she was told that the English troops had been defeated, and afterwards joined other women in making bandages for the dreadful number of wounded. The events of these months, which left General d'Arblay 'thinned and changed inconceivably' in his wife's words, by his arduous service and by the vicissitudes of the famous battle itself, play an important role in Chapter 6.

While Madame d'Arblay was anxiously awaiting her husband's arrival in Brussels, a new horse had violently kicked d'Arblay in the right leg, the injury had become infected, and he had developed a severe fever. When Frances got news of this, she set off immediately to Liège, the first stage in a long – 200-mile – journey to Trevès (now Trier), where she had learned her husband was desperately ill. This extraordinary expedition across war-ravaged territory by a sixty-three-year-old English lady, relying on the diligences (or public coaches) and the kindness of strangers, took five days, but Madame d'Arblay was finally reunited with her husband on 24 July.

After Napoleon's final defeat at Waterloo and exile to St Helena, General d'Arblay, now awarded the title of 'Comte', secured his retirement from military service, and the couple returned to Paris, but a few months later that year, not telling their French friends, went back to England. They settled in Bath, by this time a kind of genteel retirement village, where d'Arblay, whose military service had wrecked his health, was treated by a local apothecary, or unlicensed physician, George Hay. Mr Hay became an important figure in the months preceding Alexandre d'Arblay's death.

D'Arblay's pension had to be collected in person, so, though unwell, he returned to France in the summer of 1817. Dominique-Jean Larrey, whose own title of 'Barron' had been stripped from him following his emperor's defeat, was now in Paris again. After her operation in 1811, Frances Burney had kept up with Larrey's wife, and now regarded the Larreys as friends.[28] After taking other advice, to no avail, d'Arblay on his wife's urging consulted Larrey, who may have examined the general, but together with colleagues, advised against an operation. This almost certainly would mean that he thought the condition, whatever it was, inoperable and therefore fatal. On her husband's return in October, Fanny found d'Arblay 'altered – thin – weak – depressed – full of pain – and disappointed in every expectation of every sort that had urged his excursion!'[29] For the next months Burney, with the aid of Hay, took charge of his health – and as Chapter 6 shows, take charge she did. General d'Arblay died on 3 May 1818.

Two years later Burney wrote a remarkable and extended account of her husband's last months, ostensibly for their son, but as always with an eye to posterity. This document, 'A Narrative of the Last Illness and Death of

General d'Arblay', is her most extraordinary and most proleptic patho-graphic narrative. But it was not the last journal or narrative that Frances Burney composed. A few years later she was sufficiently recovered to write two more lengthy 'journals', *Waterloo Journal* in 1823, and *Journey to Trèves* two years later. Both are substantial and remarkable documents, and show no decline in Burney's ability to bring harrowing experiences home to her reader. It is tempting to include them within the purview of this book because they also certainly have pathographic elements. And because they relate events in the years before the *Narrative*, and throw some backwards light on her behaviour as related there, I briefly characterise them here.

Both pieces, but especially her reminiscences of the months leading to the battle of Waterloo, tell her own story, inseparable from the momentous historical events that determine it. As she writes near the opening of that journal, the ten years she had lived previously in Paris were 'so full, eventful, so fearful, so astonishing, the idea of Buonoparte was blended with all our Thoughts, our projects, our Actions'.[30] Soon news comes that Napoleon, escaped from Elba, is on his way north and heading for Paris. Frances fears that d'Arblay, fanatically loyal to the 'Royal Cause', is too old and too unwell to fight for the king, but he is determined. He urges her to leave: 'As the Wife of an Officer in the King's body Guard, in actual service, I might be seized, he thought, as a kind of hostage, & might probably fare all the worse for being, also, an Englishwoman.'[31]

From now on dreadful anxiety for her own fate is accompanied by much more crippling fear for her husband. A friend, the princesse de Henin, has offered her a place in her carriage, but when she arrives there the princess, usually a person of dignified serenity, is virtually mad with uncertainty whether to stay or leave. Her mind is 'absolutely disorganised' and like the Count Lally-Tolendahl (as Burney suspects, her lover) who was to come with them, totally robbed of aristocratic poise and self-control. They eventually leave in the dark, heading for Brussels, on 19 March. From this moment Frances Burney is a refugee, a displaced person. With its insistent undertow of anxiety, her narrative anticipates the accounts of many others since, forced to flee their homes in desperation, carrying only a basket or bag of possessions, and in the face of an advancing enemy. There is no comfort in travelling with her friends: 'It was every way a frightful night. Misery both public & private oppressed us all, & the fear of pursuit & captivity had the gloomy effect of causing general taciturnity.' 'No kind voice' helps to relieve the fear of danger or gives her encouragement.[32] Each of them is alone with their own terrors, hers most acutely for the fate of d'Arblay.

There is a lull in Brussels, but then in mid-June, having sent a letter off to d'Arblay in Trèves, where he is now stationed, she realises that the encounters that preceded what was to become known as the battle of Waterloo have begun. She watches the 'wounded, the maimed, the bleeding, groaning, – agonized martyrs' to the war, as they pass by in the street: even worse is 'the sight of the continually pouring forth ready-armed & vigorous Victims that marched past my Windows to meet similar destruction – '.[33] The outcome of the battle or battles is still uncertain, and Burney decides that she needs a passport. Her account of her confrontation with Colonel Jones, the British officer charged with issuing passports, shows that her capacity for recreating a dramatic scene has not diminished.

To obtain a passport, she must go to the police office where Jones has the unenviable job of refusing passports to the crowds of people besieging his office and clamouring for them. When he appeared, Burney writes, 'he was immediately attacked, envellopped, entreated, reproached, or interrogated from all quarters.'[34] She keeps her head among the 'promiscuous swarm' and goes to his office, where she figures he must soon return. There this small lady confronts him, blocking his way when he attempts to walk out, and settles on a compromise, asking him merely to sign her old passport, which he does with a very bad grace, very vividly captured. The courage, quick-wittedness, and intransigence Madame d'Arblay displays here is present too in *Journey to Trèves*. This narrative is even more gripping than the *Waterloo Journal*, filled with excruciating suspense as impediments – the refusal of officials to grant her passage until she mentions one of her famous friends, the 'cruel' slowness and endless delays of the diligences – climax in the nightmarish terror of being so horribly lost in the streets of Bonn that she nearly misses the vital coach.

Both of these remarkable documents are written with her son, Alex, in mind, and infused with her love of his father. She thinks of Alexandre d'Arblay continually throughout the travails of the journey to Brussels; her whole expedition to Trèves is a desperate expedition to be reunited with him. The tenacity of her love for d'Arblay, testified in these narratives, is illustrated again in the very different circumstances treated in Chapter 6. Her brilliant but eccentric son, who had been a constant worry to his mother, actually predeceased her, dying probably of pneumonia in 1837. Charles Burney had died in April 1814, a few days before his eighty-ninth birthday. Frances lived and wrote for many years after her husband died, and published *Memoirs of Doctor Burney* in 1832, drawing on many of her own memories of the famous, when she was eighty. She died in Victorian London at the age of eighty-seven in 1840.

Her reputation, or her afterlife, has had its vicissitudes.[35] For many years after her death, she was only thought of as the author of *Evelina*. In a generally sympathetic review by Thomas Babington Macaulay in 1834, the last two novels were described as lamentable fallings off from her earlier work, and this became the accepted view of her achievement. When an edition of the *Diary and Letters of Madame d'Arblay* was published in six volumes in 1904 and 1905, it was headed at the top of every left-hand page 'Diary and Letters' and at the top of every right-hand page 'By the Author of Evelina.' The editor was Austin Dobson, a well-known biographer and man of letters, but this edition was little more than a reprint of the edition published between 1842 and 1847 by Charlotte Barrett, and still omitted a great deal of material. But these handsomely illustrated volumes (which included fold-out facsimiles of letters) did establish Burney as an important non-fiction writer and recorder of her life and times.

'The superiority of the Diary to the Novels', as Dobson had put it, then became accepted wisdom until the later years of the twentieth century, though *Evelina* retained its currency.[36] Since that time, with the rise of cultural studies and its affiliate, 'New Historicism', in the literary academy, Burney's novels have been mined, especially in North America, for their political and social consciousness, their feminism or proto-feminism and their contribution to 'the politics of women's writing'.[37] Hence Margaret Anne Doody's influential *Frances Burney: The Life in the Works* (1988) defines 'Works' more or less entirely as Burney's fictional writings, her then unpublished comedies and gothic tragedies, as well as her novels, though Doody has some telling pages about Burney's experiences at the royal court.[38] This striking shift in focus was accompanied by the first publication in the Oxford World's Classics series of *Cecilia*, followed in the same series by *The Wanderer* in 1991. The number of books and articles published about her novels and plays has grown greatly since. The shift away from the journals was confirmed with a change in nomenclature. The author was called 'Fanny Burney' on the front cover of the Oxford volumes, but 'Frances Burney' on their title pages. 'Fanny', always used by biographers and editors until then (and still current in some British publications) is now usually replaced by 'Frances' as in the *Court Journals*, as more respectful and less disconcerting to North American readers.

In this book 'Fanny' is sometimes used when the context is familial, since her husband, her sisters and her father all called her by that name, just as she called her sister Susanna or Susan.[39] Madame d'Arblay is used when her status as a married woman is important. The focus here is almost wholly on Frances Burney's journals: her plays and novels are only alluded to when they throw light on the non-fictional works under discussion. But the question of fictionality – fictionality *within* non-fictional writing – cannot be avoided in a study concerned with Burney's journals, or – as mentioned in the Introduction – with modern illness narratives. A complication of that question occurs when, as in Burney's case, the author's original manuscripts are known to have been tinkered with (to put it lightly) both by herself and by her early editors.

Peter Sabor, the general editor of the *Court Journals and Letters*, writes that '[i]n the last two decades of her long life, from the death of her husband Alexandre in 1818 to the failure of her eyesight in 1839, Frances Burney d'Arblay strove to create an edition of her own journals and letters.'[40] She was forced to hand over the tremendous task of turning the enormous amount of manuscript material into something like a readable and coherent account of her life to her niece Charlotte Barrett, who gathered a team of helpers around her, and eventually brought *Diary and Letters* to publication in seven volumes between 1842 and 1847. In effect Barrett's edition is a creative reworking of the documents she inherited from her aunt. To call it 'creative' is to recognise the magnitude of her task, but it is hardly the word to describe the process of rewriting and cutting that first Burney and then Barrett, who was evangelically inclined, performed with their pens, scissors, and glue pot. Both worked assiduously to ensure that nothing inappropriate or damaging to the family got into the public domain. The court journals were especially tampered with. Sabor writes, for instance, that about three-quarters of the available material for 1789 was rejected.[41] This also involved, most obviously, censoring passages about the royals and giving false names to people at court, so that in Madame d'Arblay's record of those years, Colonel Digby appears as 'Colonel Fairly', and Colonel Greville as 'Colonel Welbred'. Even in the modern editions, painstakingly restored and recovered, there are words and even phrases that Burney's scoring out has made it impossible for the editors to read.

A prior process of alteration and censorship may also have taken place, one in Burney's original writing up of her memories. In *Frances Burney: A Literary Life* (2000) Janice Farrar Thaddeus notes that Burney's *Memoirs of Doctor Burney* exhibits what was by then an old-fashioned slippage between fact and fiction. 'This fluidity of discourse is reflected in Burney's memoir of her father, especially in her way of heightening scenes with detail,' she writes. Moreover, she suggests that

'Burney herself remained a palimpsest or a miscellany' of eighteenth-century habits, and a more modern dedication to veracity. It follows, Thaddeus argues, that 'the most pertinent approach to the *Memoirs of Doctor Burney* is to see it both as autobiographical and as a species of fiction.'[42] Thaddeus's remarks could apply, though perhaps in a tempered form, to all of Burney's autobiographical writings.[43] It is rare to catch Burney actually falsifying by cutting her record, but there is an instance in the account of her meeting with the convalescing king, discussed in the next chapter.

Her style, or rather more than her style, her temperamental leaning, was increasingly towards heightened phrasing and extremities of recalled emotion. Open any page of her letters and journals and you find variations on expressions like 'the torturing state of my poor heart and soul'. Was her mind calm, she asks, on one occasion with Stephen Digby: 'O No! – All was discord there! Perplexity – confusion, – contrariety! Terror!' Typically, the lancet used by the apothecary to cut the surface of her son's skin during his inoculation has a 'slaughtering design'. The effect of this habitual hyperbolic intensity, while not disabling the narrative authority (forgivable perhaps in letters to one's nearest and dearest, and often enough seemingly required by the material) is to incite her modern reader to suspect that such violent emotions cannot all be truly or accurately recalled, or rather perhaps to incite him or her to feel so much that they feel nothing precisely at all. It is hard to believe too that journals recording events that occurred months or even years before are not heightened with retrospective imagination. Nevertheless, by and large, one is compelled, as I have suggested, to accept the reconstituted journals as trustworthy records of events and emotions.

There is one apparently good piece of evidence as to the accuracy of Frances Burney's memory. This is the often-cited fact that her reports back to the court of speeches made during the sensational impeachment trials of Warren Hastings between 1788 and 1791 were deemed fuller and more accurate than those in newspaper reports. The queen repeatedly asked her to be her proxy at the sessions of the trial, so reliable were thought the memories she carried back to the court. Although remembering the gist of rhetorical and formally delivered speeches is quite different from remembering the run and play of conversations, as well as the registering of smiles, gestures, hesitations, and tones, there is no reason to think that Burney's often very long passages of remembered dialogue are actually made up. Moreover, the chapters in this book are focused on sequences in Burney's journals relating events that were in themselves highly dramatic and momentous, and might therefore legitimately arouse powerful, even extreme, emotions.

Hester Davenport, the author of *Faithful Handmaid: Fanny Burney at the Court of King George III* (2000), widely accepted as the best account of that period, imagines what Burney might have written if she had not been consigned to the court for those years, but writes that: 'To put it crudely, a novel between *Cecilia* and *Camilla* would be likely to have shared the characteristics of both: some excellent characters and dialogue, some lively scenes with social interest, but for modern readers too long, too moral and too sentimental.' Davenport adds that 'the journals offer events, characters and dialogue vivid as any to be found in a novel.'[44] This book is founded on the belief that Burney's journal writings, especially as now published, are certainly worth as much attention as her fictions. By treating four episodes under the rubric of pathography, I hope to show that her extraordinary life resulted, among much else, in some extraordinary accounts of medical experience.

Notes

1. Madame d'Arblay, *Memoirs of Dr Burney*, II, p. 123.
2. Deborah Rohr's *The Careers of British Musicians* does not discuss Charles Burney, but provides a compelling analysis of the contested, and often ambiguous, status of musicians in this period.
3. Balderston, K., ed., *Thraliana*, I, p. 329.
4. I have given an account of Burney's rendering of Johnson's conversation in '"Gay Sam, Agreeable Sam"'.
5. Balderston, K., ed., *Thraliana*, I, p. 413.
6. Spenser, J., 'Evelina and Cecilia', p. 30.
7. Cooke, S., ed., *Additional Journals*, p. 150, p 151; see also Lonsdale, R., *Dr Charles Burney*, p. 286.
8. Ribiero, A., ed., *The Letters of Dr Charles Burney*, p. 464.
9. Doody, M., *Frances Burney*, p. 154.
10. Hemlow, J., *The History of Fanny Burney*, p. 90.
11. Cooke, S., ed., *Additional Journals*, p. 181.
12. James, H., '*The Lesson of the Master*' and Other Stories, 'The Figure in the Carpet', p. 145. But note that Mrs Thrale's diary uses these markers even more indiscriminately.
13. CJL I, 8.
14. This was Charlotte Gunning, who was jealous of Burney's friendship with Stephen Digby. Clark, L., ed., *Court Journals*, IV, p. 441.

15. Sabor, P., ed., *The Court Journals and Letters of Frances Burney*, I, p. 208.

16. Ibid., p. 207.

17. Cooke, S., ed., *The Court Journals and Letters of Frances Burney*, II, p. 290.

18. Doody, M., *Frances Burney*, p. 177.

19. Harman, C., *Fanny Burney*, p. 225.

20. Sabor, P., ed., *The Court Journals and Letters of Frances Burney*, I, p. xviii.

21. 'If you can cut out a volume of Digby, it will be an improvement,' her daughter told Charlotte Barrett, Burney's first editor, in 1842: cited in Note H, p. 493 of Hemlow's biography.

22. This and subsequent references to events in 1790 will be to Dobson, A., ed., *Diary and Letters of Madam d'Arblay*, as DL. This citation is to Volume IV, p. 429.

23. JL Vol. II, p.11

24. It's an impressive list, including two royals, Mrs Siddons and a long gathering of 'Right Honourables'. Sabor, P., *The Subscription List to Frances Burney's Camilla*. Jane Austen knew Burney's novels well, and several references to *Camilla* appear in her letters.

25. Hemlow, J., *Fanny Burney*, p. 290.

26. Ibid., p. 292.

27. Harman, C., *Fanny Burney: A Biography*, p. 300.

28. *Memoir of Baron Larrey*, p. 229. No author or editor is given.

29. DL VI, 347.

30. JL VIII, 340.

31. JL VIII, 354.

32. JL VIII, 375.

33. JL VIII, 424.

34. JL VIII, 428.

35. For an excellent account up to 2007, see Clark, L., 'The Afterlife and Further Reading'.

36. Dobson, A., ed., *Diary and Letters of Madame D'Arblay*, VI, postscript, p. xiii.

37. Epstein, J., *The Iron Pen*.

38. Doody, M., *Frances Burney*, pp. 170–174. Doody uses the court diaries to throw light on Burney's tragic dramas; she does not discuss the journals in their own right, and they do not appear in her bibliography.

39. Her father occasionally also called Frances 'Fan'.

40. 'History of the Manuscripts and Early Editions', in Sabor, P., ed., *The Court Journals and Letters of Frances Burney*, I, pp. xxvi–xxx, xxvi.

41. Ibid., p. xxx.

42. Thaddeus, J. F., *Frances Burney*, p. 198.

43. Austin Dobson's treatment of this topic is worth considering. In Burney's novels, he writes, 'having invented a character, she proceeds to make it talk itself into being,' and she does the same, he argues, with living persons: 'having mentally noted their tricks of speech, their favourite topic, their line of argument, she sets about what she calls "theatricalising a dialogue" in which

they reveal themselves. In one case, fiction operates on fiction; in the other, fiction operates upon fact, with manifest advantages . . . it is probably far more convincing than History, for, however imagination may have coloured the picture, the artist's intent was to be veracious.' 'Postscript', *Diary and Letters of Madame D'Arblay*, VI, pp. xiii, xiv.

44. Davenport, H., *Faithful Handmaid*, pp. 188, 189.

CHAPTER 2

The King, the Court, and 'Madness': 1788–1789

King George III is undoubtedly the most famous 'mad' patient in British history. The most dramatic and consequential episode of his illness set in during October 1788 and lasted until late February 1789. These were five months during which the English court, the political class, and the general public were ceaselessly agitated by conflicting reports and predictions. George's frenzy or derangement, whatever it was, and however it was diagnosed, had consequences for the state and for the constitution. Since the king was unable to carry out his official duties, and it was thought possible he would never recover, his illness occasioned an extended and fierce struggle for power between the Tory Party, under William Pitt, long supported by the king, and the opposition Whigs, led by Charles Fox and patronised by the king's eldest son, the Prince of Wales. Everyone had their ideas about what was the matter and how to treat it: speculation, in both senses, was rife. Daily bulletins were issued by George III's doctors, but their patient's condition fluctuated: if the reports promised recovery, Pitt and his government were safe; if the king's condition seemed incurable, and possibly fatal, the Prince of Wales was all too ready to step into his father's shoes and to become, if not king, then regent with all of a king's authority.

Frances Burney had served as Keeper of the Robes to George's consort, Queen Charlotte, for little more than two years when the first signs of the catastrophe that was to engulf the court emerged. It was possibly the first symptoms of his illness that sent the king to try the Cheltenham waters in June 1788. In July Burney noted that the king had 'a flow of spirits at this time quite unequaled' (CJL III, 324), which might be a polite way of saying there was something frightening about his elevated moods.[1] As she was often in their majesties' company, Burney was able to observe and to record in her journals the king's increasingly disturbing symptoms, and later, when he was locked away from his family and all but a few attendants, to capture the effects of the crisis as it played out within the royal household, itself ultimately under house arrest. Burney's journals show that 'madness' metastasising through the court, affecting everyone, including Burney herself, in strange and curious ways.

Her records constitute a pathographic narrative less of the king's illness alone than of the queen's, Burney's own, and the courtiers' distress. These journals are far from the only source of information about those months, however. There are medical records, of course, letters and reminiscences of other witnesses, such as Lady Harcourt, and other diaries, including those of the Duchess of Devonshire, hostess of the Whigs, and Betsy Sheridan, sister of Richard Brinsley, who had become Fox's right-hand man. Most importantly, Colonel Robert Fulke Greville (1751–1824), one of the king's equerries, kept a meticulous and detailed, even intimate, daily record of the king's behaviour and its consequences over four months. He is the 'Colonel Welbred' – 'equal and pleasing' – of the early editions of Burney's diaries. In this chapter Greville's lesser-known reports are drawn on to supplement and contrast with Frances Burney's account of the same months.

Burney first became aware that something was seriously wrong with King George III in October 1788. Her brief note or memorandum for Friday the seventeenth reads as follows:

> Our return to Windsor is postponed till to-morrow; the King is not well; – he has not been quite well some time, – yet nothing, I hope, alarming, – though there is an uncertainty as to his complaint not very satisfactory. – So precious, too, is his Health! (CJL IV, 480)

Reading between the lines – or the dashes – there is more anxiety here than the writer will admit to herself. Burney must have heard of previous mysterious 'illnesses' that had afflicted the king, and she certainly knew of the complaints that had sent him to try the waters. His symptoms now were also physiological – a rash on his arm and excruciating pain in his stomach and bowels, as one of the queen's attendants, Lady Harcourt, reported – but they were soon followed by behaviour that was much more troubling.

The court was then staying at Kew Lodge, and expecting to leave soon for Windsor Castle, the main royal residence at that time. The next day Burney reports that '[t]he King was this morning better. My Royal Mistress told me Sir George Baker was to settle whether we returned to Windsor to Day or to-morrow' (CJL IV, 482). Baker, a distinguished physician and the king's doctor, was evidently less sanguine about his patient's condition, and the court's return in fact was delayed for a week. Frances lamented their 'detention', but her days were alleviated by a visit to her room by Colonel Stephen Digby (1742–1800), the queen's vice-chancellor, with whom she had formed a friendship at Cheltenham, and almost the only one among the courtiers whose company she found congenial.

On 22 October Baker, seriously disturbed by the king's behaviour, wrote to Pitt, the prime minister, that he had left the king 'in an agitation of spirits nearly bordering on delirium'.[2] He was at a loss for a diagnosis of the patient's symptoms. The next day, however, the king seemed better and the court was allowed to travel. Though at Windsor the king resumed his normal routine, there were ongoing symptoms of emotional instability, and Burney had an alarming encounter with him on the evening of the twenty-fifth:

> I had a sort of conference with His Majesty – or rather I was the object to whom he spoke – with a manner so uncommon, that a high Fever alone could account for it, – a rapidity, a hoarseness of voice, a volubility, an earnestness, – a *vehemence*, rather, – it startled me inexpressibly, – yet with a *graciousness*! – exceeding even all I ever met with before – it was almost *kindness* – Heaven – Heaven preserve him! – The Queen grows more & more uneasy, – she alarms me sometimes for herself, – at other times, she has a sedateness that *wonders* me still more. (CJL IV, 497–498)

During this first phase of the monarch's illness, as the medical historians Ida Macalpine and Richard Hunter claim, Burney's reports 'become at this stage paradoxically more informative than those of the royal physician'.[3] They are more than informative in the strict clinical sense. Burney here unconsciously mimics in the rendering of her own distress the tumbling, incoherent rhythmic pattern of the king's speech. Her shock, with its undertone of panic, is conveyed through the apparently incidental employment of dashes, exclamation marks and italics, none of which one would expect to find in a clinical note or case history. Through these the emotions of the observer are manifest. Havi Carel makes this a distinction between a 'naturalistic' and a 'phenomenological' approach.[4] Moreover, unlike clinical reports, focusing on the isolate patient's symptoms, Burney's account here and elsewhere presents the king in his family and cultural context, and attends, as modern pathographies so often do, to the collateral damage of a severe or fatal illness within the family. In this instance, the worst damage, as Burney, her personal attendant, was to frequently observe, fell on the queen. As royal personages, the family became an egregious example of the suffering and distortion of normal relationships that serious illness of one family member can inflict on the others. This recording of an encounter with the ill person is thus quite different from the sober, 'objective' reporting of clinical symptoms by physicians.

In a 'journal letter' to her sister Susan, begun a few days later, Burney recalls another incident that occurred more or less at the same time:

> I was present at his first seeing Lady Effingham, on his return to Windsor this last Time: 'My dear Effy, he cried, you see me – all at once – *an old man* –!'
>
> I was so much affected by this exclamation, that I wished to run out of the Room. – Yet I could not but recover, when Lady Effingham, in her well meaning, but literal way, composedly answered 'We must all grow old, Sir, – I am sure *I* do! – '
>
> He then produced a *Walking stick*, which he had just ordered: he could not, he said, get on without it: his strength seemed diminishing Hourly.
>
> He took the Bark, he said, 'But the Queen, he cried, is my Physician; – & no man need have a better! – she is my *Friend*, and no man can have a better! – she is my *Friend*, – and no man *can* have a better!'
>
> How the Queen commanded herself I cannot conceive. (CJL IV, 504)

Burney here again embeds the king's illness in the context of his family and the court. It's a dramatic encounter, this time rendering a scene in which the interplay between the four participants is an integral part of the tragi-comic medley. At the same time, it characterises the affectionate, or feverishly over-affectionate, tendency of the king's behaviour – an aspect of his personality that was to take indiscreet and exacerbated form as his condition deteriorated. In a comment a few days later, Burney sums up: 'We are all here in a most uneasy state, – the King is *better* & *worse* so frequently, & changes so Daily, backwards & forwards, that every thing is to be apprehended, if his nerves are not some way quieted' (CJL IV, 507). The feature that Burney succinctly identifies – that extreme agitation and torrents of 'mad' rambling were often followed by a period of apparent calm and rationality, and this by renewed violence – is a key aspect of the king's condition over the next months. It made the medical bulletins that were issued daily extremely unreliable, since a quiet morning might be followed an hour or two later by a reversion to crazy incoherence. But this was not the only reason why the bulletins were misleading. They were in effect political documents, and were framed with a view to their political implications.

It is the queen's distress that Burney records in these early days of George's illness. Soon she mentions that 'the Queen is almost over-powered with some secret terror':

I am affected beyond all expression in her presence, to see what struggles she makes to support serenity. – To Day, she gave up the conflict, when I was alone with her, & burst into a violent fit of tears – It was very – very terrible to see! How did I wish her a Susan or a Fredy! – to unburthen her loaded mind would be to relieve it from all but *inevitable* affliction: O may Heaven in its mercy never – never drive *me* to that solitary anguish more! (CJL VI, 507)

There is something tragic about this moment. The queen is condemned to be queenly in the presence of her inferiors; struggling to maintain the decorum and aloofness that befits her office and status, she breaks down in front of Burney, a sensitive woman who is alone with her, and who might conceivably have been a confidante and comforter. But protocol prevents Burney offering that consolation to someone so much above her, and who is struggling to deal with her anguish, even though Burney has known, as she declares, a similar lonely anguish herself. Writing to her sisters, she perhaps excusably, here and subsequently, focuses as much on her own distress as on the queen's.

Burney also records here that another famous doctor, William Heberden, has been called in.[5] (He was only the first of a string of other eminent physicians summoned to the court.[6]) But her account for this day (3 November) ends with a note that is significant for the interpretation of all that follows. She writes as to her readers, 'Ah, my dearest Friends! I have no more fair running Journal.' In other words, from this time onwards, she has no more entries fully written up the day they occurred. Instead what she now writes is dependent on the brief memoranda she kept each day, and sometimes she hasn't even these. This means that for the next months of the king's illness her journal, though apparently and designedly appearing to be a similarly spontaneous diary, is in fact written (and probably polished, elaborated, filled out, perhaps dramatised) much, probably months, later.[7] Moreover, she is dependent for news about the king's condition from secondary sources, which protocol often forbids her to disclose to her readers. What she writes about the king becomes more distant and generalised as his condition worsens, apparently less and less reliable.

On 5 November she records, obviously retrospectively, that:

At noon, the King went out, in his Chaise, with the Princess Royal, an airing. I looked from my window to see him; – he was all smiling benignity, but gave so many orders to the Postillions, & got in & out of the Carriage twice, with such agitation, that again my fear of a great Fever hanging over him grew more & more powerful.

Alas! – how little did I imagine I should see him no more for so long – so black a period! (CJL IV, 509)

That evening it is from Digby that she learns 'the whole of the mysterious horrour!' of the king's breaking out at dinner with his family into delirium and violence, driving the queen into hysterics and the Prince of Wales apparently into tears. When she is summoned into the queen's presence, she would have collapsed, she declares, if she had not been quieted by Digby's stoical and pious talk earlier in the evening (CJL VI, 514–515).

On the morning of the sixth, the atmosphere of fear and dread in the court affects Burney and she bursts into tears when the queen speaks to her:

> She looked like Death – colourless & wan, but *Nature* is infectious – the Tears gushed from her own Eyes, & a perfect agony of weeping ensued, which, once begun, she could not stop. – She did not, indeed, try; for when it subsided, & she wiped her Eyes, she said 'I thank you, Miss Burney, – you have made me cry! – it is a great relief to me. I had not been able to cry all this Night long!' (CJL VI, 517)

'Nature is infectious': it was becoming clear that the turbulence and horror of the king's condition was pervading the whole court. 'The Queen was very wretched; poor Mrs Schwellenberg all spasm & horrour, Miss Planta all restlessness; the House all mystery; & my only Informant & comforter distanced!' (CJL VI, 543), Burney wrote four days later: her 'comforter', naturally, was Digby. When considering the course and nature of the relationship that developed between Miss Burney and Colonel Digby, it is certainly necessary to consider the horribly disturbed circumstances in which they were thrown together.

The queen was still occupying a room next to the king's apartment, where he was now confined with his doctors and pages and was talking, or raving, incessantly. That same morning she commanded Miss Burney to listen in to what her husband was saying:

> Nothing could be so afflicting as this task: – even now, it brings fresh to my Ear his poor exhausted voice – 'I am *nervous*, he cried, I am not *ill*, but I am *nervous*: if you would know what is the matter with me, I am *nervous*. But I love you both very well; if you would tell me *truth*: I love Dr. Heberden best, for he has not told me a lie; Sir George has told me a lie: – a *white* lie, he says; but I hate a white lie! if you *will* tell me a lie, let it be a *black* lie!'
> This was what he kept saying almost constantly: mixed in with other matter, but always returning & in a voice – that truly will never cease vibrating in my recollection! (CJL IV, 518–519)

The word 'vibrating' captures both the thin, hoarse, wavering quality of the king's voice and its presence in Burney's memory. Though Burney characteristically emphasises her own suffering as well as the king's, no other witness records his speech during this crisis with such exactness, with its frantic, pathetic struggle to retain rationality and to keep craziness at bay. Burney's journal for the next few days conveys a still more vivid sense of the horrible anxiety and confusion that filled the castle. The queen more than once in Burney's presence 'gave way to a perfect agony of grief & affliction', crying '*What will become of me! – what will become of me!*' (CJL IV, 523).

Frances tells her sisters that she remembers things she 'never would write' and that 'all I have put down was known to other witnesses.' The questions of protocol and confidentiality mentioned here have to be borne in mind when interpreting Burney's journal records for this time. Other circumstantial evidence suggests that either Miss Burney was kept in ignorance of the details of the king's treatment or that she forbade herself from mentioning them.

Robert Greville's diary opens on that very day ('O Dreadful Day!') of 5 November 1788, when Burney last saw the king. This was a significant date because it marked the doctors' recognition that the monarch's condition was very serious and likely to get worse. So wild in fact had become his speech and actions that he was confined to his own apartment and wholly separated from the queen and his daughters. The Prince of Wales commanded that the castle should go into lockdown: no visitors were to be allowed; no letters were to be sent or received; no one in the household was even permitted to leave the building itself. Under house arrest, Burney never saw her father, her sisters, or her friends and was scarcely to breathe fresh air for three months. Greville, the king's favourite personal attendant, hurried back from London when alarming news of the monarch's dreadful state reached him, and from then onwards he kept a daily, and on many days hourly, record of the king's condition. It is apparent that his reports are written shortly after the events they record, and that they are kept at least in some respects as part of his duty – to leave an accurate and reliable testimony to events of public and historical importance.

Greville's account, headed 'His Majesty's Ist Illness in the Year 1788–9', is almost 200 pages long.[8] Like Burney's journal, his entries do not constitute a continuous narrative, but their unremitting focus on the patient and his illness certainly make his work pathographic. He notices expressions and gestures and records dramatic situations and dialogues. The scenes that Burney now writes about take place overwhelmingly in her own room; his account is largely confined to what happens within the king's apartments. Unlike Burney, and except for an occasional 'Alas!', he gives little direct expression to his own emotional life, which is mostly concentrated on his subject, his behaviour, and his attending personnel. But this impersonal quality is also quite unlike a medical record because, implicitly, his own feelings, his loyalty towards the king, and his concern for his royal master infuse almost everything he writes.

Greville pens brief notes for the first days after his arrival, but on 12 November, clearly frightened and distressed by the king's symptoms, he puts together a long and detailed account of the day and night just passed. The king had not slept at all the night of the eleventh (Greville must have been informed of this by the pages whose duty it was to watch over him), and he writes of 'constant rambling of thought' during the next day till 'At length this Extreme agitation, continued through the two last hours, caused a Violent perspiration – He called to have the Windows opened, and complained of burning' (G: 82).[9] After a little time 'He became more violent,' and 'He put Himself in a violent perspiration.' Greville sat up all night 'with H.M²' and observed with consternation his extreme shifts of mood. About three in the morning the king 'had a violent struggle, jerking very strongly with his Arms & legs, but made no attempt to rise – Three quarters of an hour after this, he became quite recollected'. Greville observes that 'He had been without sleep for above twenty-nine Hours.' Apparently the king slept after Greville was relieved at 5:00 AM. The next days too '[t]he ramblings continued' and he 'complained much of heat & burning' (G: 83, 84).

The queen, wisely in Greville's opinion, had delegated all the arrangements regarding the king's treatment to his physicians, who wanted to keep him as quiet as possible, and therefore thought that the equerries should be prevented from entering the king's bedroom. But – this is almost the last occasion when the king's wishes prevailed – two were allowed to see him, of whom Greville was one. Given that on 16 November 'H.M took a warm Bath for fifteen Minutes – Its Temperature 95°', a modern reader might wonder why the patient's own temperature was not taken, since his 'burning' fairly obviously indicates a fever and therefore an infection.[10] The doctors regularly took the king's pulse rate and were alarmed.[11]

The equerries did not enter the king's room when the physicians and surgeons were attending their patient, which explains why Greville gives little information at this stage of their treatments, most of which would have been designed to draw 'noxious humours' from the body. It seems to have been Sir Lucas Pepys, a physician called in on 18 November, who instigated blistering, which was the application of a caustic substance to the skin so that infection would develop at the site. The resulting effusion of pus was thought to bring out the toxic substances. Apparently the king's shaved head was treated on the theory that whatever was wrong with his brain would be remedied by having the bad humours drawn upwards. It is certainly clear that the king's legs and feet were blistered and that this was to cause him prolonged pain.[12] On the evening of the eighteenth Pepys ordered 'Carded Wool & Bootikins of Woolen Yarn' applied to the king's feet, probably to stop him touching the blistered flesh (G: 89).

As a hard-working and diligent head of state, the king had managed his households and estates, consulted with his ministers, and worked on parliamentary business with care. He was used to giving orders and being obeyed. One feature of his delirium was refusal or inability to give up the habit of his twenty-eight years in the job. The king 'struggles hard for Obedience', wrote Greville (G: 87). He gave cascades of directions continually, some fantastic, some sensible. But he was confronted by the equally entrenched authority of the doctors. Similarly used to giving orders and strengthened by the mandate of the queen, they decided how he should be treated, determined who might come into his room, and deceived him when they thought it necessary. On the grounds that lack of stimulus would quiet him, they did not allow him even to look through the window to see his younger children (G: 93). Greville thought this unnecessary and painful. As the king's servant, but bound to obey the physicians, he found his position stressful.

On 21 November, for example, 'HM' said he wanted Colonel Digby to sleep in his apartment, and he had ordered a couch brought into the room and prepared. Recollecting that Digby was not well (he was in fact suffering from severe gout), the king then asked Doctors Baker and Reynolds if they had any objection to Greville sleeping in his room. 'They did not give an immediate answer, but looked at each other' (G: 95). It required some adroitness on Greville's part to persuade the next physician on duty to confront the king, but he was eventually cajoled into dropping this idea, and he did order the couch removed. Next day, when Greville saw the king, he had to agree with the physicians that 'all was now very wrong indeed' (which probably means that the king's speech had become 'not free from Indecencies' – the obscene notions and foul language which, on other evidence, was to become a feature of his ravings) (G: 98). The king, 'very restless and loquacious', issued various hurried commands and instructions, impossible to carry out, and the next day was the same. The normally restrained Greville gives expression to his feelings: 'at this time what with the favor which is extended to Me, & also from the power I am supposed to hold, independent of the controul of the Doctors, I have enough to do from an unceasing string of Orders' (G: 97). Later he confesses that: 'Painful indeed are now the passing hours, & My head becomes Weary, from the continual fidget around Me, which unceasing conversations, & constant hurry of contrivances gives rise to'(G: 100). Meeting him for the first time two days later, Frances Burney thought: 'He looked very sallow & ill; these night watches, & this close attendance, disagree with them all' (CJL IV, 587). Worn down, he seemed to her hopeless about the king's condition.

The turbulent, conflicted atmosphere within the castle similarly affected the king's friend Stephen Digby. Not only was the king's behaviour violent and unpredictable, the doctors made conflicting decisions, were in disagreement about his prognosis, the Prince of Wales himself issued orders, and fear, tension and uncertainty, even, in Burney's word, 'horrour' pervaded the court. As the crisis deepened during November, Digby, who as the queen's vice-chancellor had many calls on his time and must have had many delicate negotiations to undertake, began to spend his evenings in Miss Burney's secluded apartment. There he read extracts from Cowper's *The Task* to her and, sitting at her table, composed many of the diplomatic letters he needed to write, sometimes showing her the contents. Burney wrote in her record for 23 November:

> 'I wish, he cried, while he was making some memorandums, I could live without sleep! I know not now how to spare my night.'
> He then explained to me various miscellaneous matters of occupation, & confessed himself forced to break from the confused scene of action as much as possible, where the tumult & bustle were as overpowering, as the afflic-tion, in the more quiet apartments, was dejecting. Then – by implication, what credit did he not give to *my* poor still Room, – which he made me understand, in every way but saying so directly, was his only refuge & consolation in this miserable House. (CJL IV, 581)

'Harrowed to the very soul with surrounding afflictions', Burney was confined to her room, her only regular companion the jealous, ill-tempered Mrs Schwellenberg, who still insisted Burney play cards with her for hours every evening, her only attendance on the afflicted and despairing queen, and 'without a glimpse of Light to when or how all might terminate' (CJL IV, 571). She naturally became grateful to and emotionally invested in her suave, kind, and gentlemanly visitor. When they joked together, she was glad: 'satisfied in both making & hearing a speech that, on both sides, seemed openly disclaiming all views or thoughts beyond common, though sincere Friendship' (CJL IV, 546). Something more than friendship might be hinted at here.

Frances Burney did have another friend in Dr Lucas Pepys, with whom she was to have many 'conferences'. He had been one of Samuel Johnson's medical attendants and a great favourite with her friend Hester Thrale earlier in the decade; he and Burney were old acquaintances.[13] The boot-ikins were soon removed, and the king wrote out very clearly an undoubt-edly sane memorandum forbidding Pepys 'to attend the present confinement'.[14] This was ignored, and Pepys kept on. He politely visited Miss Burney shortly after his appointment and reassured her that 'His Royal Patient would *certainly recover*, though not immediately' (CJL IV, 561). Pepys was the only physician who held to that view from this time and throughout the king's illness – a view with clear-cut political consequences. Frances found her frequent consultations with him a great comfort. Even when everyone around her, including Digby, seemed to have given up hope, he endorsed her own conviction, held from the onset of the king's illness, that the king would get well again.[15]

Another old acquaintance was the fashionable and very successful phy-sician Dr Richard Warren, who had also attended Johnson in his last illness. Baker, unable to deal with the crisis, had summoned Warren to his aid on 6 November. Meeting this doctor by chance outside the queen's apartment, Burney wanted to ask about the king, but Warren, though very courteous, 'would not enter upon that subject' (CJL IV, 538). He was a Whig, physician to the Prince of Wales, and the king adamantly refused to see him. Warren was forced to eavesdrop on George's ravings from the next room and deliver his opinion. On this slim evidence he pronounced 'the king's life to be in the utmost danger' and that 'the seizure upon the brain was so violent, that if he did live, there was little reason to hope that his intellects would be restored'.[16] The doctor lost no time in conveying this grim verdict to the rival court of the prince. Burney recognised the drastic significance of this: '*Already* to become but second, even for a king!' (CJL IV, 523) Warren's medical position, diametrically opposed to Pepys's, was also not to deviate for months.

Warren was in favour of strict seclusion, and on 24 November signed an order that only one equerry would be permitted in the king's room. When Baker found this out he cancelled it. Greville's account of the resulting 'turbulence' in the king's chamber graphically illustrates the tensions and conflicts that involved everyone in attendance on the king. Warren and Baker went into the king's apartment:

On seeing them H.M. was angry & agitated, on which Co^l Goldsworthy looking out of his Apartment, called for Two Equerries to Come in – Co^l. Manners and Myself immediately went in – We found The King violently agitated & very Angry, but more particularly with Dr Warren – Shortly after some other Gentlemen in Attendance & Pages came into the room – Dr Warren spoke to The King & endeavor'd to pacify Him – He requested at the same time that He might feel his Pulse – This the King refused & then getting up briskly He desired Dr Warren to leave the room, telling Him He had sent Him a harsh order that day, & which Sir George Baker had got altered – Dr Warren still tried to pacify H.M^y upon which the King advanced up to Him & pushed Him – Colonel Manners & Myself being at this time close behind Dr Warren, interfered, & stopped His Majesty, who on this, & seeing others coming up, He retired from Dr Warren, pale with anger, & foaming with rage. (G: 101)

On 27 November a meeting was held at the queen's lodge at which members of the Cabinet, including Pitt, the Prince of Wales and the physicians, decided that the king and the court should be removed to the other royal residence at Kew. This was ostensibly (as the king was informed) so that he might benefit from a 'change of air', but it is likely, given that his condition had drastically worsened, that what was in mind was a place of asylum. At Kew a permanently 'mad' monarch could be kept away from the public eye. What ensued was a battle of wills with an almost tragic cast. The plan was that 'her Majesty & the Princesses should go away quietly', Burney reported, '& then that the King should be told they were gone, which was the sole method they could devise to prevail with him to follow. He was then to be allured by a promise of seeing them at Kew' (CJL IV, 601). Informed of the scheme on 29 November, the king would not hear of moving. The process of persuasion or bribery was begun by the prime minister informing him that the queen had already left: the king objected that she 'had gone without leave, & that She should return to supplicate his pardon' (G: 107).[17] When Greville and Harcourt, another equerry, attempted to persuade him, the king, still in bed, abruptly drew the bed curtains and refused to listen to them. He drafted a letter to the colonel of the Welsh Fuzileers on duty at Windsor. Greville suspected that he was hoping to summon military aid.

The king's removal was planned for after 5:00 PM, 'in order to prevent his being seen by any croud'. The November day was closing in. No time was to be lost if the removal was to be carried out as planned. 'Finally a squad of four of his physicians advanced on him.'[18] The king, still in his bed, again demanded that Warren get out and, when he didn't, jumped up to punch him. Greville laid hold of the king's arm and managed to restrain him. 'On this a firmer Tone was assumed & He was plainly told that He must go, or that other means must be resorted to. ——— ' (G: 109). Greville's very long dash here expresses his distress and invites his reader to dwell on the awful significance of this moment. The king was next told that if he still resisted he would be forced. When he delayed dressing, another of the equerries, Manners, took out 'his Watch & holding it up' threatened the king to make haste. 'Finding now that he was press'd on all sides', he gave in. Holding back tears on the way, George, 'with affecting sensibility', as Greville put it, cried, '"Why am I taken from a Place I like best in the World"' (G: 111). The king had been told he would see the queen at Kew, but of course he didn't: on arrival he found he had been assigned rooms far from hers. In the days after, his condition worsened. Three weeks later, there was consternation when it was discovered that the king had been given *King Lear* as light reading.[19] But it is not the resemblance of the kings' 'madness' that strikes one: it is the similarity of the remorseless process by which the monarch is stripped of the last vestiges of authority.[20]

The 'total banishment from all intercourse out of the House, & an unremitting confinement within its Walls!' (CJL IV, 535) that had begun at Windsor was made much worse by conditions at Kew. The old palace was utterly ill prepared for the courtiers' reception: a summer residence, unfit for winter, where the king was consigned, apparently, to the coldest apartment of all. There were no carpets in many of the rooms. Digby was horrified and took on the responsibility of procuring sandbags to stop draughts around the windows and under the doors, and managed to secure carpets, or mats at least, for the royals' rooms. Burney was accommodated, with Mrs Schwellenberg next door, a long way from the queen. She feared 'inevitable destruction' (CJL IV, 623) if she was condemned each day to linger in a cold, dark and wet passage for a page to bring her a report on the king to read to her mistress.[21]

The removal to Kew was accompanied by a significant change in the medical arrangements. In her retrospective account of these early December days Burney writes that 'my poor Royal Mistress began to sink more than I had ever yet seen. – No wonder!– the length of the malady so uncertain – the steps which seemed now requisite so *shocking*! – for *new advice*, & such as suited only disorders that Physicians in general relinquish, was now proposed – & compliance or refusal were almost equally tremendous' (CJL IV, 615). She was not wrong in supposing that this step, to which the queen reluctantly consented, was to have far-reaching consequences. On 5 December the famous 'mad doctor' Dr Francis Willis (1718–1807) came to Kew with his son Dr John Willis and took charge of the king's treatment. This meant that his condition was openly acknowledged as insanity (as the king himself deduced). Greville describes Willis's first visits to the king's apartment. The king shouts at Willis, abuses doctors in general, and becoming 'violently Enraged' rushes at him:

> Doctor Willis remained firm, & reproved him in nervous & determined language, telling Him He must controul Himself otherwise He would put Him in a strait Waistcoat. On this hint, Dr Willis went out of the room & returned directly with one in his hand from the next room. It was in a paper & He now held it under his Arm. The King Eyed it attentively and alarmed at The Doctor's firmness of Voice & procedure, began to submit. He promised to go to bed & with difficulty went to the next apartment & undressed. (G: 120)

It is unusual to find verbs (as opposed to nouns) capitalised in Greville's diaries. Here the conjunction of 'The King Eyed' with 'The Doctor' and 'Voice' manages to dramatise the king's recognising the ominousness of the doctor's threat. It is the first appearance of the 'strait Waistcoat' that was to restrain him frequently over the coming weeks. This was called putting him 'under coercion'. Greville continues with a more reflective account:

> I was much struck with the proper manner & the imposing stile of the Authoritative Language which Dr Willis held on this occasion. It was immediately necessary to have this struggle. He seized the opportunity with Judgement & conducted Himself throughout this Interview with wonderful Management & force. He felt his ground with attention, He parried & attacked as circumstances required with great discernment & Energy. As the Kings Voice rose, attempting Mastery Willis raised his, & its tone was strong and decided[.] As the King soften'd his, that of Doctor Willis dropped to softening Unison, but the King still attempted to over-power in Voice, but found stronger powers in that of Doctor Willis & which on Every trial rose superior. Awed at last by the firmness of his Manner, & baffled in Every attempt to resist it, The King gave way. (G: 120)

After Willis left the king continued to abuse the rest of the physicians, 'principally as He said for not having dealt fairly with Him & and by having concealed from Him his real situation – .' After this 'the Poor Dear King', Greville writes, 'burst into a flood of Tears and wept bitterly'.

Burney had been assigned rooms in the draughty old building, where she was disturbed all night by Mrs Schwellenberg, who was ill, calling for attendance, and since she was 'beginning to grow unwell' herself, the queen graciously issued orders for a removal to take place. Her new accommodation was carpeted and much better furnished, but it was only what might be called a bed-sitting room. Though Burney was nervous because she had '*only a sleeping room above*' (CJL IV, 619), Digby promised, 'I will be much more discreet than *Peeping Tom!*' (CJL V, 625), and soon after bounded upstairs determined to visit her.

> I met him at the Door, where he stopt short, smiling, & very conscious, yet not very *repentant*, that he came an *unbidden Guest*; – 'May I – he cried, very humbly, *may* I – come in? –'
> 'You must appear, I answered, in the Character of a Physician; no one else properly visits such places as these!'
> And, then, placing him a Chair opposite to a window, I told him he must sit exactly there & make it his sole prospect, without turning to the right or the left. (CJL IV, 622)

In other words, he must not look at her bed. Is this dialogue flirtatious or not? If it is, what is Burney's purpose in recording it? Does she remember (that is, record) it because it is flirtatious? The next evening, Digby comes again, unannounced, up the two flights of stairs. He suddenly recalls that he ought to go and deliver a message to Dr Willis who is arriving that evening and then that he can get one of the surgeons to deputise for him.[22]

> I saw an arch & droll expression, at some internal idea, rising in his face, & presently, with a half conscious, half-serious smile, he turned to look at the Fire, while he exclaimed 'But I shall not tell him – I am coming back to drink Tea with – *you!*'
> I cannot say this *fact* surprised me, but its declaration did not a little, & with a stare, I cried 'Shall you not?'
> 'N – o!' he answered, – looking yet more away.
> A pause ensued, – I could not *ask* him what I could not wish told; but yet, I thought him *almost too sincere* in acquainting *me* with this intention! (CLV 628).

In Greville's reports of events in the king's apartments, rough usage and physical violence between men is a regular event. It takes different forms: pages forcing the king into the straightjacket, strapping him down in his bed, his assaults or attempted assaults on his attendants and doctors, his equerries turning bouncers as they shoulder in to ward off the enraged and demented patient's attacks. Greville reports facts, actions, in a direct, factual prose. In Burney's narratives of the meetings in her room, the content is nuance, gesture, velleities of significance to be inferred from tones, looks, smiles, and the slightest of movements, and the underlying significance is that these are dialogues between members of the opposite sex. Here, Digby treats as a joke the danger of the rest of the court knowing about his visits, with the subsequent notions about romantic assignations that this might provoke. What is implied in his 'declaration' and his looking away? Certainly the effect of Burney's reporting of this moment is to hint to her readers that *something* (to borrow her own style) is in the air.

Burney became constantly anxious that Digby's frequent visits to her room might become the substance of court gossip. She later learned through Digby himself that even the king has teased him about his frequent visits to 'learned ladies'. She repeatedly records her surprise that a man so courteous and diplomatic should be unaware of the consequences to her reputation if a flirtation between this aristocrat and a humble commoner is suspected. Nevertheless she becomes dependant on his visits for congenial company (and matter for her journal). He shares with her his despondency about life, and she becomes increasingly gratified at his willingness to confide in her – his 'confidence', which in the usage of the time means his sharing of private or secret information, almost certainly about the king, and the various quarrels throughout the castle. 'The comfort of being thus relieved from painful ignorance of all things till they are over,' she writes under the date of 16 December, 'puts me under an obligation to him I can never, I think, forget. He seems indeed to hold back his confidence in nothing' (CJL IV, 661). These confidences or shared secrets naturally become a bond between them.

Digby probably saw the queen every day, and could not have been unaware of Her Majesty's own deterioration and suffering. But it is precisely this knowledge between Miss Burney and Digby that is unavailable to the reader of her record.

Digby's next evening visit on 18 December was so momentous for Burney though that her account of it covers eleven pages in the modern edition (CJL IV, 663–674).[23] Digby tells Miss Burney that he is going away, and almost extracts from her a promise that she will write to him. This makes her anxious enough, and when he goes on to ask her, in a discussion about prayer, what are her own prayers, she parries the question.[24] He then asks to see her prayers, which Burney finds impossible to grant him. She then represents a conversational duel or tug-of-war in which he persists, sometimes in great earnestness, with his request, apparently seeing nothing amiss in what she perceives as an intrusion into her private life. The softness with which 'he pressed on his advantage', with a 'gentleness which had so much interested her on their first acquaintance', she finds unnerving. Though, as she avows, she deeply respects him, she declares she would be 'foolishly exposing' herself to grant him his request and stands her ground.

In the prolonged and anguished rumination that follows, Frances finally confesses, 'my dear Friends, I am writing as if I gave you a window to my Breast – that Mr Digby has conceived an attachment of a far more serious sort than I had believed compatible with the state of his mind' (CJL IV, 675). Recently bereaved, Digby had as early as June discussed with her whether 'second attachments' were permissible, and might even equal the first in strength and happiness – this being couched as a merely theoretical question, accompanied by the denial of the possibility of any such future attachment for himself. Burney has heard a Maid of Honour, a Miss Gunning, mentioned, but is convinced by Digby's manner that any remarriage is out of the question. But perhaps that has changed. 'Whether with a convicted, or an unconscious influence, – whether with any plan, or only some vague idea of forming one', she thinks (without actually saying it) that he might propose to her. It is at least surprising in light of this that the next evening Digby says he has forgotten her Christian name (CJL IV 681). Was it she with whom he read 'Moir'? he asks a day later, and Burney is amazed that he's forgotten.[25] As Lorna Clark writes, 'FB avoids the obvious conclusion, that Digby had recently been reading the same work to another lady or ladies.'[26] Burney certainly (and in her isolated and straitened circumstances, understandably) thinks more about him than he thinks about her.

The day the Willises had arrived in early December Digby gave Burney an account that made her 'quite long to see them' (CJL IV, 639). Their first encounter with the king, as he had reported it, she found 'interesting, curious, extraordinary!, – Full of promise & Hope!' By mid-January she was writing, 'This Morning the news was very chearing, & I have begun now a great Friendship with Dr. Willis & Dr. John. They are most delightful people, all originality, openness, & goodness' (CJL V, 48). The Willises's methods, which involved frequent recourse to tying the patient in the 'strait Waistcoat' for long periods, can seem horrific to modern readers, but their rationale was not (as the king must have perceived it) punitive, but adopted as a means of facilitating his sleep. Whether Burney had learned about the Willises's methods with the king seems unlikely, or perhaps she understood this rationale. As Greville noted, before the Willises arrived the king had sometimes and on more than one occasion had, in addition to the waistcoat, his legs tied as a penalty for violent outbursts.[27] Colonel Digby may not have actually witnessed this treatment of the king, though he must have heard of it, possibly in detail, from Greville or Dundas, the chief surgeon, or one of the pages. If he did

tell Burney of it, this might be one of the 'confidences' she could not share
with her readers.

Burney's entry for Monday, 22 December, begins, 'With what joy did
I carry this morning an exceeding good account of the King to my Royal
Mistress!' (CJL IV, 690). On this day the king's doctors, led by Willis,
reported that he was much improved, which probably enabled the government in the House of Commons to defeat a motion to grant full regency
powers to the Prince of Wales. Digby called into Burney's room to say
goodbye before he took a holiday to see his family: that he should trouble
to take leave of her delighted her. On the twenty-eighth Burney wrote
joyously to her father of the king's recovery. 'The fair signs yesterday were
such as to make my *Anchor* [Sir Lucas Pepys] declare that he now saw *The
understanding was sound* and that '*convalescence* was the word' (CJL
IV, 695).

Both the Willises's notes and Greville's record for this week tell
a different story and cast doubt on the doctors' bulletins.[28] On
Christmas day, for example, Greville wrote, the king 'became troublesome
& turbulent, & so much so that recourse to Coercion became necessary . . .
& when He was reported quiet, He was as deranged as possible, & had
been so for some time –'. 'These were proofs too strong', he added, 'that
a turn was given how these [things] were to be thought of' (G: 133).
Greville's 'turn' is today's 'spin': Willis, in other words, was a spin doctor.
Greville suspected that the violent Tory allowed his politics to determine
his medical bulletins. Willis had in fact sent a positive report to Parliament,
as the Whig Duchess of Devonshire wrote in her diary for the twenty-third:

> Dr Willis on Tuesday tho' he knew the K was in a strait waistcoat sent an
> express to Pitt which was to have found him at the house saying ye K was
> better and wd recover for Willis is a great Pittite and thought it might
> influence the division. Warren reproached him with this and he own'd it.
> Warren said he disgrac'd his former character a Clergyman and his present
> one a Physician by becoming a political note writer.[29]

These were the days, as Betsy Sheridan put it, of 'Wars among the Medical
Tribe'. 'There is not a day now, in the course of which I do not perceive
symptoms of prevailing Jealousies . . . Nothing in my Opinion can be
More prejudicial to H.M.[ys] true Situation,' Greville wrote (G: 132). He
suspected that the Willises kept other medical men away from the king lest
they should disagree with their optimistic assessments. It is certain that the
bulletins were couched in such a way as to further the government's policy
of warding off the prospect of a regency as long as possible. Warren

remained convinced that the king would never recover. On 2 January he refused to sign an optimistic bulletin and said '[h]e could not see that things were mending' (G: 148).

The Willises, Burney's new friends, became in Digby's absence her sources of information – optimistic and heartening information. On 4 January 1789 she wrote that 'all is now promising and fair,' but Greville's journal for that day again suggests that is too optimistic. Though the king was sleeping longer and had periods of calm, it required a lot of dexterity to keep him off dangerous subjects and to control his rages. Greville wrote dryly that 'the day rubbed on without a crash' (G: 152). Despite her joy 'in the great, great point' that the king was still amending, Burney now wrote that her day was 'scarce endurable'. Her journal is filled instead with the horrors of her forced companionship with Mrs Schwellenberg. 'I can give no other interpretation to the <almost constantly> insulting mode of present behaviour except the incapacity of bearing with patience the gloomy confinement inflicted on all the House: which renders a Temper, naturally irascible, fierce & furious even to savageness' (CJL V, 10).[30] After a session of such attacks, a visitor is shocked at her appearance and asks 'what [has] made [her] so *pale & thin* all at once' (CJL V, 9).

During these days in January 1789 the opposition and the Prince of Wales, concerned that their chance for power was slipping away, subjected the physicians to interrogations designed to show that any evidence of remission did not alter the long-term prognosis of madness. They pushed on with the proposal for a regency with full powers to the prince. One historian suggests they hoped 'that with luck, the knowledge that his despised son had been made Regent, might render the King's madness permanent'.[31] Sir Lucas Pepys was questioned on 7 January. In response to the question whether he could 'speak with more certainty . . . when you say His Majesty will recover?' he replied, 'Yes, I think I can.' Willis confirmed his view; Warren stuck to his. But the king was in fact improving and was soon allowed, under escort, to take walks in the Richmond and Kew palace gardens. The queen's name was dragged into the inquiry when it was assumed that she had colluded with the Willises to make the daily bulletins more optimistic. Burney wrote on the tenth: 'my poor Royal Mistress now droops, – I grieve – grieve to see her! – but her own *name & conduct* called in question! – who can wonder that she is shocked & shaken? – Was there not enough before, firmly as she supported it?' (CJL V, 11).

The queen summoned Colonel Digby back that very day. He spent the evening with Miss Burney, and her journal resumes its protracted recording of every detail of their conversation. Digby renews his pleas to see Burney's prayer, 'the most serious request', he calls it. She protests that she would have thought that, in his long time away, he would have forgotten it. He replies, 'very serious' again, 'No! – I have thought of it ever since!' This is enough to set Burney wondering again if he has 'more than a simple meaning'. Her meditations on this point end with the enigmatic statement that 'the *situation*, with all its strangeness, – is common, is nothing, to the *internal* strangeness of the *Person* so situated' (CJL V, 17).[32] When, a few evenings later (on 21 January), they are talking about Burney's friends the Lockes, 'with a most singular smile – half open, half subdued – he precipitately exclaimed "I believe – I shall settle near Leatherhead myself – if ever I settle at all!"', Burney is able to construe this as a 'fervent' declaration of a desire to settle 'in the bosom of *my* friends' and presents herself worrying half the night over whether this 'singular smile' is not evidence that he does not 'in defiance of all obstacles, nourish indeed a regard that threatens either [his] peace or [his] prosperity' (CJL V, 57–58, 59). It is not uncommon for a person in love to read into the slightest, or the apparently ambiguous speeches and behaviour of the beloved, the desired and longed-for signals that they must be loved in return. Burney is perhaps caught in this hapless state, but she seeks to rescue her own independence or agency by telling herself that if he proposes she is honour bound – presumably because of the difference in their stations – to refuse him.

The weather grew warmer (it now became one of the mildest winter months on record) and the king continued his walks with the Willises and their men. But out in front of Kew Lodge on 27 January he caught sight of Robert Greville:

> & eagerly calling for 'Greville' approached Me hastily. Perceiving that I was both seen & known, I advanced towards H. M.[y] Mr Willis was at this time with Him – The King locking My Arm in his, said I should walk with Him, & that He would not part with Me again during the day. (G: 193)

'The first thing He proposed with earnestness to Me', Greville continues, was 'Remember your promise to be my Friend.' The king then asked Greville 'What I would have. Would I have the Treasureship of the Household?' A week later, Frances Burney also met the king in the gardens by accident. 'Sir Lucas Pepys still persisting that exercise & Air were absolutely necessary to save me from illness', she took a walk in either Richmond or Kew Garden every morning. On 2 February she asked

Dr John Willis where she might walk 'in safety', and he told her she would be safe in Kew Garden. This led to the encounter which is deservedly the most reprinted passage of reportage in Burney's court journals – featured, for instance in Roy Porter's *Faber Book of Madness* under the banner 'Fanny Burney meets the madly amorous George III.'[33]

Her report of this incident, in a letter to her sister, takes eight pages in Volume V of the *Court Journals* (though there are extensive notes) (103–111). It is a detailed, dramatic and polished account, evidently from a quick memo made on a scrap of paper soon after the event. As Kate Chisholm, in whose biography of Burney this note appears, writes, in it she describes 'the king's appearance in very different terms from those she eventually used'.[34]

> He is muffled wrapped & disguised
> But the indignant voice
> Terrific . . . met my eye
> Clamps instantly are taken off
> Approaches – & salutes.

It is clear that Burney kept from her sisters any 'confidences' from Digby, any details of the king's harsh treatment that came to her knowledge. This is an example of such censorship. The king 'had been manacled like the inhabitant of a lunatic asylum', as Chisholm writes.[35] Burney's finished account begins dramatically and as if it is a spontaneous recollection: 'Monday 2d. What an adventure I had this morning! one that occasioned me the severest personal terror I ever experienced in my life.' She relates that 'I suddenly perceived, through some Trees, two or three figures,' one of whom she thought must be the king. Then:

> Alarmed past all possible expression, I waited not to know more, but turning back, ran off with all my might – But what was my terror to hear myself pursued! – to hear the voice of the King himself, loudly & hoarsely calling after me 'Miss Burney! Miss Burney!'

She is terrified on two counts. The rule is that no one is to come anywhere near the king, lest she or any other courtier provokes him, so she is frightened both of the doctors' and the queen's displeasure. She is also terrified by the possibility of a close encounter with the king, because she knows about the volatility of his moods and, if (as is possible) Digby has confided them to her, about his unpredictable acts of violence. (Only a few days before, the king had suddenly without provocation seized one of the Willises's men by the hair and dragged him by it [G: 196]). When George

calls out to her, she is caught between these two terrors: to approach him is
to break an edict that everyone has to obey; to flee from him is an
unthinkable discourtesy to the sovereign. She tears away as fast as she
can, but the voice of the king pursues her. He is running after her, with his
attendants running after him. But when one of them yells, 'Dr Willis begs
you to stop!' and then 'You *must*, ma'am, it hurts the King to run,' she has
no alternative. 'Heavens how I ran, – I do not think I should have felt the
hot lava from Vesuvius! – at least not the hot Cinders, had I so ran during
its Eruption.' This vivid simile might be an accurate reflection of how she
felt at that moment, but it might more likely be the writer's later
embellishment.[36]

For even though she is tearing away in terror, one feels that there is some
release, even exuberance, in the physical activity, so that it becomes, in her
recall and writing, a celebration, in a strange sense, of the liberated body, as
well as the liberated writer. Though she depicts her terror, she is in
possession now of a subject, a great dramatic and important subject.
'Still ... on I flew, – & such was my speed, so almost incredible to relate,
or recollect, that I fairly believe no one of the whole party could have
overtaken me.' This exhilaration is detectable too in her account of what
follows:

> When they were within a few yards of me, the King called out 'Why did you
> run away?'
>
> Shocked at a question impossible to answer, yet a little assured by the
> mild tone of his voice, I instantly forced myself forward, to meet him –
> though the internal sensation which satisfied me this was a step the most
> proper, to appease his suspicions & displeasure, was so violently combatted
> by the tremor of my nerves, that I fairly think I may reckon it the greatest
> effort of personal courage I have ever made.
>
> The effort answered, – I looked up, & met all his wonted benignity of
> Countenance, though something still of wildness in his Eyes. Think, how-
> ever, of my surprise, to feel him put both his Hands round[37] my two
> shoulders, & then kiss my Cheek! – I wonder I did not really sink, so
> exquisite was my affright when I saw him spread out his arms! –
> Involuntarily, I concluded he meant to crush me: – but the Willis's, who
> have never seen him till this fatal illness, not knowing how very extraordin-
> ary this action was from him, simply smiled & looked pleased, supposing,
> perhaps, it was his customary salutation!
>
> I have reason, however, to believe it was but the Joy of a Heart unbridled,
> now, by the forms & proprieties of established custom, & sober Reason. He
> looked almost in *rapture* at the meeting, from the moment I advanced; & to
> see any of his Household thus by accident, seemed such a near approach to

liberty & recovery, that who can wonder it should serve rather to elate than lessen what remains of his disorder! (CJL V, 105–106)

Burney has described her flight and her terror so powerfully (the two form a visceral experience impossible to separate one from the other) that the moment she halts and confronts the king is an enormous relief for the reader. The king's greeting is not 'madly amorous'. On reflection, Burney describes it exactly as an impulsively warm and affectionate gesture, and the paragraph explaining it that follows (a retrospective understanding) is a piece of analysis so convincing because of Burney's imaginative identification: her own experience of imprisonment and now release is present in her empathy with the king at this moment.

They walk side by side, Burney 'not completely *composed*', the king talks, and another moment of extraordinary insight follows: 'Every thing that came uppermost in his Mind he mentioned; he seemed to have just such remains of his flightiness, as heated his imagination, without deranging his Reason, & robbed him of all controul over his speech, though nearly in his perfect state of mind as to his opinions' (CJL V, 106). A moment later she says she is giving an account of the king's talk that, she implies, may be confronting, but 'no accident can render of much consequence what a man says in such a state of physical intoxication.' These remarks come closer than any others to the sympathetic perception that there is something organic or 'physical' wrong with a man whose symptoms and pressures his 'reason' struggles to overcome: certainly he is not, or is no longer, wholly consumed by his disease or disorder.

In the ensuing talk, the king assumes the role of ruler that his illness and his doctors have stripped from him – he is the benevolent patron of Burney and her family. 'I am your Friend,' he declares, and treats her just as he had treated Greville, promising advancement to her father and protection for her against Mrs Schwellenberg. He attempts to sing bits of Handel (he has been singing Handel with his family during these weeks, though Burney wouldn't know this), but his voice is 'so dreadfully hoarse, that the sound was terrible'. The Willises try several times to break up the dialogue, fearing he is entering a manic state, but each time, as Burney puts it, the king 'conquers'. He certainly seems to work himself up, and a more troubling element comes into his talk: a Lear-like 'I will do such things'[38] emerges when he declares he will 'form an entire new Establishment' and throw out Lord Salisbury, and, pulling a memorandum from his pocketbook, declares, 'I shall be much better served: – & when once I get away, – I shall rule with a rod of Iron!' (CJL V, 110) 'This was very *un*like himself,'

Burney writes. Insisting 'I here pledge myself to be your Friend' and saluting her 'just as at the Meeting' (with a kiss on the cheek), he is taken away.

Burney seems to have found pleasure not only in the king's ameliora-tion, but in reporting and then writing up both the incident and her own heroic behaviour. It was a gift to a novelist, and so the king's 'near recovery' is accompanied by a different kind of recovery for Burney, as the dramatic vividness, shaping and verve of her reporting that has made the incident famous testifies. (Her run also suggests that this small and apparently frail woman had great reserves of strength.) She spared no time in telling the queen about her encounter and soon told Robert Greville too, whose curiosity, she says, she 'never saw equally excited'. Greville merely noted less excitedly that '[t]he kindness with which She was received, & the composure which She saw, dissipated Her alarm, & She reported that The King had talked very collectedly, & more so, than She had any idea of' (G: 203).[39] He added that 'this seems to have been among the very best days He has passed since He has been at Kew.' The next day the Willises were 'inexpressibly happy themselves', Burney writes, 'in the delightful convic-tion given me, & by me spread about, of the near recovery of their Royal Patient' (CJL V, 112). It was about this time, as Charles Trench notes, that regency medals were struck, with the exact day of His Royal Highnesses' accession on 'February _ 1789' left blank.[40]

But the rejoicing at court was also premature. The king was improving and sleeping better and was calm for longer periods. On 6 February he was allowed 'for the first time to have a Knife & Fork' (G: 209). But there were still violent rages, crazy projects poured from his mouth, and he still had to be restrained. (The opposition now renewed efforts to push through a regency bill.) On the seventeenth, though, the bulletin signed by his doctors for the first time announced 'a State of Convalescence'. Greville remained sceptical and cautious, writing 'sorry am I to be so sure as I am at this moment, that the Dear King was by no means well at that day, when the joyfull News of his Convalescence was announced to The Public' (G: 231). During mid-February he found that his reservations were shared in talks with his friend Stephen Digby. Nevertheless, George did become gradually calmer and more continuously rational, and when Greville saw Dr Warren on the morning of the twenty-third, 'he spoke very favourably of every thing' in the king's conversation (G: 242). A measure of his recovery is that on 3 March, attended by Colonel Digby and Dr Willis, the king took a long walk to the New Workhouse at Richmond, where 'The Master of the Workhouse, having shewn the Apartments alloted to

The Poor in it to H. My., asked Him if He would see their Madhouse. To this He conducted Him, & there passed a Conversation respecting it, & in which, the mention of Strait Waistcoats every now & Then was introduced' (G: 256). Greville was glad to learn that the king was apparently not at all disturbed! On 14 March the king returned with his entourage to his beloved Windsor.

With the court back at Windsor, Digby renewed his visits to Miss Burney's rooms and her recording of their exchanges resumed. But it now seems as if she could no longer ignore the approaches and hints that might suggest he was on the brink of making a proposal. A reader, however, might be as perplexed as before. Nothing Digby says to Burney can't be explained as the solicitude of a friend who finds, in this undoubtedly very clever lady, a precious intellectual companion. Burney, however, reposes meanings in her reiterated descriptions of Digby's facial expressions that are designed to suggest something more. To give one example: 'while speaking of his hopelessness of amending, he very suddenly, & with an expression of extremest flattery, turned full upon me, & exclaimed Unless *you* . . . would undertake to make me better!' (CJL V, 161) 'Good God – how I started!' Burney adds. Having on a later occasion, in March, cornered her in company, he asks her whether she'd like 'to . . . *settle*'.

> I turned quick towards him, amazed, to *see* his meaning in his Countenance, – it was very expressive – but did not let me *examine* it much, as he sedately added – 'not steady enough – to settle . . . for life? – ' There was something in this too . . . what can I say? for a slight answer. (CJL V, 198)

Is he asking about her readiness to stay with the court, or about her readiness to accept a proposal from him – or both – or neither? A few pages later, he is enquiring after her health, bends forward and 'lowering his voice, while his Eyes *fixed* me steadily', he asks if she is not ill, and 'When I looked at him, to answer in the negative, the expression of his countenance was so earnestly enquiring, so deeply investigating, & so filled with the most marked personal kindness, that there was no standing it.' Burney is very aware, as usual, that this is being noticed by others, 'but still he would not remove his Eyes' (CJL V, 201). By mid-March she is able to find that 'not common was the manner, nor common were the looks of Mr Digby; on the contrary, I have never yet seen both so marked with strong, open, undisguised partiality' (CJL V, 231).

Geoffrey Sill's volume of the *Journal Courts and Letters* includes a notable five-paragraph 'memorandum' under the date of 19 March, which appears, as he suggests, to be written retrospectively and was plainly inserted later into Burney's papers. Its style is quite different from the previous pages. In it she describes her account of the last 'busy & conflicting 4 Months', as a 'minute & faithful narration'. Now she is offering a summary or defence of her feelings and behaviour which (it seems) is designed to prepare her readers for the events to come. She writes that Digby's 'conduct, his high Character, his solicitude for my confidence, his reproaches for my with-holding it . . . in short, – an assiduity to secure my friendship, esteem, sympathy, & confidence, so unweariedly exercised for now so long a time, – since at Cheltenham it was perpetually evident, – all this, concurred to satisfy me *His Heart was Mine*' (CJL V, 232). But she could not reciprocate, she implies, because her 'conscience demanded the opening of a painful old story', which must mean her still lingering feelings about or for Cambridge.

Some readers have taken a far less sympathetic view of Digby's behaviour than the one implied in the account I have given. Susan apparently called him 'Mr Feignwell': Kate Chisholm characterises him as a 'debonaire officer . . . practised at putting on the mask required of a courtier'.[41] The affair invites moral judgements, but what must also be said is that the many pages covering these four months are remarkable pieces of reportage. They seem to take Burney's readers into the intangible arena that exists between two people conversing. In conversation one is attending to the other, while performing an inner activity of understanding and interpretation at the same time. So is the other person. This dialogic interplay is rendered by Burney's acute and finite presentation of Digby's speeches and their accompanying gestures, together with her own less specific, more ambiguous responses. Thus one can understand Digby's solicitude – his repeated enquiries about Burney's health, for example – as actual responses to her own responses, which appear to him to be a lack of vivacity or energy, which is true, because she is troubled by feelings that she can only declare in her writing. His responses in turn foster her impression (and perhaps her unacknowledged wish) that he is seriously courting her.

Free for a moment at last, Frances and her sister Susan attended the thanksgiving service held to celebrate the king's recovery at St Paul's Cathedral on 23 April 1789. Everyone including Burney believed that Dr Willis and his sons had brought about this miraculous restoration to health, and they were handsomely rewarded. But the fallacy *post hoc ergo propter hoc* is in operation here: there is no necessary causal relationship between events that follow one another in time, though the sequence of remission or even cure after sickness is especially likely, depending on the period, to be credited to whatever is widely believed to work, as in this case the Willises' treatment apparently did. But it may have had nothing to do with the king's recovery, especially if he was suffering from an undiagnosed, and at that date undiagnosable, organic condition.

Retrospective diagnosis, though widely practised, is another field in which conclusions are drawn from dubious logical premises. Physicians usually make diagnoses on living subjects whose symptoms can be verified, and upon whom treatments and their results can be tested. The diagnosis of someone dead for more than 200 years – George III (or Samuel Johnson, for example) – rests not on the authority of the body, but on witness accounts like Burney's, Greville's, and the physicians': in short, on the authority (or otherwise) of texts. In 1961, Ida Macalpine and Richard Hunter, however, published *George III and the Mad-Business*, in which they argue that 'a retrospective diagnosis can be strongly supported if the disorder presents a characteristic clinical picture, if it is rare and above all if it is hereditary. Porphyria almost uniquely fulfils all these criteria.'[42] Porphyria, of which there are several strains, is a rare inherited blood disorder, with a key symptom of discoloured urine. Their case, which in effect disputed any assessment of 'madness' or insanity, was widely accepted. But in what reads like a replay of the eighteenth-century doctors' disputes, their interpretation of the clinical evidence has been recently vehemently contested by the psychiatrist Timothy J. Peters and his peers. Peters asserts that 'they manipulated their quotations from their source material' and were 'either woefully ignorant or deliberately dishonest'.[43] Instead he and his colleagues propose the alternative diagnosis of 'bipolar disorder' or 'manic depressive psychosis'.[44] At the same time, Peters concedes that if the diagnosis of porphyria is discounted, 'the causes of [the king's] "madness" remain an unsolved mystery.'[45] Another mystery is why he recovered. John Brooke's biography *George III* (1972) traces the history of the ascription of 'madness' to the king by historians from Louis Namier onwards, and concludes that: 'On the basis of our present evidence we can say that the King was not mentally ill. The myth of King George III's insanity is exposed.' Convincing as Brooke's argument is, his conclusion was certainly premature.[46] Can the diagnosis of manic depressive psychosis account for the symptoms of burning heat that the king suffered from for many days?[47]

In the months following the king's recovery the court travelled and Digby was absent for much of the time. When he and Miss Burney met, there was evident deterioration in their relationship, but she continued 'to scrutinise every incident and to change her assessment of his feelings with weathercock frequency', as Hester Davenport puts it.[48] It seems certain that Digby became uncomfortable in Burney's presence and treated her with dismaying inconsistency. The conclusion of this troubled affair came in November 1789. On the eighteenth of that month, Miss Planta rushed into Burney's room exclaiming, 'Have you heard the news? ... Mr Digby is going to be married!' and on the twentieth regaled Frances with the information that 'it's all declared – & the Princesses wished Miss Gunning joy yesterday in the Drawing Room' (CJL V, 459). Though she had all along been sure that the rumours about Miss Gunning were false, Burney could not now deny that Colonel Digby and Miss Gunning were to be married. The shock and bitterness were terrible. 'He has risked my whole Earthly peace, with a defiance of all integrity ... He has committed a breach of all moral ties <&> with every semblance of every virtue!' she wrote in her journal.

> My Hand, indeed, he has never requested, but never can any Heart have been more assiduously assailed; whatever was most likely to take it, appeared to invest it; – honour, delicacy, simpathy, generosity – the utmost semblance of openness & frankness, the most earnest & anxious desire of trust and confidence, – the most undaunted avowal of distinguished preference ... all the refined flattery of participating in all my tastes and opinions, & of endearing to himself all my friends & favourites. (CJL V, 461)

On Digby's behalf, it might be argued, as Burney herself allows, that her demeanour, her own resistance to any closer intimacy between them, might justify him in supposing her unharmed. There is a conversation about 'Blue Stockings' not long before the announcement of his engagement to Miss Gunning in which (as Burney reports) Digby speaks apparently approvingly about her. Burney protests that she '*belongs* to no society' and he replies, 'I protest I do not know them! – There's Miss Gunning, indeed, – she has had a very good education – but she has nothing of the *Blue-Stocking* in her, – no pretensions to it.' It's as if he assumes she must know about his association (CJL V, 229). He might well have thought that she must have heard, from gossip at the court, of negotiations with Miss Gunning's family, and she certainly knew of his visits to Sir Robert Gunning's estates (CJL V, 147). It might also be true that nothing like the significance that Burney wants to read into his gestures and 'countenance', from both literary and personal motives, can be justified. Perhaps she, who in her novels had made so much play with the distinctions between genteel and vulgar manners, did not wholly understand aristocratic lifestyles.[49] It is likely too that her imagination, like her own style, saturated with the hyperbolic intensities of the literature of sensibility with all its focus on female susceptibility, led her (both in actuality and in writing) to invest in or project emotions which had no secure grounding in ordinary life and conduct. But it must also be true that, in his own exigency during the months of the king's illness, Digby had allowed himself to confide too much in a woman who he should have known would have felt flattered and aroused by their intimacy. Digby's need of refuge or sanctuary combined with Burney's need for friendship, reassurance, and love had created the conditions for a sad, ultimately destructive misunderstanding, with results for her that are the subject of the next chapter.

George III was not to suffer a bout of his illness for another ten years, and it was twenty before the Prince of Wales became regent. Presumably the medals celebrating his accession in 1789 were melted down.

Notes

1. Clark, L., ed., *The Court Journals and Letters of Frances Burney*, Vols. III and IV, are subsequently cited in the text in the form (CJL III, 324).
2. Clark, L., ed., *The Court Journals and Letters of Frances Burney*, IV, p. 491, fn. 363, citing the Baker Diary and Correspondence in the library of the Royal College of Physicians.
3. Macalpine and Hunter, *George III and the Mad-Business*, p. 22.
4. Carel, H., *Illness*. 'Because of phenomenology's focus on the subjective experience of the ill person, it sees illness as a way of living, experiencing the world and interacting with other people' (p. 10).
5. Heberden was greatly respected. He had attended William Cowper (Cowper, W., *Memoir of the Early Life of William Cowper*, p. 40) and Samuel Johnson (Redford, B., ed., *The Letters of Samuel Johnson*, IV, p. 149). Dr Heberden soon withdrew, however: he practised in London during the winter months.
6. Seven attending physicians – Baker, Warren, Willis, Pepys, Reynolds, Addington, and Gisborne – were examined by a committee of the House of Lords on 11 December 1788. Apothecaries and surgeons were also in attendance, one of whom, Dundas, is a source of information for Greville.
7. Lorna Clark's note 418 mentions that 'the entries were not sent to SBP [Susan Burney] until more than a year later, probably not long after they were composed' (CJL IV, p. 508). See also her important article 'Epistolarity in Frances Burney'.
8. Bladon, F. McKno, ed., *The Diaries of Robert Fulke Greville*, pp. 77–260.
9. This is the form in which Greville's *Diaries* is cited in the text.
10. The thermometer had been brought into use in the early eighteenth century by the great scientist Herman Boerhaave and his student Anton de Haan, but

technical difficulties prevented its wide adoption (the early thermometers seem to have been a foot long, and needed twenty minutes to determine a patient's temperature). Pearce, J. M. S., 'A Brief History of the Clinical Thermometer'.

11. Sir John Floyer published *The Physician's Pulse Watch* in 1707: 'The Chinese Art of Feeling the Pulse is describ'd, and the Imitation of their Practice of Physick, which is grounded on the observation of the Pulse is recommended.' Taking the pulse became routine in the later eighteenth century; William Heberden published 'Remarks on the Pulse' in the *Transactions of the Royal College of Physicians* in 1772.

12. 'Why should not Sir G. B. be honest enough to impute the King having bad nights to the blisters drawing on his legs?' wrote Lady Harcourt (*Harcourt Papers*). 'Lady Harcourt's 'Memoirs of the Year 1788–89' are available at https://archive.org/stream/harcourtpapersooharc/harcourtpapersooharc_djvu.txt.

13. Boswell, J., *Life of Johnson*, IV, SJ's letter to Taylor, 17 June 1783: 'I have been accustomed to bleed frequently for an asthmatick complaint; but have forborne for some time by Dr Pepys's persuasion, who perceived my legs beginning to swell.' 'I do love Mr Pepys with a degree of preference to all the World almost', wrote Hester Thrale Piozzi (*Thraliana*, I, p. 417) (7 January 1780).

14. It is reproduced in the 1930 edition of Greville's diary, opposite p. 88.

15. 'I think, in my Heart & my Conscience, that it will **all end well**,' Burney wrote to her father on 16 November (CJL IV, 560).

16. Macalpine and Hunter, *George III and the Mad-Business*, p. 27, citing 'Memoirs of the Years 1788–89'. By Elizabeth, Countess of Harcourt, ed. E. W. Harcourt. In *Harcourt Papers*, pp. 15–16.

17. The source of this information is unclear. Greville occasionally reports conversations at which he was not present.

18. Guttmacher, M. S., *America's Last King*, p. 209.

19. This was when Willis and his son had made some progress in moderating the king's condition.

20. *King Lear*, Act II, scene 4. Here Gonerill and Regan progressively conspire to deny their father the attendance of even one of his own household, a sequence that ends with the king crying, 'O Fool, I shall go mad!' (l. 280).

21. About 3 January, Betsy Sheridan wrote in her journal: "Tis a bitter day and I expect to be frozen. Nothing can equal the severity of the weather. They say it is beyond the year 40', Le Fanu, W., ed. *Betsy Sheridan's Journal*, p. 144.

22. Burney's account suggests that Willis arrived the evening of the fourth; Digby says the fifth.

23. There are two pages missing from the source, at p. 670.

24. As Jane Austen's *Sense and Sensibility* (1811) makes clear, letters between a gentleman and a lady would be construed as having romantic implications.

25. This would be the clergyman John Moir's *Gleanings: Or, Fugitive Pieces* (1785) (Clark's fn. 646, p. 629).

26. Fn. 718 on page 684. Clark's illuminating note traces a connection between Digby, Moir, and Sir Robert Gunning, Miss Gunning's father.

27. 'This restraint was designed to end the over-excitement that [Willis] believed caused madness' (Black, J., *George III, America's Last King*, p. 278). Even in 1940, a psychiatrist wrote that: 'Today, even in the poorest public institutions, the application of restraint is no longer permitted as punishment, but reserved almost entirely for the purpose of preventing the patient from hurting himself or others' (Guttmacher, *America's Last King*, p. 226).

28. 'I begin to think Dr Willis is rather too incautious a Man for his present conspicuous and responsible situation – At the least he is certainly unguarded and imprudent, & too much so for a Man who strongly leans to a Political Party– . . . He attacks Mr Fox and the Opposition with as much zeal as any Partisan I know' (G: 126); Lorna Clark's edition includes a page from John Willis's notebook (IV 695) for 24 December, which records the length of time the king was kept in the 'strait Waistcoat'. It was taken off at noon on the twenty-third, but put on again two hours later and not taken off again until nine the next morning. Willis records also that the king had had only two hours of sleep.

29. Sichel, W., *Sheridan*, II, p. 420. 'Great Wars and Rumours of Wars among the Medical Tribe', wrote Betsy Sheridan in her journal for this day, before giving more detail about Willis. 'In the course of the debate a Note from him was deliver'd to Mr Pitt informing him that within a few hours the K– had had a very great and sudden change for the better and that he had continued some hours in that state of amendment and that he (Dr Willis) had now the strongest hopes of a recovery in a very short time.' Warren rode off to Kew and elicited from the 'Attendants' that the king 'had never been worse than during the precise point of time that Dr Willis had marked as the period of amendment' (Journal, p. 138, 139.)

30. Sill, G., *The Court Journals and Letters of Frances Burney*. This is the form in which this volume is subsequently cited in the text.

31. Trench, C. C., *The Royal Malady*, p. 145.

32. This is one of the many hints in the journal that Burney is thinking of George Cambridge, and possibly that she still nurses strong feelings for him.

33. Porter, R., ed., *The Faber Book of Madness*, pp. 465–468, 465.

34. Chisholm, K., *Fanny Burney*, p. 150. The source is given (p. 308) as 'box of 417 miscellaneous scraps in the Berg collection (198300B) N.Y. Public Library'.

35. Ibid., p. 151.

36. Geoffrey Sill, editor of Volume V of the *Court Journals*, gives a penetrating account of this incident in his introduction (pp. xvi–xviii). The account given here differs in several respects from his. He writes, for instance, that as Burney runs she is 'imagining as she does so' that she is running over hot lava.

37. Originally 'over', amended to 'round' above the line (CJL V, 206, fn. 254).

38.
> 'I will do such things –
> What they are yet I know not; but they shall be
> The terrors of the earth.' *King Lear* Act II, scene 4, ll 275–278

39. This is the only time Burney appears in Greville's record.
40. Trench, C. C., *Royal Malady*, p. 171.
41. Chisholm, K., *Fanny Burney*, p. 143, p. 154.
42. Macalpine and Hunter, *George III and the Mad-Business*, p. 195.
43. Peters, T. J. and Wilkinson, D., 'King George III and Porphyria', pp. 7, 9.
44. Peters, T. J. and Beveridge, A., 'The Madness of King George III'. The authors draw on Greville's diary for illustrations of the king's behaviour that support the diagnosis of 'Mania with Psychotic Symptoms (F30.2)' (p. 28).
45. Peters, T. J. and Wilkinson, D., 'King George III and Porphyria', p. 3. See also Peters, T., 'Fitzpatrick Lecture 2014'.
46. Brooke, J, *King George III*, p. 341.
47. These matters are discussed further in Chapter 7.
48. Davenport, H., *Faithful Handmaid*, pp. 143, 132.
49. By 'lifestyle' I mean not just gracious manners, but the assumption, similar to a caste system, that the treatment of persons in classes below one does not entail the same obligations as treatment of persons of the same status.

CHAPTER 3

Aftermath: 1789–1791

Digby's betrayal was, Burney wrote, a 'catastrophe'. She determined not to reveal her distress or even to show concern within the court, keeping her misery and turbulent conjectures about Digby's motives to her letters. Claire Harman wrote in *Fanny Burney* (2000) that 'Digby, in the time-honoured way of the male in such circumstances, avoided Fanny like the plague thereafter.'[1] The full publication of the *Court Journal* for 1789 in 2016 reveals that the very reverse of this is true. Digby persisted in seeking occasions for conversation with Miss Burney over the next year. In fact he paid Burney a visit ten days after she heard the news of his engagement to Miss Gunning: she received him with grim and chilly formality. This visit and his later persistence only deepen the mystery of his motives. He tries to make light conversation – asks about her friends, her health, whether she had liked Weymouth (where the court had travelled for the king's health and where he had actually proposed to Miss Gunning) and so on, but Burney responds briefly and dryly, recording his nervousness – 'he twisted his riding stick twenty ways' – with palpable malice (CJL V, 468–470). Perhaps Digby did think that a reconciliation might be possible or that she would understand what he had done, and even that he did not feel himself to be especially at fault. But for Burney the friendship was utterly violated. A letter to her sister, written about a week after the news of Digby's engagement had broken over her, sums up her situation:

> True, my Susan – & too true, – 'it is a malady of which we shall not cure' – & true, too, 'Time has hitherto but irritated the disease.' – A disease of 3 Year & nearly an half's standing, – what can touch it? Is not the greatest wonder remaining that the fabrick bears it?
>
> One anodyne – for a while, I thought I had met – & how thank fully I grasped at it! – It came, too, at the time it was most needed – just when the only truly medicinal balm to my disorder was withdrawn – forever! – & now even this anodyne is withdrawn also – My dearest Friends will already read

this intimation with concern – but as the catastrophe is now complete, it would be useless to hold it back. (CJL V, 476–477).

The 'disease of 3 Year & nearly an half' is the period of her time at court; the 'truly medicinal balm' must have been Mrs Delany's friendship; the 'anodyne' is Digby's company. Here Burney casts herself as a patient, or to put this in other terms, entertains the thought of herself as a pathological subject, sick with a now permanent, incurable malady. Later in the letter she says that she is 'well' and that 'the Fabrick' is 'strong', making a brave distinction between her physical and her psychological state, a separation which was to become unsustainable over the months that followed. For it is impossible not to speculate that not only was the anodyne withdrawn, it might have turned into a kind of poison. The loss of Digby's companionship, and of whatever hopes she may or may not have entertained of him, meant, she had earlier written as she struggled to understand his behaviour, the end of 'all hope, all view of solace to my official toils'. It left her, 'just as usual, – obliged to finish every Evening with Picquet! – & to pass all and every afternoon, from Dinner to Midnight, in Picquet company!' Then she added a line that her editor brackets as an 'uncertain reading' because the words have been blacked out: 'Laborious – *painful – useless life!*', which might well be interpreted as a cry of despair being repressed (CJL V, 463). There can be little doubt that the loss of the only man with whom she could spend time away from Mrs Schwellenberg in congenial company and conversation would contribute to the depressive illness that overwhelmed her over the next year and a half.

But worse was to follow. In December she tells her sister she has heard still more 'black intelligence', coming from a source that she does not reveal. This woman (someone at court, obviously) began by asking '*when I had seen Mr Digby*? & then quickly added *You made that match!*':

> Miss Gunning, she said, had hung back, in the beginning, & disclaimed the report; & desired *her*, among others, to contradict it; – but, from the time of the King's illness, she heard so much of his attentions & visits elsewhere, that she grew in evident uneasiness & alarm & when – she was amidst the general assembly of the Queen's Ladies, waiting in the Japan Room, Mr. Digby was enquired for; & hearing the answer given that *he was with Miss Burney*, she took out her Salts, – &, the moment he entered the apartment, Fainted away! – (CJL V, 485)

Frances later heard a similar account from Mrs Ord. This gossip revealed that everyone in the court knew of the frequency of Digby's visits to Miss Burney (even the queen, it seems certain). She began to think that he had only used her as a decoy, that his visits were 'made, only that [Miss Gunning] might hear of them'. She entertained paranoid thoughts that Digby had only cultivated her friendship so that he could excite Miss Gunning's jealousy, that he had borrowed personal documents from her only to show them to the woman he was really courting. Though this seems unlikely, it also seems that everyone else at court thought so too. No one told her; no one (except her servant Colomb, who made his suspicions of Digby apparent) warned her. There could not be a clearer demonstration of the class divisions among the royal household, and Miss Burney was reminded cruelly thereby of her position as a commoner, her role little more than a menial's.

If one is to understand the decline in Burney's physical and mental state over the next months, these bitter experiences cannot be disregarded. They followed the long months of anxiety, tension, fear, and imprisonment which the king's illness had brought about and from which she had probably never recovered. Sir Lucas Pepys had in January 1789, Burney wrote, 'declared my confinement menaced my Health' and charged her to 'take air & exercise very sedulously', which she had tried to do. It had then been three and a half months since she had gone 'without Doors' (CJL V, 78, 79). Following the king's return to health the courtiers were released from their imprisonment. Digby, as the queen's vice-chancellor, was permitted to take a long leave, but Burney, also a devoted servant of her mistress, was not so fortunate, and instead was required to continue as usual with her onerous daily duties. She was allowed no holiday, given no chance to recuperate. It is not so surprising that on 21 May 1789 she wrote to an enquiring acquaintance, Mrs Dickenson, 'I have not been quite well some time, – which you will not wonder to hear, for my long confinement, &c have robbed me of some *robustness*; & I had not much to spare' (CJL V, 285). Apart from her other troubles, she had earlier in the month, as she wrote to Susan, been 'grievously ill with a pain in my Face'. She tried 'a blister, in vain': leeches were applied, and either, as she conjectured, because one of them was 'noxious' or another 'certainly bit a nerve' (CJL V, 289), the pain became agonising. Though no doctor is mentioned, she may well have been attended by Dr Gisborne, physician to the royal household and probably an apothecary, who would have treated her trouble with the leeches. She certainly was in desperate pain.[2] It is possible, as her statement that she had lost robustness would imply, that she was severely weakened and therefore liable to such symptoms as mouth ulcers. The pain was so bad that Burney feared she would die from the infection, but it seems that, except for 'that extremity which, for 3 days, incapacitated me for any thing but moaning outwardly, & settling solemn Adieus inwardly' (in other words, imagining death), she continued her 'official attendance'. The queen visited her, she wrote, in what is apparently a later addition to the record, not knowing 'in what anguish I appeared before Her long ere I could appear no more!' Her Majesty's attitude during these months does not seem to have been especially cold, but her unawareness of her attendant's feelings was to continue, and was, as Burney had ruefully learned, what you might expect from her rank and status.

Lorna Clark, who must be considered an impeccable authority, reads, as I have mentioned in the Introduction, Burney's very extensive accounts of her conversations with Digby unsympathetically, arguing that she was constructing a romantic narrative out of them, seeing and presenting herself as a sentimental heroine, and drawing on many of the tropes of epistolary fiction. She concludes that when the 'narrative construct nourished over so many months' collapsed with the news of Digby's engagement to Miss Gunning, 'the complete mental and physical breakdown of the narrator is the result. Burney's depression of spirits manifests itself psychosomatically and leads to her decision to resign from court, convinced that her very existence is at stake.'[3] This may well be true: what is certain is that more than a year after Digby's 'betrayal', Frances Burney was to suffer a collapse, the exact nature of which remains unknown.

It would be a mistake, though, I believe, to attribute Burney's tribulations in the next eighteen months wholly to the disappointment over Digby. It is more as if the emotional resources in their relationship that enabled her inner self to defend against anguish, frustration, and despair were withdrawn, leaving her unable to think of herself as other than what I have called a pathological subject, someone who is going to be always ill. But these thoughts were not irrational or quite pathological. Burney was a woman with a powerful intellect and, as her subsequent life was to demonstrate, much stamina and drive: the thwarting of her intellectual energy and the restrictions on her will must have taken a psychic toll. Her daily work was arduous and completely unrewarding, there was a constant need for discretion in all aspects of behaviour and speech within the court, there were very frequent disappointments when a chance to see her family and friends outside the court was abruptly cancelled by the queen's change of plans – all these, let alone the long hours which she was compelled to spend with the bad-tempered bully Mrs S – these deprivations were enough in themselves to lead almost anyone to a state akin to despair. And when she did try to exercise agency, as the next months would show, she was always to be thwarted.

In the months after his marriage, and the purchase of a house in London, Digby visited the court often, for three days at a time, and always, according to Burney's accounts, was looking out for a chance to catch her and to initiate a conversation. One such occasion was on a walk back from the Sunday service chapel in Windsor Castle, when he goes ahead of the other gentlemen to speak to her alone: 'he hastily said "will you – allow me only five minutes conversation with you? – "' She replies 'dryly': 'I am so much engaged I have hardly any time.' 'Some *other* time then? *any* time?' he pleads. The next day Colomb brings Miss Burney a letter:

> I cannot help thinking, Miss Burney, that your manner to me is so *wholly* altered, that you must have taken something ill; & being perfectly at a loss to conjecture what it can be that may have given offence, I do beg of your candour & fairness to let me know it.
>
> I must protest it was far, – very far from my intention to have given you any cause of ill will towards me. – Feeling – as I do, – perfectly innocent – & having long conceived a regard & esteem for your character, I cannot refrain from letting you know how much your coolness – too marked to be misunderstood – hurts me. If it were not the case, I should scarcely take this step; but it is part of my character to be fair, open, & explicit; & I trust you will not be less generous to explain wherein I have offended, & to suffer me to do away impressions injurious to me.
>
> I have taken the liberty of writing, as you seemed unwilling to give me an opportunity of speaking to you.
>
> If this request should appear impertinent, or you should be averse to grant it, – I must in silence submit: but I can scarcely repent having the best & fairest means to restore that footing of friendly intercourse I had wished might ever have subsisted between us.
> With much concern –
> your sincere & obliged
> Humble servant
> Sunday, May 16th.
> S. D. (CJL VI, 117–118)

Isn't this an extraordinary letter for a blackguard to write? But the words 'perfectly innocent' and the description of his own character as 'fair, open, & explicit' are enough, Burney writes, to fuel her indignation, which she expands upon for a page or so. She adds, 'I thought of him no more than he forced me to think – yet so delusive was his conduct, that he had surely broken my Heart, from the reliance he excited upon his regard, had not Nature happily fortified it with an impenetrability scarce accountable' (CJL VI, 119). It is difficult to match the claim that she thought of him no more than he forced her to think, with her very full and minutely attentive recording of their conversations. It may be that Digby did believe himself to be quite innocent: since everyone seems to have been aware of his interest in Miss Gunning, he might well have assumed that she would know about this too. In November 1788 he had made his association with the Gunnings quite clear to her, mentioning 'his visit & detention at Sir Robert Gunning's very openly & unaffectedly, yet, I thought, with a kind of *solicitude to name it*, lest it might be supposed a secret' (CJL IV, 514). (These are Burney's italics). (It is true, though, that when the king teases him with Miss Gunning's name, not long after Digby tells Burney that he assured him 'there was nothing in it') (CLV IV, 585).[4] He did not make any approaches to her that an independent witness would construe as amorous. (The nearest to it would be a moment after Frances has spoken of her life with Mrs Schwellenberg, when he 'suddenly – & apropos to nothing – took hold of my Hand' (CJL IV, 542). Her relish in denying his requests for a few words with her, and reporting this, is revenge, which means that she almost certainly had felt passionate attraction to him, though she had repeatedly disguised this from herself and her sisters. She may have written about their relationship in an idiom derived from the sentimental novel, but this does not mean that the feelings of which that idiom was the vehicle were false: her attention to every nuance of his speech and behaviour is plain enough evidence of her emotional investment.

It seems plausible to suggest that through 1790 she began to display symptoms for which the term 'psychosomatic' is only an opening towards diagnosis. Her physical symptoms were accompanied by, or sometimes indistinguishable (as she recounts them) from, a mental state of deep depression. There was a crucial occasion that year, though, when she avowed her despair. During the court's sojourn in London (during which she had been courteously, or perhaps cruelly, visited by Digby's new wife), Fanny contrived to meet her father at a packed performance of Handel's *Messiah* in Westminster Abbey on 20 May. There was some discussion of Frances's court duties and of her access to friends and family. A Frenchwoman who was present exclaimed 'Mais, monsieur, es-ce possible! Madamoiselle votre fille n'a't-*telle point de vacance?*' (CJL VI, 142). This was the opportunity for his daughter to reveal to Charles Burney how she felt about her life at court:

> I spoke my high & constant veneration for my Royal Mistress, her merits, her virtues, her condescendsion, & her even peculiar kindness towards me: but I owned the *species* of life distasteful to me, – I was lost to all private comfort, dead to all domestic endearment, – I was worn with want of rest, & fatigued with laborious watchfulness & attendance. My time was devoted to

official duties, & all that in life was dearest to me – my friends – my chosen
society – my best affections – lived now in my mind only by recollection, &
rested upon that with nothing but bitter regret. – with Relations the most
deservedly dear, with Friends of almost unequalled goodness, I lived like an
orphan! – like one who had no natural ties, & must make her way as she
could by those that were factitious. Melancholy was the existence where
Happiness was excluded, though not a complaint could be made! where the
illustrious Personages who were served possessed almost all human excellence, – yet where those who were their servants, though treated with the
most benevolent condescendsion, could never, in any part of the live-long
Day, command Liberty, or social intercourse, or repose! (CJL VI, 142)

This appears to be a summary of what she actually said, probably modified
in the writing. In the versions of this paragraph in her niece's edition of
Burney's *Diary and Letters* (1854) and in Dobson's edition of 1905, the
punctuation is altered, the capitals are removed, and the dashes are largely
replaced by commas. This enhances the impression of carefully structured
and formal speech – highly unlikely in the circumstances of a public
concert. In the original document as now reproduced in Volume VI of
the *Court Journals*, the dashes, the exclamations and the tripartite sentences, with their insistent repetitions ('where . . . where . . . where'),
convey the almost reckless urgency with which a long-meditated inner
narrative is being drawn upon to seize the attention of her father and to
force him out of his illusory belief that her life at court was even tolerable.
Her relation of her father's response then creates a dramatic context which
works to imply the authenticity of the speech that has gone before:

> The silence of my dearest father now silencing myself, I turned to look at
> him, – but how was I struck to see his honoured Head bowed down, almost
> into his bosom, with dejection & discomfort! – We were both perfectly still
> a few moments; but when he raised his Head, – I could hardly keep my seat,
> to see his Eyes filled with Tears! 'I have long, he cried, been dissatisfied – and
> thought you far too good for your office – though I have not spoken; . . .
> but . . . if you *wish* to *resign* – my House – my Purse, my Arms – shall be
> open to receive you back!' (Barrett, V, 106–107; D IV, 392, VI 118)

Perhaps Dr Burney did speak like a character in one of her novels. And just
because Burney's speech appears more spontaneous in its original tran-
script does not mean that it was spoken in just these words. Though there
had been some preliminary discussion of her circumstances in response to
the Frenchwoman's astonishment, here it seems Frances forbears to tell her
father, who was instrumental in placing her at the court, any details of her
life there (no mention of Mrs Schwellenberg) and is careful to emphasise

her regard for the royals that he had so slavishly admired. The queen did
not always treat her with benevolent condescension.

But Frances had seized her opportunity and broken her silence. Charles
Burney agreed that she should write a petition or 'memorial' to submit to
Queen Charlotte asking for her release, and seems to have rallied his friends
to do what they could to influence the court. But Burney's conscientiousness – now not only her loyalty to the royals, but loyalty to her family –
prevented her from obeying her other instinct, her desperate need, to
escape. It was months before she gathered her courage to approach the
queen.

She did, however, take a small step. It concerned her younger brother
Charles, fondly known as 'Carlos'. These were the days of the trial of
Warren Hastings in Westminster Hall, which had begun in February 1788,
but continued intermittently for years. Burney is sent by the queen to listen
to the proceedings, now renewed, and to report back to her. As Clark
points out, there is very little in the journal about the trial's proceedings
and a great many pages relating teasing dialogues between herself and
William Windham (he being on the side of Burke and the prosecution,
she being loyal to Hastings, an old acquaintance supported by the court).
Windham was another previous acquaintance (he had assisted Samuel
Johnson in his last days) and a member of the Literary Club to which
many eminent and influential men, such as Sir Joshua Reynolds, belonged.
She took the opportunity to enlist Windham in the scheme to present
a petition (another 'Memorial') to the Archbishop of Canterbury seeking
his worship to reinstate Charles Burney Jr as a minister of the church.[5] This
was a long-meditated project. To have any success, the 'Memorial' would
have to include an explanation of why such a request was necessary, and
this would mean disclosing that in 1781 the Bishop of London had refused
him ordination because Charles had been expelled as a student from
Cambridge for having stolen books from the university library. As Joyce
Hemlow writes, to bring up this matter would have been 'very painful', not
to say humiliating, for the family.[6]

During these summer months of 1790, Frances made strenuous efforts
to fulfil what she knew was her family's expectation – that when she
entered the court her position would give her the leverage to advance the
careers of both Carlos and her elder brother James, a naval officer currently
without a ship to command. The queen could be asked to intervene on
Charles's part with the archbishop. Frances had been long reluctant to
approach her mistress over this matter, but now she decided that she
would, since with her father's support now gained, she was seriously

contemplating a plan to leave the court. It would be an acid test: if Her Majesty spoke to the archbishop, and if the archbishop then reinstated her brother as a minister of the church, she would feel that her dreary life of self-sacrifice was in some degree worthwhile. If the attempt failed, she might feel released from her obligations to the queen.[7] In a letter to Charles she described the effort this cost her: 'I did! I opened the affair . . . The next morning I more explicitly told the brief heads of the unhappy tale, – though I could not yet explain the particulars, – my voice *would* not give them.' But she does manage to relate the crucial story and make clear 'that the interference of the Archbishop was *all or nothing*'. The queen seemed to understand, and to feel 'some concern and compassion, but whether to any effect, I know not'.[8] Eventually many eminent men were persuaded to sign the petition on behalf of Charles. After encouraging Carlos to expect that these efforts would succeed, and lingering in ignorance for weeks, in July the mortifying news came that the archbishop had refused the petition. Further attempts were made to get him to change his mind, but in vain (CJL VI, 145–6).

The wearing tension preceding this bitter disappointment was soon followed by another crisis. In fact during these months – months when Digby is still trying to get Miss Burney to talk to him, and therefore reminding her of his 'betrayal', months when she is getting thinner and thinner and more and more exhausted – Burney's sorrows came not in single spies but in battalions. In August her faithful servant Jacob Colomb became seriously ill. Dr Gisborne and Mr Keate, the court surgeon, 'did what was possible for him', but because his disorder was 'A swelling upon the Liver!' (which as she intimates, but does not say, meant cancer) and needed constant attendance, Gisborne arranged for him to be sent to St George's Hospital in London.[9] Poor Colomb asked Miss Burney to keep ten guineas in trust for him, as well as wages due. 'Scarce able to stand, and already fit for a shroud', he went off to St George's. He seems to have entrusted her with the whole management of his financial affairs, and she drew up a document that would make this official. But he died the third day after his arrival at St George's.

Unpredictably, a complicated and taxing sequel unfolded. A Swiss friend of his told Burney Colomb's last wish was to leave 'everything' to his sisters, which was in complete contradiction to what he had arranged with her. Then a rascal calling himself 'Peter Bayond' emerged with a claim that he possessed Colomb's will, leaving Colomb's estate to him: Frances was sure this was forged, but it seemed to be signed and sealed at 'Doctor's Commons' and therefore legitimate. Burney was 'almost ill with the shock and horrour' of this business, and dreaded having to go to court to prosecute the 'wretch' CLJ VI, 184. Bayond hired an attorney who demanded that she pay *forthwith* the sum Colomb had left in trust with her. Then she was filled with terror at having to face being prosecuted herself (CLJ VI, 195). She sought help from her father and from Horace Walpole, one of whose servants was a Colomb, but with Bayond's lawyer persisting in his threats, and apparently following her 'with incessant menace', she was forced to accede to another lawyer's advice that it would cost her double the whole of Colomb's estate to defend her case, and gave in: Bayond got half of Colomb's savings; the other half went to his cousin (CLJ VI, 197–8). This was another failure to use her position in the court to do good.

It is during these months that Frances Burney was planning and composing closet tragic dramas. *Edwy and Elgiva* had been begun as a diversion from her miserable confinement in 1788–1789, but was picked up again and more or less completed during this renewed period of intense distress. Two others were written and a fourth drafted, but their bombastic style and melodramatic plots make them difficult to read. They may well have relieved her mind, but these plays can also be read as symptoms: pitifully disguised and distorted reflections of her own tragic circumstances and conflicts.[10] But now that her father had understood her situation and was encouraging her, she also drew up a 'Memorial', her petition to the queen asking for release from the court.

Writing it was one step, but presenting it to the queen was another. People who saw her, including Windham, who declared, 'I knew indeed . . . that it was a situation perfectly unworthy of Miss Burney – but had never conceived any species of *hardship* belonged to it' (VI, CLJ VI, 203), and the devout royalist Mrs Ord, were evidently appalled at the onerousness of her life and the toll it was taking on her health. 'Miss Goldsworthy declared she thought my looks so altered as scarcely to be known again.' There was, she writes, a general fear that Miss Burney might die – that 'resignation of place, or of life, was the only remaining alternative' (VI, 226). She was 'ill' again in November. She writes that: 'This month will be very brief of annals: I was so ill, so unsettled, so unhappy during every day that I kept not a memorandum . . . languor, feverish nights, & restless days were incessant. My memorial was always in my Mind: my courage never rose to bringing it from my Letter Case' (CLJ VI, 214). She felt that if she presented it, the queen would have been shocked, 'wholly unprepared':

It is true, my depression of spirits, & extreme alteration of person, might have operated as a preface: for I saw no one, except my Royal Mistress & Mrs Schwellenberg, who noticed not the change, or who failed to pity & question me upon my Health & my fatigues: but as they, alone, saw it not, – or mentioned it not, that afforded me no resource ... And thus, with Daily intention to present my petition & conclude this terrific struggle, night always returned with the effort unmade, & the watchful morning arose fresh to new purposes that seemed only formed for demolition! And the month expired as it began, with a desire the most strenuous of liberty & peace, combatted by an ill will unconquerable to give pain, displeasure, or distress to my very gracious Royal Mistress. (CLJ VI, 214)

This is a classic account of the psychological dilemma Gregory Bateson and his colleagues identified in the 1950s as the 'double bind'.[11] Bateson coined the phrase to define the conflict that ensues when a small child is always being issued with conflicting alternatives by their parents (mother saying, 'you mustn't play in the garden, you'll get dirty,' and then father exclaiming, 'why don't you go out into the garden, it's so sunny out there?' and this pattern being endlessly repeated). One message negates the other; the child has no way of resolving the dilemma or of opting out of the situation. Bateson argues that the result is severe, possibly enduring, mental distress, even schizophrenia. Like a child trapped within such a family, Burney is caught in the court. To put this perhaps too simply, everyone (most importantly now her father) is telling her she must leave the court, while the other authority figure (the mother), the queen, is communicating by her demeanour the opposite: 'though I was frequently so ill in her presence that I could hardly stand, I saw she concluded me, while life remained, inevitably hers' (CLJ VI, 226).

Looking back to December 1790, three months later, she described her condition in more physical terms (and this emphasis must have relevance to the breakdown that occupied those previous months, but was unrecorded):

My loss of Health was now so notorious, that no part of the House could wholly avoid acknowledging it. – yet was the terrible picquet the catastrophe of every Evening! though frequent pains in my side forced me, 3 or 4 times every evening, to creep to my own Room for Hartshorn & for rest. And so weak & faint I was become, that I was compelled to put my Head out into the air, at all Hours, & in all Weathers, from time to time, to recover the power of breathing, which seemed not seldom almost withdrawn. (VI 224)

A very different woman, Mary Wollstonecraft, marooned in Ireland as a governess and desperately miserable, wrote the same year to her sister of her 'spasms and disordered nerves' and incurably broken heart. As Clare Tomalin writes: 'There was talk of a "constant nervous fever", violent pains in the side, difficulty in breathing, fits of trembling, a rising in the throat and faintness.'[12] In that year too the painter Joseph Wright wrote of himself that 'no disease more completely debilitates the frame than a Nervous or putrid fever,' and in 1792, 'for the week past I have been so indisposed wth a pain in my side and Breast (a serious complaint in my nervous constitution).'[13] Serious emotional distress can certainly manifest itself in such physical symptoms as shared by these three writers.[14]

Retrospective diagnosis, as I have emphasised in George III's case, is full of pitfalls. But some attempt must be made to elucidate Frances Burney's symptoms, if only because the suspicion arises that there was an unconscious motive behind them, that is to say something more powerful than the conscious desire to escape the court. In her biography Claire Harman suggests a range of possibilities around which this suspicion hovers. 'Fanny was fading dramatically', she writes, 'displaying psychosomatically enhanced symptoms of a cough, breathlessness, fever and weight-loss that were redolent of both consumption and a wasting disease, such as anorexia nervosa.'[15] 'Anorexia nervosa' raises the possibility that Burney's 'illness' was a hidden expression of power, 'the body as a weapon for autonomy', as a modern anorexic has put it, the only resource of the otherwise powerless.[16] Unconsciousness also seems to be the implication of Hester Davenport's comment that '[i]llness was Fanny's only effective strategy in her campaign for release; that is not to say that it was a tactic deliberately adopted.'[17] Margaret Doody gives a similar diagnosis: 'Nearly total debility offered the only way out of the impasse; Frances Burney's subconscious obliged by supplying her with the major symptoms of tubercular consumption.'[18] (Neither Burney nor any of the observers concerned about her appearance seem to have mentioned the possibility of tuberculosis.) I would argue that Burney herself was right: the 'anodyne', the only alleviation of her 'disease', having been withdrawn, the conditions of her dreary, exhausting, loveless, sexless 'marriage' to the court were enough in themselves to bring her into a state of unremitting exhaustion and misery. Added to this was the failure of her loyal actions: to assist Charles, followed by the bizarre consequences of her kindness towards her servant. Most destructive was the inner conflict between her conscientiousness and her wishes, the world outside the court saying, 'you must leave,' the queen saying 'you must stay': both powerful forces but pulling her in different directions and paralysing her. She had in fact depicted the physical cost of such psychological conflicts in *Cecilia*, nearly a decade before.

Finding her inability to present her petition to the queen 'unconquerable', she cast around for other avenues (CLJ VI, 226). She wrote to her sister Charlotte, who had met Clement Francis, a surgeon and former medical officer in the East India Company, to ask Mr Francis to give his professional opinion. 'Will you tell him, my Charlotte, that I find [my health] sensibly declining, without any ostensible illness that points out a road of cure, by coming to any crisis?' Then she described her symptoms in careful detail: she had spent four months during which she 'could scarcely keep awake', but 'I am now *never* sleepy, not even on my latest nights, not even on my earliest mornings, not even in the ennui of card playing, or conversation hunting' (she means the hours spent in Mrs Schwellenberg's company). She goes on:

> But, meanwhile, my appetite goes, & my strength diminishes, as well as my flesh. Without taking bitters, I had *rather not* eat at all.
> So extreme is my weakness, that the slightest thing I do fatigues me even to pain: & those long walks which used so much to refresh & revive me, are now absolutely impracticable ...
> I have frequent pains in my side & chest, but they move from place to place, & give way to hartshorn & water. And my complection looks *jaundiced*, so sallow it has become, & so fishy my Eyes – All conditions of people notice my attired appearance (CLJ IV, 227: possibly 'altered' is meant). (269)

She then lists the medicines she has tried (a sad list of useless household 'remedies'): saline draughts, nitre, bitters, camphor, 'Rhubarb – peppermint water – Colmba – all have had their turn.' Then she concludes that: 'It seems, therefore, as if the *life itself* was more than my frame is formed for sustaining. I have two thoughts about myself; one is, that broken rest by *force* is now become broken rest by *nature*, – & that my constitution is essentially altered & injured – the other is, that all these nervous & wearing feels, & this extreme sleeplessness, are but symptoms of an approaching long fever' (CLJ VI 228).

Mr Francis had written to her father, apparently 'exhorting instantaneous resignation, as all that stood before me to avert some dangerous malady' (CLJ VI 226). When it came to, she told the queen that she had consulted him, but could not voice Francis's categorical opinion and instead said lamely that he was not able to 'prescribe at a distance'. She hoped the queen would take the hint, but she only looked perplexed. Next day, she managed to say that she had something 'of deep consequence' to herself to give in writing to Her Majesty. This was the 'Memorial', expressed in the most flattering terms and enlisting her father's support (CLJ VI, 230). The ground had apparently been prepared, but then the queen, seconded by the king, proposed that Frances see the court physician. The next day when she returned to her room she found Dr Gisborne waiting. 'Think if my mind, now, wanted medicine the most!' she cried despairingly to her sister. Gisborne prescribed 'opium and three glasses of wine in the Day' and told her she *surely* required *rest*, & a *vacation*, to restore my shattered nerves' (278, 281). Burney offers no comment on these suggestions, so like those often made to people suffering psychological misery even today.

This was the beginning of a complicated negotiation. The queen wanted to retain Frances Burney's services; Burney desperately needed her resignation to be accepted. Burney saw it as a kind of duel: her mistress was kind and apparently conciliatory, but it was clear to Fanny that she has 'an expectation of *parrying the Coup*' (VI, 240, 20 December). It is obvious that these days of anxious suspense would only make her 'nervous' symptoms worse. She asks her father to write a letter to the queen making clear that a holiday to 'recruit', or get back her strength, is not what is necessary: only retirement. But when his letter comes it quotes a letter from Francis, in which he writes that Burney's retirement must be 'speedy', which she thinks might offend the queen, so she doesn't deliver Charles's letter. And she cannot bring herself to divulge how intolerable life with Mrs Schwellenberg is because the woman, after all, is a faithful old servant (CLJ VI, 245, 6 January).

The official celebration of the queen's birthday on 18 January 1791 was now approaching, but early in the morning of the seventeenth, Burney experienced the beginning of a 'terrible illness' that was apparently to last for several weeks. It is difficult to reconstruct or to imagine what happened in these weeks. A document apparently dated at the end of February and addressed to her sister is almost all we have to go by:

> February.
> 1791.
> This month, my dearest Susanna, has no memorial but in my Heart –
> which amply you supplied with never-dying materials for recollection.
> End of February. (CLJ VI, 255)

The emptiness of the record is eloquent enough. But since this appears to be issued from the queen's lodge at Windsor, it can be assumed that someone in the court (probably Dr Gisborne) summoned her sister to come and to care for a patient who now very evidently needed nursing attendance in her private room. It seems that Susanna enlisted their friend Frederica Locke, which might suggest the urgency for round-the-clock nursing care. When she was recovered Burney called this her 'grand seizure', 'seizure' meaning what could be called an 'attack' today – the terms not necessarily, but possibly, implying a physiological event. Possibly too the pains in her side and the difficulty in breathing mentioned in her retrospective summary were so intense that she became actively hysterical. Or perhaps she collapsed.[19] This drastic illness, of which Her Majesty was certainly informed, was the turning point.

A letter dated '22 February' (1791) (but quite possibly later) sent to her father thanks him fulsomely for a letter of his own, in which Charles Burney, drawing on one from Mr Francis – whose categorical medical opinion is their strongest card – formally requests the queen to release his daughter. In April, having marginally recovered and returned to her duties, Frances succeeds in making clear to the queen that she is determined to retire and that she expects the king's birthday, 5 June, to be her last day. But the duel is still not won. 'It would be useless to attempt telling the scenes I go through', she writes to her sister, 'the efforts used to dissolve my plan, & the exertions to affirm it' (323). When she has a relapse, the queen advises her 'in a very kind manner' to try riding. She also tells her father that she's been told that the queen thought '*till lately*' that the trouble was 'want of *will* to be better!' (325). It appears that the queen now accepts that Burney will leave her soon, but in the meantime requires her to fulfil her duties to the utmost – including attendance at the trial of Hastings, now resumed.

In May she is visited in her apartment by Dr Francis Willis, surprisingly back at the court. This interview, as Frances records it, is interesting. She tells him that there is no medical advice 'in the whole World, which would have such assistance with me from faith as his', but fears offending 'Dr Gisborne':

> 'Why now I really think, cried he, which you'll say is very vain, that I could cure you: & why should we not consult without [Gisborne's] knowing it? I give you my word I would not offend any man, none whatsoever, – but you may take my word for it, for all that, I would affront all the College of Doctors, & all the world beside, rather than not do you good if it is in my power.'
>
> When I thanked him for this most exceeding kindness, which was uttered with a cordiality of manner that doubled its warmth, he said, 'Why, to tell you the truth, I don't quite know how I could have got on, at Kew, in the King's illness, if it had not been for seeing you in a morning. I assure you

they worried me so, all round, one way or other, that I was almost ready to
go off. But you used to keep me up prodigiously. Though, I give you my
word, I was afraid sometimes to see you, with your good humored Face, for
all it helped me to keep up, because I did not know what to say to you, when
things went bad, on account of vexing you.' (CJL VI 283)

The novelist's talent is displayed here: Burney is able to convey Willis's
'noble open heart' through her capture of his speech rhythms. Just a visit
from this man, embraced with his warmth, his comedy, his friendship,
would do her good. He fortifies her by reminding her of the time when
she fortified him. His cheerfulness, his faith in his own gift, is a reminder of
the role these might well have had in the king's recovery. He also prescribes
medicines, which the patient finds too 'violent' to take in her weakened state.

Though she had condescended to seek a replacement, the queen more or
less demanded on 1 June that Miss Burney attend the current session of the
Hastings trial in Westminster Hall, when Hastings himself was to deliver
his defence, and to report what she heard back to her. Burney says in her
journal that many of her former acquaintances there did not recognise her
at first, 'but I saw they read the history of my long illness in my Face' (CJL
VI 288). In the last week of her residence, the queen's cordiality rather
diminished, as Burney bitterly wrote, 'from an opinion I ought rather to
have struggled on, live or die, than to quit her' (VI 303).

But a replacement had been found, and Mlle. Jacobi arrived on
3 July. Burney comments that 'I am again falling so unwell, that I had
fully expected, if the delay had been yet lengthened, another dreadful
seizure for its termination'. She still had to attend the queen at the
public occasion of the Drawing Room at St James's. Frances Burney
finally left Queen Charlotte's service on 7 July 1791. The queen told
her, over her protests, that she would give her a pension of half what
she was presently receiving – £100, a munificence that Frances had
never expected, and which was to prove vitally important to her future
happiness. It is possible that Her Majesty, despite the behaviour
towards Burney that makes one think of her as a capricious tyrant,
was genuinely fond of and grateful to her attendant, who had become
so necessary to her during the terrible times of the king's illness. Now
Burney looked forward, she told her father, to

> such rest as that, with peace, my long postponed medical trial of Dr W's
> prescription, & my own most wished regimen of affection in domestic life,
> will do all that can be done towards recruiting my shattered frame; & the
> frequent gentle changes of air, with such a skilful directress as Mrs Ord, will
> be giving me, indeed, every possible chance. (CJL VI, 307)

In these last days, Frances Burney was in company with Digby again, at tea with several other gentlemen. She seems to enjoy writing that: 'With Mr Digby I proceeded as usual, – distant, impenetrably distant, & cold, invincibly cold: he too proceeded as usual with me; attentive, submissive, serious, meditative, & vigilantly watchful for opportunities he never found' (365). So that was the end of that. Mrs Ord kept her promise to take her on an excursion to the west country, which began her convalescence. Two years later, fully recovered, she met a man who, like Digby, was an aristocrat with military service, General Alexandre d'Arblay. The difference was that he loved her and unequivocally meant to marry her.

Notes

1. Harman, C., *Fanny Burney*, p. 221.
2. The passages describing this occasion in Geoffrey Sill's volume are problematic, and his text is assembled from fragments. An illustration on page 291 shows the state of the manuscript and is an illuminating demonstration of the amendments, cancellations, paste-overs, and additions that confront Burney's modern editors.
3. Clark, L., 'Epistolarity in Frances Burney', p. 213.
4. The context of this remark (Digby's wish to head off the king's joke about his familiarity with 'Learned Ladies', and his subsequent demeanour – as reported by Burney – fixing his eyes on the fire, not looking at her and then saying, 'I am glad however *she* does not hear him!') makes it difficult to interpret.
5. Charles Burney Jr had been sent down from Cambridge in 1777, but went to King's College, Aberdeen, in 1778 or 1779, and there obtained an MA. In 1781 the Bishop of London refused him ordination. (Hemlow, J., *The History of Fanny Burney*, pp. 72, 75, 144). His fortunes changed, and in 1807 the orders against him were rescinded; eventually, in 1812, he was awarded the degree of Doctor of Divinity.
6. Hemlow, J., *The History of Fanny Burney*, p. 214.
7. This is my interpretation of a passage from a letter to Charles given in Hemlow, J., *The History of Fanny Burney*, p. 214.
8. Hemlow, J., *The History of Fanny Burney*, p. 214. Footnote 1 on page 493 gives references to letters concerning promotions for her brother James and Charles held in various library collections, but the date of this letter is not clear.
9. St George's Hospital was established at Hyde Park Corner in central London in 1733. All folllowing CJL page numbers in brackets are to Nancy E. Johnson, ed., *The Court Journals and Letters*, Vol. VI, Oxford, 2019.
10. A full account and interpretation of these difficult works is given in chapter 5, 'Love, Loss and Imprisonment: The Windsor and Kew Tragedies', in Doody, M. A., ed. *Frances Burney*, pp. 178–198.

11. Bateson, G., Jackson, D. D., Haley, J., and Weakland, J., 'Towards a Theory of Schizophrenia'.
12. Tomalin, C., *The Life and Death of Mary Wollstonecraft*, p. 81.
13. Wetherall Dickson, L., ed., *Depression and Melancholy, 1660–1800*, pp. 221, 223.
14. I owe this assurance to Dr David Mushin.
15. Harman, *Fanny Burney*, p. 223.
16. Macleod, S., *The Art of Starvation*, p. 66.
17. Davenport, H., *Faithful Handmaid*, p. 143.
18. Doody, M. A., *Frances Burney*, p. 193.
19. A letter from Charles Burney dated 10 January was annotated 'last note before a very dangerous seizure of fever' (CJL VI 247). To Susan she writes of the 'various adventures' of her illness, and of her 'kind and tender nurses.' (CJL VI 253 and footnote 808).

CHAPTER 4

An Inoculation for Smallpox: 1797

This is an extract from Robert Greville's diary for Christmas Day, 1788:

> The Report of this Morning stated that H. M^y had had about 5 hours sleep, & the Bulletin mentioned that He had a good Night & was quiet in the Morning. Afterwards in the course of the day He became troublesome & turbulent & so much so that recourse to Coercion became necessary & He was confined on his Couch – Such sudden transitions appeared strange to Me, but I was informed on the best authority, Mr Dundas, that in the Morning when in bed, & when He was reported quiet, He was as deranged as possible, & had been so for some time – Among his extravagancies of the Moment He had at this time hid part of the Bed Clothes under his bed, had taken off his Night Cap, & got a Pillow Case round his head, & the Pillow in the bed with Him, which He called Prince Octavius, who He said was to be new born this day.[1]

Octavius had been George III's very favourite son, some compensation, perhaps, for the king's disappointments with his rascally older brothers. When he was four years old Octavius had been inoculated against smallpox in April 1783, along with his sister Sophia, two years older. 'Princess Sophia is in the finest way possible,' a nurse in the royal nursery reported a week or ten days after the inoculation. This means that the spots or pustules which would signify the virus had taken hold had appeared, and that the normal course of the treatment was occurring. But Prince Octavius was said to be not 'in so forward a state'. About a week later, to the horror and devastation of his nurses, the child died.[2] Princess Amelia, born only months after the death, and to become Frances Burney's favourite, was nevertheless subject to the dangerous procedure, though years later, in August 1790. The operation was successful, one of the child's sisters soon being able to write to their brother Augustus that '[d]ear little Amelia has got through her inoculation remarkable well – She has no spots in her face and not altogether thirty about her body.'[3] 'We had all much interest about this time in the welfare of the dear little Princess, who was innoculated,' Burney wrote: 'Thank Heaven, All prospered, & she suffered nothing' (CJL VI 162). Austin Dobson's 1905 edition of the *Diary and Letters of Madame d'Arblay* appends a curious note to this statement: 'This ... seems to have been regarded as a very serious matter.'[4]

It *was* a very serious matter, and this chapter sets Burney's letters, which give an account of the 1797 inoculation of Alex, the d'Arblays' small son, within its historical contexts, both medical and cultural. The disease was greatly feared, and there was great risk in the procedure that offered to safeguard against it – dread and risk that Burney's writing makes palpable. Alex's operation ironically happened to coincide with developments in medicine that would eventually banish smallpox entirely. Edward Jenner, the pioneer of vaccination, had first experimented with the counterintuitive procedure of injection by cowpox a few months before, and it was ironically only a year after Alex's inoculation before Jenner published the undeniably successful results. Though informal, Burney's report belongs to a crucial moment in the history of the disease and offers a glimpse of a vanished moment in patienthood.

George III's grandmother Caroline of Ansbach had been an early champion of inoculation as a preventive treatment for smallpox, and when she became queen she had all of her children undergo the procedure. Given this heritage, and the many deaths from the disease in various, more remote branches of the royal family, the king's determination to treat all of his own children is not surprising.[5] Frances Burney must have known about this tradition and about Octavius's death. Three years later, on 28 November 1793, she had to write to Marianne Waddington, Mrs Delany's niece, with whom she had formed a friendship at court, to offer condolences for a 'sad & unexpected stroke' – the death of her daughter. Mary Anne, aged one year and seven months, had also died from an inoculation for smallpox, 'that terrific [i.e. terrifying] disorder'. Burney later wrote to her father that '[p]oor Mrs Waddington is broken Hearted by this blow' (JL III, 20, 39).

The eradication of smallpox that the World Health Organization was able to proclaim in 1980 – one of the greatest achievements of medicine – makes it impossible for modern readers to comprehend the dread and fear the disease inspired for centuries. (Fifty years after the Compulsory Vaccination Act of 1853 was passed by Parliament, Dobson's footnote suggests, its memory had already faded.) The very name 'smallpox' seems to denote a minor ailment. But as a medical historian puts it, 'if you wanted to invent a curse to terrorise your worst enemy, the horrors in [smallpox's] repertoire would be hard to beat.'[6] Michael S. Gurney, a medical practitioner, provides an account of the clinical history of the disease:

> Once the virus takes hold there is a variable latent period of four to fourteen days. A two-to-four day prodrome [a premonitory period] then occurs, characterized by high fever, headache, muscle aches, and severe malaise ... After the prodrome, a rash appears, which evolves over several days to the characteristic pustules. These then crust over, and finally clear after two to three weeks. The illness itself varies in severity. Variola minor is a mild illness, with a less extensive rash and only one percent risk of death. Variola Major, however, is the more common and severe variety, with a mortality rate of 20 to 40 percent.[7]

Gurney continues with a description of 'the badge of smallpox infection, the pockmarked scarring': 'The rash and its subsequent scars were more prominent over the extremities and face than the trunk. The scars were deep, four to six millimeters in size, and there was a predilection for lesions to develop over bony prominences or tendons. In the facial area, this included the forehead, bridge of the nose, cheekbone, and the chin.' Mortality rates were high then among those who contracted the *variola major*; worse, as many as four out of five children with smallpox died. Even if the patient survived, they would most likely be disfigured for life, since the pustules, which could number in hundreds crowding over the face and limbs, left such terrible scars and cavities.

It was during the eighteenth century in England, instigated by Lady Mary Wortley Montagu's championing of the procedure, that inoculation became gradually accepted and practised as a prophylactic against the disease. Lady Mary had seen her brother die of smallpox, and eighteen months later, in 1715, had herself suffered a ghastly attack, which ruined her once-famous beauty. When her husband, Edward Wortley Montagu, was made ambassador to Turkey in 1717, Lady Mary accompanied him to Adrianople. From there she wrote letters to inform friends in England about the local custom of inoculation. As her biographer Isabel Grundy writes: 'She had found it practised by both the local cultures, Turkish and Greek; and she probably found it not by chance, but because she was looking. She was primed both by personal experience and by intellectual contact as an Enlightenment researcher.'[8] One of her letters describes what she had seen:

> The small-pox, so fatal, and so general amongst us, is here entirely harmless by the invention of *engrafting*, which is the term they give it. There is a set of

old women who make it their business to perform the operation in the month of September, when the great heat is abated. People send to one another to know if any of their family has a mind to have the small-pox: they make parties for this purpose, and when they are met (commonly fifteen or sixteen together), the old woman comes with a nut-shell full of the matter of the best sort of small-pox, and asks what veins you please to have opened. She immediately rips open that you offer to her with a large needle (which gives you no more pain than a common scratch), and puts into the vein as much venom as can lie upon the head of her needle, and after binds up the little wound with a hollow bit of shell.[9]

Lady Mary then describes the mild sequel of the operation, and adds, There is no example of any one that has died of it; and you may believe I am very well satisfied of the safety of the experiment, since I intend to try it on my dear little son.' True to her word, six-year-old Edward was inoculated in March 1718 by the surgeon to the British Embassy, Charles Maitland, who used his own instrument, the lancet (commonly called the scalpel today). The boy did well, and the Montagus' daughter was also inoculated by Maitland in London in April 1721 where, as John Smith mentions, there had been 3,229 smallpox deaths in 1719 alone.[10] Caroline, the Princess of Wales, the future consort of George II, had her daughters inoculated a year later.

There was immediate opposition and vituperation in the press, from both clerics and doctors, one of whom wrote that he could hardly conceive how 'an Experiment practiced only by a few *Ignorant Women*, amongst an illiterate and unthinking People, shou'd on a sudden . . . so far obtain in one of the Politiest Nations in the World, as to be received into the *Royal Palace*'.[11] Lady Mary intervened with an article published in the *Flying Post* of 13 September 1722, 'A Plain Account of the Innoculating of the Small Pox'[12] in which besides describing the procedure she expressed her contempt for the medical profession. Already it seems what had been a simple and effective procedure in Turkey was being usurped by doctors who insisted on a long period of preparation, with the administration of the usual repertoire of vomits, purgatives, bleeding, and fasting, as well as a lengthy period of recovery (under medical supervision). One of the patients who suffered this regime was eight-year-old Edward Jenner, a friend of whom later recalled that '[h]e was bled, to acertain whether his blood was fine; was purged repeatedly, till he became emaciated and feeble; was kept on very low diet, small in quantity, and dosed with a diet drink to sweeten the blood.' The boy was then removed to 'one of the then inoculation stables, and haltered up with others in a terrible state of disease'.[13] This was in 1757, and Jenner very nearly died as a result. The 'inoculation stable' might have been, in effect, one of the 'Houses', or private isolation hospitals established by entrepreneurial doctors on the pretext of the widely acknowledged fact that post-inoculation patients remained contagious until they recovered and had to be kept apart from the populace.

After Maitland inoculated Lady Mary's children, he carried out an experiment in the presence of many eminent doctors, inoculating six condemned prisoners in Newgate. They all survived. Smith argues that Maitland must have made deep incisions (fearing possibly that the lymph would not take) and that this 'inexplicable break with the procedure he had seen in Turkey marks the beginning of a severe form of inoculation that was to be used in Britain until the 1750s'.[14] The prevalence of this practice led to many deaths, especially among children. The reason, as now known, is that the immune system (a term only current since the 1960s) is keyed to resist skin lesions and will be brought into action quickly to fight any damage to the surface tissue of the body. The smallpox virus would otherwise target the lungs and the lymphatic system and the immune defences would take much longer to come into play, usually failing to defeat the virus.[15] The abandonment of the method of superficial scarification by many practitioners was a key factor in retarding the adoption of inoculation for the next thirty or more years.

What also retarded the general acceptance of inoculation was the high cost of treatment, most probably as a result of the five weeks or more that the patient was required to be under medical supervision. It becomes clear that, although after 1750 more and more people became inoculated, the poor or working classes, among whom smallpox was rife, could not afford the fees most doctors, or the apothecaries who increasingly took up the practice outside the metropolis, thought fit to charge. It did, however, become gradually accepted that universal inoculation of the populace might be a good idea. The governors of the Foundling Hospital decided to inoculate their charges in 1744. When the first fourteen children to be inoculated did well, the procedure became compulsory for all of them over the age of three.[16] A writer in the *Gentleman's Magazine* in 1752 maintained that:

> [B]efore [inoculation] can come into general use, it must be done in a less expensive way. The charge of it, as it is now managed, must necessarily exclude a great part, nay I may say the greatest part of mankind, from the benefit of it. The poor in general are absolutely cut off from all share in it . . . And not only the very poor people, but multitudes of others, many farmers

and tradesmen, cannot be at the expense of so much a head for their whole family, as is at present demanded, merely for the operation of inoculating, besides the other additional charges, which must necessarily accrue.[17]

Thus the medicalisation of inoculation, which often brought huge profits to doctors, excluded the less well-off: smallpox effectively became a disease of the poor.

An important development soon took place when between 1755 and 1761. Robert Sutton, a surgeon in a Suffolk village, refined and propagated a return to the Greco-Turkish technique advocated by Lady Mary thirty years before. His 'new method' was really the old one revised. Following Maitland, it seems to have been the current belief among practitioners that besides deep cuts by the lancet, the insertion into them of matter from mature pustules was necessary to produce large, suppurating lesions. Sutton advocated the use of lymph taken from a pustule in its earlier stage of development, usually about the fourth day, and the insertion of a very small quantity on the point of a lancet, raising the cuticle as little as possible. No dressing, fewer pustules and a shorter period of isolation would follow. This reduced costs considerably, but inoculation still only began to be mandated when epidemics swept small towns and villages. Sutton's son Daniel modified his father's techniques and developed a profitable business among families who were above the poverty line. He was so successful in fact that at the end of his first year of independent practice (1764) he had apparently made 2,000 guineas. Outside the areas of jurisdiction of the Corporation of Surgeons and College of Physicians, Sutton, an unqualified practitioner with no medical degree, was free to practice in rural towns and villages. Burney's friend Hester Thrale described him as 'a Fellow of very quick Parts I think, though as ignorant as dirt both with regard to Books and the World'.[18]

One of Daniel Sutton's clients, the lawyer and politician Bamber Gascoyne, left an interesting account of the inoculation of his three sons, and a servant he called Moor, in May 1766.[19] This was at his estate in Essex, where that year the disease was widespread. The preparations and procedure took place in one of Gascoyne's tenants' houses, safely away from the manor. The boys and Moor were put on a strict diet of fruit and vegetables, water and milk, and purged frequently. After a few weeks of this, they were judged ready for the procedure, and Gascoyne wrote that '[m]y children were pretty well considering they are starved. Moor looks as if he had slip'd the chains from a gibbet ... My fears I need not express.' On the designated day, Sutton arrived with two ladies, one of whom was 'the infected person':

> [S]he had about seven pustules with large white heads on them. The doctr. thrust a lancet in one of them which he immediately applied to the arm of Bamber [the eldest son] and put so small a part of the point under his skin that he was not sensible of the point's touching him. Then he put on his cloaths, without plaister rag or any covering whatever; and so practised upon the others.

About a week later, Bamber and Moor both developed a fever and spots began to appear; the other boys soon followed the same course, though Moor suffered severe inflammation. Sixteen days after the operation, they were 'perfectly well' and a few days later were able to go home.

Much less successful was Sutton's inoculation of Mrs Thrale's son Ralph in 1774. 'He is a fine boy & will do well I doubt not,' she wrote in her 'Family Book' on 20 November, after the procedure had taken place. A week later she wrote, '[h]ere I am well paid for my presumption. The Child is vastly ill indeed – dying I think – the Confluent Sort, Sutton never Saw any thing so bad himself: Oh Lord Oh Lord! What shall I do!?'[20] The 'confluent sort' means that the pustules were so many and so large, they wholly covered his face and, presumably, his body. A month later, she wrote that Ralph was 'so altered one could not know him'. Ralph's case, like Octavius's, is a reminder that the procedure might have terrifying consequences. He was to die in July the next year.

Usually easier, simpler, and more effective, though, the 'Suttonian' system had become widely adopted. A former army surgeon with a medical degree, Dr Thomas Dimsdale, who was as well connected as Sutton was not, adopted the system and in 1767 published a widely read book, *The Present Method of Inoculating for the Small-Pox*. In 1775 George III requested that he inoculate Omiah, the native chief of 'Otaheite', and the procedure was successful. Daniel Sutton published a rather truculent book in response called *The Inoculator, or Suttonian System of Innoculation, Fully Set Forth in a Plain and Familiar Manner*, in 1796.[21] But some practitioners in the later years of the century were apparently still performing operations that penetrated the dermis beneath the skin surface (the epidermis), believing that a deeper penetration would be more effective. Edward Jenner wrote in 1798 that 'I have known an inoculator, whose practice was "to cut deep enough (to use his own expression) to see a bit of fat", and there to lodge the matter. The great number of bad Cases ... and the fatality which attended this practice was almost inconceivable.'[22] The deeper the cut, the more likely the patient would suffer a severe attack of the virus, which could, and quite often did, lead to death. The belief that a period of near-starvation was needed to prepare the patient for the procedure would not have helped either.

Frances Burney had thoroughly researched the scourge in the years previous to the writing of *Camilla*, which was published in July 1796 (JL III, 291). The fruits of her study are apparent early in the book. In its first chapters Sir Hugh Tyrold, a baronet who has 'resided upon the hereditary estate of the family in Yorkshire', leaves it to live near his brother and his family on a country estate in Hampshire. In chapter 2 his sister-in-law Mrs Tyrold considers inoculating her youngest daughter, Eugenia:

> The extreme delicacy of the constitution of Eugenia had hitherto deterred
> Mrs Tyrold from innoculating her; she had therefore scrupulously kept her
> from all miscellaneous intercourse in the neighbourhood: but as the weak-
> ness of her infancy was now promising to change into health and strength,
> she meant to give to that terrible disease its best chance, and the only
> security it allows from perpetual alarm, immediately after the heats of the
> present autumn should be over.[23]

But the Tyrold children long to go to a fair, so their soft-hearted and foolish uncle carries them there in his coach. Burney would have learned that markets and fairs were dangerous places, crowded sites where small-pox, which was extremely contagious, might easily be contracted.[24] Annual fairs and even weekly markets were often cancelled for this reason when smallpox was in the neighbourhood. Lavinia, Eugenia's older sister, begs her uncle not to let them out of the vehicle. Sir Hugh agrees to this and instructs the footman to 'ride on first, and keep a sharp look out that nobody has the small pox,' but remarks, '[a]s to the small pox, . . . he had no notion of people's taking diseases upon themselves' (in other words, being inoculated with the pox). '"Besides", continued he, "she will be sure to have it when her time comes, whether she is moped up or not; and how did people do before these new modes of making themselves sick of their own accord?"'[25] These sound like very eccentric remarks, but probably Burney is trying to capture the fatuousness of many statements made by conservative resisters to the procedure.

On arrival at the fair the little girl tearfully begs to follow the other children to 'some straggling booths'. Sir Hugh gives in and takes her into a booth where there are trinkets to buy, and tells her she can have 'as many playthings as she could carry'. 'Her grief now gave way to ecstasy, and her little hands could soon scarcely sustain the loaded skirt of her white frock.'[26] Eugenia's white dress is not only a signifier of gentility (ordinary people would not wear white clothes), but simultaneously of purity. This pure, genteel little girl is now in a poor or working-class site, conceived and dreaded as a place of contagion. As Eula Biss suggests in her *On Immunity: An Inoculation* (2014), fear of disease is essentially fear of other people, and 'the bodies of the poor' were very often seen 'as a liability to public health, as dangerous to others'. 'It is difficult to read any historical account of smallpox', as she remarks, 'without encountering the word *filth*.'[27] Soon 'the innocent voice of Eugenia' calls out 'Little boy, what's the matter with your face, little boy?' Edgar, the young hero of the novel, 'at the same instant saw the same dreaded sight, darted forward, seized Eugenia in his arms, and, in defiance of her playthings and her struggles, carried her back to the coach'. The boy's face must be displaying an array of pustules, which would mean he was highly contagious. Lavinia, hysterical, 'ran up to the little boy, and crying out, "O go away! Go away!" dragged him out of the booth, and, perfectly unconscious what she did, covered his head with her frock'. Everyone fears that Eugenia 'must now be as full of contagion as the poor object who had just had the disease'.[28]

Eugenia nearly dies. 'The disease bore every prognostic of fatal consequences, and the fond parents soon lost all hope, though they redoubled every attention': but there is 'a sudden and happy turn' and she does recover. But though she survives, the child is 'seamed and even scarred by the horrible disorder'. Lest the reader should miss the point, Burney elaborates: Sir Hugh rushes up to her bedroom 'that he might kneel, he said, at her feet, and there give thanks for her recovery: but the moment he entered the room, and saw the dreadful havoc grim disease had made on her face; not a trace of her beauty left, no resemblance by which he could have known her; he shrunk back, wrung his hands, called himself the most sinful of all created beings, and in the deepest despondence, sunk into a chair and wept aloud'.[29]

If Mrs Tyrold had meant to give smallpox 'its best chance, and the only security it allows from perpetual alarm' by having the child inoculated, it is clear that the d'Arblays felt the same way. They decided that Alexander, just three in February 1797, and their only child, should undergo inoculation without delay since smallpox, as Frances put it, was 'a dread that ... hung cruelly' over their happiness. She wrote to her father on 26 February that 'the many objects the little soul must perpetually see this summer, from our building & removal, makes all delay hazardous' (JL III, 279). Under the supervision of d'Arblay, workmen were soon to begin constructing the 'Camilla Cottage' that the success of the recently published novel had enabled the d'Arblays to afford. 'Objects' is a strange, highly class-inflected term for other people, their workmen, but it's the same one used of the infected poor boy in *Camilla*. In Burney's documentary account of inoculation, as in *Camilla*, the bodies of ordinary folk are conceived as a threat to a purity that is inseparable from class status. As Biss argues throughout her book, 'vaccination' in all its forms tends always to be loaded with symbolic significance. It is also surrounded with superstition.

Burney's brother-in-law Clement Francis (the surgeon who had intervened to insist that Frances must leave the court in 1791) had died the previous year, so the d'Arblays arranged that William Ansell, an apothecary from nearby Dorking, 'the first man for such business in this neighbourhood', should come over and undertake the operation. Burney's letter to her sister Susan about the procedure and its aftermath, written a fortnight later and dated 'March 14', is a valuable pathographic document that brings to life a lost era in medical history. Burney presents a dramatic scene involving four actors – the child, the nursemaid Betty, the mother and the doctor – all of them clustered together in a momentous, concerted and fearful, even intimate, medical moment. But it is interesting that, in contrast to Gascoyne, Frances Burney brings no donor into the picture. There might have been one present, or at the very least nearby: possibly he or she was one of those 'objects' not thought worth mentioning.

> I would not awaken useless inquietude in your kind bosom by telling you our fixed design of innoculating our little love this spring – but Mr Ansell was bespoke a Week before this Letter was begun, & the last Day of last month he came – & performed the dreaded operation. The dear little soul sat on my lap, & he gave him some Barley sugar; this made him consent to have his Frock taken off. Mr Ansell pressed me to relinquish him to Betty; but I could not to anyone but his Father, who was at his field. When the Lancet was produced, Betty held him a favourite Toy, of which I began discoursing with him ... But, while listening attentively, he felt Mr Ansell grasp his arm to hold it steady – he turned quite away from his Drummer, & seeing the Lancet, shrunk back. Mr Ansell bid me help to hold him tight, – he then shriekt, & forcibly disengaged his arm from my hand – but, to my utter astonishment, held it out himself very quietly, & looked on, & suffered the incision to be made without a cry, or any resistance, only raising his arm to Mr Ansel, with an expression of the most superlative wonder at his proceedings. Mr A. forced out the blood repeatedly, & played upon it with the Lancet for some minutes, fearing, he said, if particular caution was not used, the little soul was so pure his blood could not be infected. The Child still made no resistance, but looked at the blood with great curiosity,

in the most profound silent rumination. Mr Ansel still was apprehensive the disorder might not be imbibed, from the excessive strictness of his whole life's diet: he therefore asked my leave to innoculate the other arm also. I left it to his own decision, – & he took off the shirt from the other arm. – The little Creature fixed him very attentively, & then turned to me, as if for some explanation of such conduct; but still made not the smallest resistance, & without being held *at all*, permitted the second wound. (JL III, 282–283)

This is an example of Burney's ability to present such an event as an interactive drama: the three nervous adults in concert around the three-year-old, the comic quality of the child's innocence and independence giving the whole scenelette its amusing poignancy. It is clear that Ansell, though 'playing' upon the blood on the arm, is following the Suttonian method, and has not penetrated the skin deeply. The successful sequel of the operation may confirm this conclusion. Despite Ansell's forcing out blood repeatedly with what Burney calls in a later letter to her father, the 'slaughtering design' of the lancet, the wound is only superficial, and almost painless (JL III, 289). As early as the inoculation of Lady Montagu's son, Maitland was boasting that, when performed with a lancet, the procedure caused 'so little Pain to him, that he did not in the least complain of it'.[30] Much later in the century, an observer of Daniel Sutton's procedure stressed that '[t]he operation is performed on most without their feeling or knowing it: and in a minute afterwards, the puncture is scarce visible.'[31] Madame d'Arblay, like any mother watching her child's body being invaded, exaggerates the infant's heroism. On the other hand, she does report that Ansell said that he had never seen so young a child so brave.[32]

Mr Ansell's idea that 'the little soul was so pure his blood could not be infected' is both a physiological or pseudo-medical proposition and a social, class-bound one. In *Emma*, twenty or so years later, the heroine reflects with some satisfaction on the marriage her sister has made to 'a family of such true gentility, untainted in blood and understanding'.[33] 'Pure blood' is a sign of that 'gentility' that preserves you from taint. Ansell's remark, presuming that Burney remembers it exactly, would have been music to the ears of Alexander's acutely class-conscious mother. Not just the child's blood, but his 'little soul' by implication is 'pure'. His 'whole life's diet', the implication seems to be, has conferred upon him a kind of angelic immunity.

At any rate, it seems that Burney later seeks explicitly to associate the child's courage with his 'blood' in the sense not of the bodily fluid, but of his breeding, his 'blood' line. She remarks on the unfortunate absence of 'his Father, to whom the actual view of this infantine courage & firmness would have been such exquisite delight'. More emphatically, in her account of the operation to Charles Burney she writes, 'I shall never cease being sorry his Father did not see him, to clear my character from having adulterated the chivalric spirit & courage of his race.'[34] On a later visit, Mr Ansell 'took from his little Arm 4 *Lancets of matter* – & the dear darling Hero suffered the 4 cuts unmoved, except, as before, by astonishment and curiosity. He would not be held, & his Father, this time, had the satisfaction to see I have not spoiled his race' (JL III, 289). Alexandre d'Arblay was both a soldier and a count: Burney is, half-subtextually, confounding her son's stoicism with his 'blood'.

Her account to her sister continues with the sequel of Ansell's treatment:

> This stroke was given on the Tuesday; & on the following Sunday, after Breakfasting with us in a gaiety the most animating, & with Eyes and Cheeks brilliant with health & spirits, he suddenly drooped, became pale, languid, hot, & short breathed. This continued all Day, & towards evening increased into a restlessness that soon became misery – he refused any food – his Eyes became red, dull, & heavy, his breath feverish, & his limbs in almost convulsive tribulation. His starts were so violent, it was difficult to hold him during his short sleeps, & his cries from pain & nameless sufferings grew incessant. – I expected a fit – & indeed my terrour was horrible. (JL III, 289)

This was the most dangerous and distressing phase of the inoculation process. Burney is describing the sudden onset of high fever or elevated temperature that Gascoyne also noted, which indicated the virus had become active. In her *Account* Lady Montagu had stressed that after the procedure 'the children or young patients play together all the rest of the day, and are in perfect health to the eighth. Then the fever begins to seize them, and they keep their beds two days, very seldom three.' This feverish phase was followed by the emergence of the 'pocks' or pustules on the face, 'very rarely', she claimed, more than twenty or thirty, 'which never mark'.[35] Everything seems to have been normal for Alex: he was able to sleep a little at night, but after three 'very suffering' days for both mother and child 'the spots began to appear' and a fortnight from the operation Fanny reported to her sister

> that *now* all is deliciously well! They began to turn yesterday, and this Day, which marks but the fortnight from the operation, many of them are already fading away, – his appetite is returned, his gaiety is revived, all fever is over,

& if his face was not changed, the disorder would not be suspected. I know how you will feel for our excessive joy at this conquest of a dread that has hung cruelly over our best happiness. (JL III, 284)

'None of it dangerous, as I *now* know,' Burney told her father on 16 March, 'though I was frequently & dreadfully of another opinion in the progress of the business' (JL III, 290). On Alex's face there were only thirteen of 'these frightful boutons', the pustules – signifying a very mild infection. 'Mr A says this is recompense of his state of blood,' a non-Suttonian remark that seems to suggest that the 'low' diet his parents had long kept Alex on was contributing to his recovery. On his second visit, Mr Ansell was able to assure Burney that 'all was safely & happily over as to the distemper' (JL III, 285).

The family now became concerned about Alex's appearance, keenly aware, of course, of the disfiguring scars the pustules often left. But as Burney assured her sister, '[w]e have been so much frightened, that we would have compromised with fate for the loss of all his personal recommendation, to have *ensured* his life' (284). She would not have been so sanguine about this 'personal recommendation', meaning his good looks, if Alex had been born a girl. In *Camilla*, Sir Hugh, overcome with remorse, alters his will to favour Eugenia, on the assumption that her ruined face means she can never marry. 'As to the mere loss of beauty, pretty as it is to look at, I hope it is no such great injury, as she'll have a splendid fortune, which is certainly a better thing, in point of lasting,' he says in his usual bumbling manner, and then he goes to kiss her, but pulls back, saying, 'I shall never think I know her again, never as long as I live!'[36] Burney seems here to recognise what, as David E. Shuttleton shows in his *Smallpox and the Literary Imagination 1660–1820*, was a common assumption: 'While the scarred woman was condemned to a desexualised "after life", her male counterpart not only expected to remain socially active, but his pock-marks might even be seen to enhance his sexual allure.'[37] In Alex's case, completely different from Ralph Thrale's, only one of the spots had 'risen in order', the others dying away 'for want of nourishment' (JL III, 284, 285). His looks would remain undamaged. Inoculation did not always safeguard the patient for a lifetime, and one drawback, belatedly recognised, was that during the fever stage the patient could infect others. There was also the possibility that the lymph on the lancet, in the days before Lister and antiseptic surgery, would transmit other infections besides smallpox. But the operation the d'Arblays had gambled on and Burney had dreaded was a success.

Nine months before Mr Ansell operated on Alex, another, but far more important, procedure had been undertaken by Dr Edward Jenner, as he reported in his 1798 pamphlet *An Inquiry into the Causes and Effects of the Variolae Vaccinae, or Cowpox*. In this case:

> [M]atter was taken from a sore on the hand of a dairymaid, who was infected by her master's cows, and it was inserted, on the 14th of May, 1796, into the arm of the boy by means of two superficial incisions, barely penetrating the cutis, each about half an inch long. On the seventh day he complained of uneasiness in the axilla, and on the ninth he became a little chilly, lost his appetite, and had a slight headache. During the whole of this day he was perceptibly indisposed, and spent the night with some degree of restlessness, but on the day following he was perfectly well.

The boy was James Phipps, the eight-year-old son of a poor Gloucestershire labourer; the 'matter' was lymph from a dairymaid, Sarah Nelme, who had caught cowpox while milking with a slight scratch from a thorn bush on her hand. (It seems to have been known long before in farming communities that milkmaids, whose healthy clear complexions were legendary, were likely to have obtained immunity from smallpox by handling infected cows' udders.)

The crucial test came about five weeks later:

> In order to ascertain whether the boy, after feeling so slight an affection of the system from the cow-pox virus, was secure from the contagion of the smallpox, he was inoculated the 1st of July following with variolous matter, immediately taken from a pustule. Several slight punctures and incisions were made on both his arms, and the matter was carefully inserted, but no disease followed.[38]

This was gambling with the boy's life if the experiment failed. But Jenner was confident. That 'no disease followed' was what he had 'ventured to predict'.[39] His *Inquiry* lists fifteen cases earlier in which a previous infection by cowpox had apparently guarded the patient from infection by smallpox, but this is what we today would call anecdotal evidence. James Phipps in contrast was an experimental subject. His case was clear evidence for Jenner's claim in *Inquiry* that 'the cow-pox protects the human constitution from the infection of the smallpox.' The crucial fact that Jenner had demonstrated via Sarah Nelme and James Phipps was that cowpox could be transferred from one human subject to another. On 27 March 1800 Jenner was presented to Queen Charlotte at St James's Palace. As Richard B. Fisher remarks, given the death of Octavius almost seventeen years before, '[t]he promise of security with safety would have had strong personal meaning to her.'[40]

That same year, Jenner published *A Continuation of Facts and Observations Relative to the Variolae Vaccinae* in which he claimed that vaccination had now been proved and offered the promise of 'extirpating from the earth . . . the severest scourge of the human race'. If a brief mention of 'Dr Jenner's pamphlet on the cow pox' being read aloud in one of Jane Austen's letters of 20 November that year is evidence, his work was becoming widely known among the literate classes.[41] In 1802 Jenner was awarded 10,000 pounds by a grateful House of Commons, and early in 1803 the Royal Jennerian Society was formed, with the queen as its patron. The Society opened vaccination stations in London and apparently more than 12,000 vaccinations were carried out in the first year. The aim of the vaccination lobby was, from the first, to persuade the government to legislate to make vaccination compulsory. Despite a report by the Royal College of Physicians to Parliament in 1807 making the crucial point that individuals 'consulting the gratification of their own feelings' were in effect contributing to the 'constant recurrence' of smallpox and hence 'doing mischief to their neighbours', a bill designed to ban inoculation failed, 'as injurious to personal freedom'.[42]

From the start there was violent opposition to the practice. Dr Benjamin Mosley, a physician to the Royal Medical Hospital in Chelsea, to give just one example, violently attacked vaccination or 'Cowmania' in a work published in 1799. 'Can any person say what may be the consequence of introducing the *Lues Bovilla,* a bestial humour – into the human frame?' he asked. 'Who knows besides what ideas may arise . . . from a brutal fever having excited its incongruous impressions on the brain?' Cartoons appeared lampooning the new practice; one by Gillray published in 1802 shows unfortunate patients of Dr Jenner who have developed horrible animal protuberances or grown horns.[43] There were, perhaps inevitably, cases where vaccination failed, and these were given much publicity. Essentially, though, the most obdurate opposition came from vested interests, especially from the legion of medical practitioners (mostly surgeons and apothecaries) who saw a steady and sometimes lucrative source of income vanishing before their eyes. Moreover, inoculation had been extended gradually to the poorer classes as fees had diminished, and people were reluctant to adopt another strange – or even stranger – practice, since inoculation had certainly seemed often effective.

Not until a terrible epidemic between 1837 and 1840 swept across England and Wales and claimed more than 42,000 lives, mostly infants and young children, was 'An Act to extend the Practice of Vaccination' passed. This made universal treatment free, but many parishes, entrusted with overseeing the programme, apparently offered a choice between inoculation and vaccination. Habit prevailed and inoculation and small-pox persisted. This is what makes it plausible that in Dickens's *Bleak House*, first serialised in 1852–1853, the heroine Esther Summerson catches smallpox from Jo, the crossing sweeper, more or less the lowest of the low. Esther survives, but is severely disfigured. Dickens's novel may have had some influence: in August 1853, an Act was passed making it compulsory for parents to vaccinate their children before they reached the age of three and instituting fines for those who did not comply. This aroused great opposition and resistance, both from the poor, who had other things, like getting a living, to be concerned about, and from middle-class families, who may have resented this first intrusion of state authority into their lives. Resistance persisted for decades, perhaps partly because compulsory vacci-nation was thought to be a violation of what John Stuart Mill's classic *On Liberty* (1859) was famously to proclaim as an individual's sole 'sovereignty' over their own body. At the same time some churchmen continued preaching against what one called, even in 1873, 'such an unnatural proceeding as deliberately cutting through the skin, and planting in our system an evil disease of a beast'.[44]

The resistance of many people in the nineteenth century to com-pulsory vaccination, and the rhetoric of those who opposed it, has many echoes in present-day Western societies. ('Vaccination' as a comprehensive term for inoculations against many diseases was proposed by Louis Pasteur in 1881 as a tribute to Jenner.) But resis-tance to inoculation in some pockets of the modern world is far more irrational than the resistance to inoculation, or even vaccination, in earlier centuries. Leaving aside the fact that few people have even heard of smallpox, let alone its horrors, the prevalence of superstitions about inoculation demands explanation. Biss's *On Immunity* is a recent attempt to comprehend why some mothers still campaign against having their children vaccinated, and as her subtitle *An Inoculation* suggests, to offer sensible and well-researched arguments to dispel them. Biss writes that 'it seems inevitable that vaccination would become emblematic: a needle breaks the skin, a sight so profound that it causes some people to faint, and a foreign substance is injected into the flesh. The metaphors we find in this gesture are overwhel-mingly fearful and almost always suggest violation, corruption, and pollution.'[45] Perhaps the phrase in Burney's letter to her father describing the lancet as 'the slaughtering knife' catches, unconsciously, some of this involuntary terror. It is strange that this fear, and the fear of contamination of the 'pure' by the impure, should persist. What was well founded in 1797 approaches paranoia in 2019. As Biss and many others have argued since the College of Physicians in 1807 condemned those who in 'consulting the gratification of their own feelings' were in effect contributing to the 'constant recurrence' of smallpox and hence 'doing mischief to their neighbours', a decision not to inoculate your child dangers their whole community.

Frances Burney's recreation of that intimate domestic scene, and her chronicling of the days of acute anxiety that followed, can bring back to our consciousness how momentous and frightening was a procedure, however essential if a life was to be saved, that must have taken place thousands of times in eighteenth-century England. Her ability to catch, however briefly here, the nervous tension of the scene, the dramatic interplay of the participants, is greatly intensified in her account of the much more drastic surgery that is the subject of the next chapter. Alexander d'Arblay never contracted smallpox, though his health remained a frequent source of anxiety to his possessive mother. A teenager in Paris with his parents in 1811, he was employed to copy out Frances's detailed record of an operation designed to cure a disease – cancer – that has replaced smallpox as the most dreaded malady in the Western world. Alex managed to copy only the first two-thirds of the document before he handed over transcribing to his father. Perhaps he found his mother's narrative too disturbing to carry on.

Notes

1. Bladon, F. McKno, ed., *The Diaries of Robert Fulke Greville*, p. 133. 'Mr Dundas' was sergeant surgeon to the king.
2. This information is taken from Hadlow, J., *The Strangest Family*, p. 294. This nurse, Louisa Cheveley, was adamant that the death was not the result of inoculation.
3. Fraser, F., *Princesses*, p. 143.
4. Dobson, A., *Diary and Letters of Madame d'Arblay*, IV, p. 415, n. 1.
5. Baxby, D., *Jenner's Smallpox Vaccine*, p. 13.
6. Williams, G., *Angel of Death*, p. 50. Macaulay's description is often cited: 'Smallpox was always present, ... tormenting with constant fears all whom it had not yet stricken, leaving on those whose lives it spared the hideous traces of its power, turning the babe into a changeling at which the mother shuddered, and making the eyes and cheeks of the betrothed maiden objects of horror to the lover' (Baxby, D., *Jenner's Smallpox Vaccine*, p. 14).

7. Gurney, M. S., 'Disease As Device', p. 85.
8. Grundy, I., *Lady Mary Wortley Montagu*, p. 144.
9. Letter to Mary Chiswell, April 1717, quoted in Smith, J. R., *The Speckled Monster*, pp. 30–31.
10. Ibid., p. 32.
11. Grundy, I., *Lady Mary Wortley Montagu*, p. 216.
12. Ibid., pp. 217–218.
13. Fisher, R. B., *Edward Jenner*, p. 14.
14. Smith, J. R., *The Speckled Monster*, p. 33.
15. Williams, G., *Angel of Death*, pp. 152–154.
16. Smith, J. R., *The Speckled Monster*, p. 38.
17. *Gentleman's Magazine*, xxii, November 1752, p. 511.
18. Balderston, K., ed., *Thraliana*, I, p. 176.
19. This material is from Smith, J. R., *The Specked Monster*, pp. 75–77.
20. Hyde, M., *The Thrales of Streatham Park*, pp. 109, 110.
21. Sutton, D., *The Inoculator*.
22. *An Inquiry into the Causes and Effects of . . . the Cow Pox*, p. 58, cited in Razzell, P., *Conquest of Smallpox*, p. 20.
23. Bloom, E. A. and Bloom, L. D., eds., Burney, F., *Camilla*, p. 22.
24. In *The Specked Monster* Smith mentions the cancelling of annual fairs at Great Oakley and Earls Colne in 1773, Dedham in 1773 and 1785, and Boxted in 1798, all villages and towns in Essex (p. 21).
25. Bloom, E. A. and Bloom, L. D., eds., Burney, F., *Camilla*, p. 23.
26. Ibid., p. 23.
27. Biss, E., *On Immunity*, p. 78.
28. Bloom, E. A. and Bloom, L. D., eds., Burney, F., *Camilla*, p. 24.
29. Ibid., p. 29.
30. Grundy, I., *Lady Mary Wortley Montagu*, p. 162.
31. Hulton, R., *A Sermon . . . in Defence of Inoculation*, 1767, cited in Razzell, P., *Conquest of Smallpox*, p. 18.
32. JL III, 290.
33. Cronin, R. and McMillan, D., eds., Austen, J., *Emma*, p. 389.
34. JL III, 290.
35. Razzell, P., *Conquest of Smallpox*, p. 10.
36. Bloom, E. A. and Bloom, L. D., eds., Burney, F., *Camilla*, p. 33.
37. Shuttleton, D., *Smallpox and the Literary Imagination*, p. 158. See Shuttleton's two chapters, '"Beauty's Enemy" and the Disfigured Woman' and '"Enamel'd not deform'd": Manly Disfigurements' (pp. 113–258).
38. See Edward Jenner, *The Three Original Publications on Vaccination against Smallpox*, Harvard Classics, Vol. 38. Part 4, Case XVII, paras 42, 45 [www.bartleby.com/38/4/1.htm] accessed 8 November 2016.
39. Fisher, R. B., *Edward Jenner*, p. 67, citing a letter in the Royal College of Physicians.
40. Ibid., p. 99.
41. Le Faye, D., ed., *Jane Austen's Letters*, p. 62.

42. Smith, J. R., *The Speckled Monster*, pp. 108–109.
43. The quotation from Mosley is given in Fisher, R. B., *Edward Jenner*, p. 93. No precise source is given. Three cartoons are illustrated in Smith, J. R., *The Speckled Monster*, pp. 100–102.
44. Smith, J. R., *The Speckled Monster*, p. 126.
45. Biss, E., *On Immunity*, p. 12.

CHAPTER 5

A Mastectomy: 1811

Since its first publication in 1975, Frances Burney's account of the mastectomy of her right breast in September 1811 has been more studied and written about than any other of her journals or letters. One obvious reason for its currency is that, unlike smallpox, breast cancer has not been eradicated, and may be even more common today than it was then. The story Burney tells has several aspects that might be recognised by a woman in the twenty-first century suspecting, diagnosed with, or combating the same condition. And because this document is both almost unique as a patient's description of the experience of amputation surgery without anaesthetic, and is at least to some extent an account of a battle of wills between a female patient and her attending medical men, it has become a rich site for exploration by feminist scholars focused on the sexual politics of the occasion.[1] These intricated aspects make Burney's 'A Mastectomy' a pioneering pathographic narrative. Its belated circulation happened to coincide with the publication of many other more recent autobiographical patient narratives, and subsequently with the instauration of the genre in academic studies.

The document headed 'A Mastectomy' by its modern editors takes the form of a long letter written to Frances's sister Esther in England when Burney and her family were stranded in Paris during the Napoleonic wars.[2] At many points in the narrative Frances (or Fanny) addresses her sister directly, as if she were confiding in her and needing her imaginary presence to strengthen her own will to recall and write about a very terrible episode. There is a 'P. S.' appended to the letter, in which she reassures Esther that she is now (presumably in June 1812 when writing the letter was finished) well. Burney continues: 'Read, therefore, this Narrative at your leisure, & without emotion' (JL VI, 615). Two hundred years later, it is as impossible to give this dreadful document one's attention without emotion, as it must have been for Esther.

A way to begin to deal with this emotion is to consider the circumstances surrounding the actual operation, and which, through Burney's careful and apparently inconsequential recitation, generate the gripping suspense that is such a powerful feature of 'this Narrative'. To follow the fears and unavailing self-medications, the complications, procrastinations, and delays that precede the surgery leads, as it happens, to the more central questions of medical ethics and authority which play a crucial role in the central drama of the surgery scene itself.

There's nothing unusual about accidents and apparently unaccountable delays preceding a patient's urgent surgery. An almost contemporary letter concerning a breast cancer operation, written in 1814 by a Quaker woman called Susanna Emlen in New Jersey to her father in England relates a similar trajectory of anxiety, self-treatment, false hopes, and final reluctant decision to undergo a surgery – without anaesthetic – that was held up for weeks. This is an interesting document to compare with Burney's because, as Susan Garfinkel, who discovered it, writes: 'Within a single narrative [Emlen] is able to integrate into a descriptive chronology of external events her own personal experience of these events, with the emotions, attitudes and beliefs that inform them.'[3] Much the same, though with the enhanced dramatic skills of a practised writer, may be said of Burney's apparently private and spontaneous letter.

Emlen, like Burney, first felt something was wrong many months before the actual surgery was undertaken. She wrote that '[i]t was about the middle of the last twelfth Month [i.e. December 1813] that I first perceived a tumour in my left breast, irregularly shaped, about the size of a partridge egg ... My terror when I had fully ascertained the fact is not to be express'd.'[4] She confided in her husband only after several weeks, but in preference to consulting a surgeon, they settled on a course of treatment using a patent 'Logan's salve'. This did not prove effective. Nor did a low diet, which she tried next. As it happened her brother-in-law was a man who is often called the father of American surgery, Dr Philip Physick (his real surname). Physick, like Burney's surgeons, was highly skilled (he had spent three years in London under the renowned John Hunter). The Emlens knew he would advise an operation, but Susan confesses that 'I had not yet suffered enough to endure the thought of so terrible a measure.'[5] In April 1814 they travelled to Philadelphia, where he was eventually consulted, and first prescribed a low diet, and then bleeding by the lancet and leeches, blistering, and a mercurial plaster on the tumour. Not surprisingly, these did not help, and four doctors in consultation, including Physick's nephew, then decided that surgery was the only option. About a month later Physick, with his sister, daughter, and a nurse came down from Philadelphia to stay with the Emlens and to perform the operation, but while Susan was making her preparations he himself fell ill, with 'a cholick more violent than he had ever had' and the plan was suspended till he recovered. This delay of several weeks was what she described to her father as 'a time of complicated affliction'.[6] The other physicians came to see her and, as she wrote, 'I was willing the business should proceed, but the young men hesitating to perform it, it was judged best to delay the matter' until Physick was well enough to take it on. The recovered Physick arrived back from Philadelphia on 3 June to perform the operation the next day. But he again was too unwell, so his nephew Dr Dorsey acted as principal surgeon. Susanna Emlen then submitted to the surgery on 4 June 1814.

Delays and impediments caused Frances Burney her own complicated afflictions. In her case they seem to be a combination of her reluctance to undergo 'so terrible a measure' and her determination to retain some control over events, complicated by disagreements and difficulties of protocol among her doctors. She relates that she became first disturbed by pains in her right breast in August 1810. Her husband and friends pressed her to have an examination, which she was reluctant to undergo, but several months later she saw a Dr Jouart, who gave her 'some directions that produced no fruit'. She grew worse and M. d'Arblay insisted that she should see Dr Antoine Dubois, who had attended her previously in 1807. He was, she writes, 'the most celebrated surgeon of France', and at that time *accoucheur* to Empress Josephine (JL VI, 559). His 'constant attendance' at the court made this difficult, but sometime before the empress gave birth on 20 March 1811, he found an opportunity to visit and presented Frances with 'a prescription to be pursued for a month'. Then Dubois conferred privately with her husband, and it seems plausible to suspect, in view of later events, that, keeping his prognosis from the patient, he told d'Arblay that he feared the case was hopeless. As Robert A. Aronowitz remarks, at this time '[d]octors and most lay persons were deeply pessimistic that surgery – or anything else – could cure cancer in the breast.'[7] At any rate, when Frances saw her husband, she writes, 'his whole face displayed the bitterest woe. I had not, therefore, much difficulty in telling myself what he endeavoured not to tell me – that a small operation would be necessary to avert evil consequences!' (JL VI, 600). She followed Dubois's instructions, but her symptoms became steadily more serious.

Enter Dominique-Jean Larrey. Mutual friends persuaded this admired and eminent army surgeon to call on the d'Arblays. Larrey happened to be enjoying an interval in the capital between campaigns, using the time to write a book intended to be useful to younger surgeons. He also was famous, especially for the speed and skill with which he had performed amputations of injured limbs on the battlefield, often under fire, including at the battle of Austerlitz (1805).[8] He visited Madame d'Arblay, but 'very unwillingly, & full of scruples concerning M. Dubois'. Larrey was a surgeon, not a physician, and for all his distinction, this was a transgression of medical ethics. Dubois was ten years Larrey's senior, and previously to his position at the court had been professor of anatomy and a year later professor of surgery at the newly founded Ecole de Santé in 1794. So he asked Burney herself to write a formal letter to Dubois – a placatory and flattering letter – requesting that she be made over to Larrey. The d'Arblays were in fact fortunate to secure his services: Larrey's time between 1810 and 1811 in Paris was a rare interlude in a military career which would soon to lead to his being appointed surgeon-in-chief to the Grande Army and accompanying Napoleon on the famous, disastrous campaign against Russia in 1812.[9]

Burney writes that she was 'now put on a new *regime*, & animated by the fairest hopes' (JL VI, 601). The arrival of Larrey is followed in her letter by a character sketch (more or less a panegyric) of Larrey, and it is very likely that, just as anxiety and fear had made her painful symptoms more palpable to consciousness, her admiration and liking, amounting almost to love, of Larrey, 'this singularly excellent of men', lifted her mood, so that refreshed by 'the fairest hopes' her awareness of pain diminished, and she was able to experience some recovery. But soon Larrey, she writes, 'forced' her to see another doctor, the outstanding anatomist Francois Ribe, because with characteristic scrupulousness he suspected that his desire to save her from the drastic and dreadful surgery might have clouded his judgement (JL VI, 602).

Then Burney learned of the death of her favourite Princess Amelia (apparently from tuberculosis, in November 1810[10]), the subsequent recurrence of King George's 'mad' symptoms, and – through a brutally short message – the death of her close friend William Locke. 'Three such calamities', she later wrote, 'overwhelmed me' (JL VI 706). Larrey, shocked at her regression, called on Ribe again, and the two of them seem to have firmly proposed the operation. Frances pleaded with them, 'the weather was not propitious to any operation' (this must now be in the summer of 1811), and they gave her more time. Susanna Emlen, following the consultation among four doctors that decided on surgery for her, was to write of their 'awful sentence'.[11] After Larrey, Ribe, and a younger doctor,

Moreau, had discussed her case, Madame d'Arblay was, as she too put it, 'formally condemned to an operation by all Three'. Both women were grimly comparing themselves to a prisoner in the dock.

Larrey now 'proposed again calling in M. Dubois', which Burney reluctantly agreed to because of what Larrey, she writes, called his 'super-skill and experience'. (There might well be a 'safety in numbers' element in this request.) This resulted in further delay – 'What an interval was this!' – before Dubois could spare the time to visit (JL VI, 604). Burney's remark that on his arrival he 'behaved extremely well, no pique intervened', like Larrey's deference in bringing him on board, suggests a tension between the two, both recently created 'Barron' by Napoleon, which throws light on Larrey's demeanour as reported by her during the ensuing surgery. There is furthermore a clear conflict of opinions or attitudes, as a later letter of Burney's mentioning Larrey illuminates. He was a man, she wrote, 'to whom I owed my almost restoration to life, through the skill, courage, & Judgement with which he performed a difficult & doubtful operation against an incipient cancer, in opposition to the opinion of his Rival, Dubois, that the evil was too deep for extirpation' (JL VI, 623). This rivalry (if that is in fact the word) was to run as an undercurrent throughout Burney's account of the operation.

After another delay, Burney is summoned to meet the assembled medical men, all of whom, including Larrey, are silent until she exercises her authority – as the patient who is also in a sense their patron – and calls upon them to speak. Dubois takes the lead and delivers 'a long & unintelligible harangue, from his own disturbance', but in the end makes clear that the operation must go ahead (JL VI, 604). It is obvious (and understood by Burney) that the surgery is dreaded almost as much by her doctors as it is by her. It is also possible that Dubois's speech was nervously crammed with medical terms and qualifications because he was compelled to disguise his own doubts about or opposition to the procedure. A few moments later, when Burney asks that her husband be kept in ignorance of the scheduled day until the operation is over, there is another disagreement: 'M. Dubois', writes Burney, 'protested he would not undertake to act' if M. d'Arblay were present. Larrey 'looked dissentient but was silent'. Has he resolved to let Dubois have his way as the price for his collaboration? Her word 'protested' might convey the intuition that Dubois's speech emerges out of another dispute, though she does not actually know Dubois's views yet.

Once the decision is made, Burney expects, as any patient would, that the operation is to be scheduled very soon; instead she is left to linger three weeks in misery before Larrey tells M. d'Arblay that the doctors are awaiting a formal summons from her. In fact, the delay, Larrey later informs her, is due to Dubois's continued reluctance. In a passage of retrospective narration enclosed in the letter, she learns that 'M. Dubois had given his opinion that the evil was too far advanced for any remedy; that the cancer was already internally declared; that I was inevitably destined to that most frightful of deaths, & that an operation would but accelerate my dissolution' (JL VI, 607). The Hippocratic injunction 'First, do no harm' must have been in play here: Dubois thinks that the cancer has metastasized, 'internally declared', and that they will be inflicting terrible pain without any hope of a cure. It's a dispute over medical ethics, but Larrey resolved his own fears, he tells Burney, by remembering the patient's wishes, and, respecting them, determined to 'make the attempt' to save her life. Larrey was known for the resolution with which he performed amputations on the battlefield and was convinced, as he wrote, that:

> However cruel that an operation may be, it is an act of humanity in the hands of the surgeon when he can save the life of the injured, in danger, and the more the danger is great and pressing, the more the response must be prompt and energetic. *Ad extreme morbos, extrema remedia exquisite optima* (Hippocr.). In this circumstance, the man of the art does his duty, and absolutely does not think about his reputation.[12]

The ethic of the military surgeon and the ethic of the physician, in this case, collide. The day and time for the operation is finally settled: one o'clock on the last day of September. But when one o'clock arrives, the news comes that Dubois can't attend until three. Burney captures her own emotions during this last, cruel, delay:

> This, indeed, was a dreadful interval. I had no longer anything to do – I had only to think – TWO HOURS thus spent seemed never-ending. I would fain have written to my dearest Father – to You, my Esther – to Charlotte, James – Charles – Amelia Lock – but my arm prohibited me: I strolled to the Sallon – I saw it fitted with preparations, & I recoiled – But I soon returned; to what effect disguise from myself what I must so soon know? – yet the sight of the immense quantity of bandages, compresses, spunges, Lint – Made me a little sick: – I walked backwards & forwards till I quieted all emotion. (JL VI 609)

Burney conjures up helpless violent agitation and distress in her words and phrasing. She conveys her turning from one unavailing resource or thought to another through the relentless employment of dashes which, replacing the formal punctuation that signifies order and rationality, generates a convincing simulacrum of jagged, restless thoughts and movements trying to fend off unappeasable dread.

This deployment of the dash continues, now consciously dramatic, when the doctors arrive at last: 'the Cabriolets – one – two – three – four – succeeded rapidly to each other in stopping at the door.' Then her room, 'without previous message, was entered by 7 Men in black, Dr Larry, M. Dubois, Dr Moreau, Dr Aumont, Dr Ribe, & a pupil of Dr Larry, & another of M. Dubois. I was now awakened from my stupor – and by a sort of indignation – Why so many? & without leave?'[13] As Madame d'Arblay, a well-connected gentlewoman of nearly sixty, she must have felt, as I have suggested, in some degree the patron of her doctors, with equal weight in making decisions. This was now a huge violation of protocol. She had been asked to authorise the operation, but had not been told how many doctors to expect and when they would enter her private dwelling. (This is the period in French medicine that Foucault described as 'the birth of the clinic'. The unauthorised inclusion of pupils may be a sign of a shift, more advanced in post-Revolutionary France than in England, to a 'new medicine', in which the balance of power between patient and physician has altered.)[14] Since no fees are ever mentioned, it may be that the doctors understood it as their right to bring along pupils. '*Already* to become but second, even for the King!' (CJL IV, 523) Burney had cried at a crucial moment of George III's illness: now she similarly registers the shocked revelation that she has become second to the doctors.

Madame d'Arblay does not accept this new position without a struggle. She seeks throughout the preparations for the surgery to make her own will known (she has already succeeded, with great address, in concealing the imminence of the surgery from her husband – he is safely away at his office). She writes, with some hostility, that 'M. Dubois acted as Commander-in-Chief' but a few minutes later when she describes him as trying 'to issue his commands *en militaire*', as if she were a soldier in the inferior ranks, she says she 'resisted all that were resistable' (JL VI, 610). She is, however, 'compelled' to disrobe, in front of these men, and this she finds so distressing that Dubois 'softened, and spoke soothingly'. This struggle for power or authority between the doctor and the patient takes place in an atmosphere already tense with apprehension. Burney responds to Dubois's changed tone with an attempt at conciliation, and this leads to one of the most critical moments in the narrative:

Can *You*, I cried, feel for an operation that, to *You*, must seem so trivial? – Trivial? he repeated – taking up a bit of paper, which he tore, unconsciously, into a million of pieces, *oui – c'est peu de chose — mais–*' he stammered, & could not go on. No one else attempted to speak, but I was softened myself, when I saw even M. Dubois grow agitated, while Dr Larry kept always aloof, yet a glance shewed me he was pale as ashes.[15]

It is worth pausing over what this speech, assuming that Burney recalls it exactly, reveals. The operation is not 'trivial' for Dubois. He is presiding over a scene to which he has consented against his conscience. He is trying to reassure the patient, saying 'it's not much really', for a professional man, she is invited to assume, of great experience in such things. But – *'mais'* – this surgery is in fact quite different: an operation, surrounded by danger, momentous in its consequences, to be performed by a military surgeon, on an elderly gentlewoman in her own home, and moreover a gentlewoman who has already made plain that she is no passively acquiescent patient. His tearing of the paper 'unconsciously' does not belong to the same order of nervous action as Stephen Digby 'twisting his riding stick' twenty ways: 'unconsciously' here signals what would be in psychoanalytic terms a symbolic action, and what it may actually symbolise is Dubois's despair; he's found himself compelled to do something, it is very 'little', nothing much, but it may mean the destruction of the patient, it might be a hopelessly destructive action, just as his bit of paper is reduced to fragments. It discloses what he cannot say, faced with the emotional authority that Burney so powerfully projects. What the paper was and what may have been Dubois's conscious impulse to destroy it are intriguing questions.

The result of this moment is that Burney now understands that the doctors are, so to speak, on her side, convinced that 'danger was hovering about' her and that 'this experiment alone could save me from its jaws'. Italicising the word *'experiment'*, in his reading of this scene Aronowitz suggests that Burney may have sensed her 'doctors' pessimism about the effectiveness of breast amputations in saving women's lives', and calls this, for her, 'an enduring, existential bet'.[16] At this point she takes conciliatory action and mounts onto the bed, 'unbidden', as she writes, thus acting autonomously and committing herself to the surgery. Susanna Emlen's nurse spread a handkerchief over her face, but she could see through it the preparations for her surgery; Dubois now, perhaps in a gesture of kindness, does the same for Burney. The cambric, though shielding her eyes from the doctors, is so thin it means she can see 'the glitter of polished Steel': Larrey's lancet. Dubois's action must have another intended function, loosely analogous to anaesthetic: it seeks to erase the patient as a person, an identity, so that the operation might be carried out simply on a body. This moment too is strikingly symbolic, since the thin cloth dramatises the porosity, or transmission of affect that nevertheless continues to play between Madame d'Arblay and these physicians. This transmission, rather than the collision of doctors and patient, is, at least until the climactic minutes of the surgery, the key dynamic of this occasion.

These tensions and unspoken conflicts between the medical personnel, and between the patient and her doctors, suggest that the relations revealed within this medical encounter are more complex than some readers imagine. Since Julia Epstein's ground-breaking reading of the narrative, which argued 'the entire letter depicts and metonymizes a dynamic of male-female power relations, a play of professional authority against female autonomy as symbolized by the sacrosanct female body here to be defiled' and that writing her account of the operation allowed Burney to defuse 'the framework of domination and submission that she found as oppressive as the physical pain', it is common to read the situation as a sustained conflict between hostile genders.[17] Burney is depicted as the female patient struggling against a dominant, coercive 'masculinist' medicine. It has been asserted, for example, that Burney's 'own desires are completely ignored by the doctors' or, extending this suggestion, that Burney is 'like helpless prey to the hunter-doctors'.[18] More temperately, Kate Chisholm writes that the '"7 men in black" burst into her bedroom . . . conspiring against her to remove her breast in a sign language all their own'.[19] But as Annie Précastaings writes, 'readers of Burney's mastectomy letter should resist the temptation to cast her in the role of impotent victim only.'[20] There is a continual interplay of will and emotion between the doctors and their patient; it is her ability to capture and to recall this that makes Burney's account so remarkable.

Précastaings offers a quite different reading, in which Burney is strong, but the men, including her husband, cannot control their emotions. She argues that 'throughout the letter Burney contrasts her control of affect with the reactivity of the men who surround her.' Burney is able to 'seal in her emotions' while allowing, in her narrative, the men 'to give free rein to their emotional reactivity'.[21] Thus Burney, she argues, exemplifies the stoicism propagated by post-Revolutionary theorists. 'Burney's insistence on her own Stoicism, while the men around her indulge their sensibility, amounts to a daring role reversal,' she claims. While it is certainly true that Burney is far from passive during the whole sequence, Précastaings is still proposing an adversarial or polarised view of the patient–doctor relationship. The doctors are weak; the female patient is the heroine.

This insistence on the doctors' 'emotional reactivity', however, fore-closes the question of what they are reacting to. When Burney, desolated by the bad news from England, for example, seems much worse, and Larrey, she reports, cries 'Et qu'est il donc arrive?', it is clear that he is reacting in response to Burney's own changed looks. When she describes his face 'as pale as ashes' or his tone as 'nearly tragic', it is as well to remember that these are Burney's words, and that it is she who perceives them (or projects them) onto the subject. She is deeply sympathetic to Larrey, and will read him through her own feelings. Just before Dubois's resort to the tearing of the paper, Burney has dramatised her distress at having to disrobe: 'Ah, then, how did I think of My Sisters! – not one, at so dreadful an instant, at hand, to protect – adjust – guard me – no one upon whom I could rely – my departed Angel! – how did I think of her! – how did I long – long for my Esther – my Charlotte!' (JL VI, 610–611). Here it must be clear that Dubois does not just react; he 'softens' as a kindly human response to her very apparent distress, and that for a moment there is the mutual human contact which leads to that resolution of the patient to share the 'experiment' with her doctors.

So nuanced and compelling is Burney's account of these preparatory negotiations that it is relevant at this point to compare Susan Emlen's report of the prelude to her own mastectomy:

> About one oclock, Nurse Hooke came into the chamber I was in to tell me the Doctors waited my coming in my own room. She cover'd my head with a handkerchief, as she led me in, hoping it might save me the sight of the preparations – I however saw Dr Dorsey with his sleeves tuckd up and his cloaths coverd with a large apron, and had a slight view of the other four: of whom Dr Tucker held my arm, while my Aunt supported my head, and at times gave me something to smell.[22]

This setting differs markedly from Burney's. Physick and his nurse, as well as Dorsey, are guests in Emlen's home. Dr Tucker is her local doctor. While Burney feels desperately alone and vulnerable surrounded by seven men (in a country at war with hers, and the leading doctors intimate with Napoleon, the dictator she hates), Emlen's chief surgeon is her brother-in-law, Dr Dorsey is his nephew, and she has the presence of a nurse and her aunt – apparently throughout the operation – to comfort her. Quakers, they share their religious faith; the community, the enclosed domestic, familial context makes some difference between what she and Burney underwent.[23] But at this point, Emlen's account of the procedure 'breaks down'; as Susan Garfinkel writes, 'her painful experience overwhelming her ability to narrate the scene'. Whatever were the details of her surgery, they are erased, either in her memory or because she was sparing the father who would read her account. She now simply continues: 'My suffering was severe beyond expression, my whole being seemed absorbed in pain – the tumour was taken out in 25 minutes, but it was an hour before I was in bed.' Garfinkel comments that 'Though the focused subject of her suffering and the motive for her narrative, the operation itself is the most undescribed section of her letter.'[24] As I have mentioned in the Introduction, writing about an amputation of the foot without anaesthetic in 1843, another patient had recourse to the same gesture: 'Of the agony it occasioned, I will say nothing. Suffering so great as I underwent cannot be expressed in words, and thus fortunately cannot be recalled.'[25]

When she first realises that an operation will be necessary, Burney writes to her sister, 'Ah, my dearest Esther, for this I felt no courage – my dread & repugnance, from a thousand reasons *besides* the pain, almost shook all my faculties' (JL VI, 600). It is usually assumed that here she is referring, not so much to the possibility of death, as to the violation of her modesty – the repugnance felt is that of an elderly lady compelled to expose her breast to the gaze of male strangers. But having consented to the operation by mounting the bedstead, Burney makes herself into the co-operative and maybe indeed 'stoical' patient. Dubois places her on the mattress and spreads the cambric over her face. He does not tell her that he is going to do this or why. The room is silent, 'during which, I imagine, they took their orders by signs, & made their examination – Oh what a horrible suspension! – I did not breathe – & M. Dubois tried vainly to find any pulse. This pause, at length, was broken by Dr Larry, who, in a voice of solemn melancholy, said "Qui me tiendra ce sein?"' (JL VI, 611). (An instance perhaps of Larrey's instinctive tact: not 'the breast', as if it were the possession of the medical fraternity, but 'this breast', this right breast, that is this woman's.) No one answers, 'at least not verbally'. It is the doctors' silent sign language throughout the operation that draws even calm readers, like Chisholm, to feel that they are 'conspiring against her', when it is more plausible to suggest that they are acting as a disciplined team, wholly focused on the terrible task at hand.

Larrey's words lead Burney to fear that they intend the amputation of the entire breast, a fear which is confirmed when 'again through the Cambric I saw the hand of M. Dubois held up, while his fore finger first described a straight line from top to bottom of the breast, secondly a Cross, & thirdly a circle; intimating that the WHOLE was to be taken off.' At this moment Burney throws off what she now calls her 'veil' – renouncing her modesty – and cries 'C'est moi, Monsieur!' – 'I will, Monsieur!' 'I will support the breast for you.' She holds her hand under her breast, in effect, as Ann Dally notes in *Women under the Knife*, 'even offering to hold her breast herself to keep it still while the surgeon operated', so that 'she can be somehow, or at least in part in control of herself and her body'.[26] She is offering to engage with the doctors in the surgery.

Burney then speaks: she

> explained the nature of my sufferings, which all sprang from one point, though they darted into every part. I was heard attentively, but in utter silence, & M. Dubois then re-placed me as before, &, as before, spread my veil over my face. How vain, alas, my representation! immediately again I saw the fatal finger describe the Cross – & the circle – Hopeless, then, desperate, & self-given up, I closed once more my Eyes. (JL VI, 612)

'Representation' here must mean a claim: she is not just showing her breast, she is claiming a unique knowledge. All patients must recognise this impulse to contribute their own experience, to present oneself as a person, when surrounded by doctors or when confronted with the imminence of surgery. Thus this moment is a fiercely dramatic and indeed classic enactment of the schism between patienthood, the patient's identity and the other world of medical authority and power. Moreover, by the silent communication by signs, suggesting the esoteric language of the initiated, her description of the circle above her, and by the phrase 'the fatal finger', Burney has managed to intimate her unconscious or subconscious sense that she is being sacrificed, the female victim of a male cult – a vibe that communicates itself, as I have shown, to many readers. After her courageous intervention, she is 'heard attentively', but it is clear that, from the medical perspective, the procedure has already been initiated, and will be carried through. What Larrey knew as the surgeon's 'cruel . . . act of humanity' has begun.

At this point, Burney briefly breaks off to address 'My dearest Esther' and with the phrase 'this doleful ditty' seeks, unhappily, to make light of the operation, perhaps to introduce some distance from it. Yet she very soon resumes her narrative, and there is no sparing of her sister at all. For a brief moment Burney seems to be adopting the tactic Emlen and others adopted – saying that her terror 'surpasses all description', but then the writer sets to work and employs everything she knows about rhythm and phrasing to make the experience cut through to her readers: 'Yet – when the dreadful steel was plunged into the breast – cutting through veins – arteries – flesh – nerves – I needed no injunctions not to restrain my cries.

I began a scream that lasted unintermittingly during the whole time of the incision – & I almost marvel that it rings not in my Ears still!' (JL VI, 612). Relating her son's subjection to the apothecary's lancet years before, she had written to her father of the instrument's 'slaughtering design': what was then a brief hyperbole now becomes deliberately made a 'design', step by step present in her prose. Now it becomes a prose exceptionally precise and focused, with metaphors that make a reader flinch, as if with pain: 'When the wound was made, & the instrument was withdrawn, the pain seemed undiminished, for the air that suddenly rushed into those delicate parts felt like a mass of minute but sharp & forked poniards, that were tearing the edges of the wound.' Madame d'Arblay has fought to retain her position as a lady throughout the preparations for the surgery, but one cannot call her description modest or delicate or genteel. There is a ruthless determination or commitment in the writing. While she ensured that her father or her closest friends did not get to hear of the operation, Burney is apparently sparing her sister nothing as she relates her experience of the surgery with as much graphic detail as she can recall.

The horror for the reader, as for the sufferer, is increased by the interruptions of the surgery. Larrey, she notices, must swop one hand for the other because he is 'describing a curve, cutting against the grain' (a different action, possibly, from the surgical strokes of amputation on the battlefield that Larrey was inured to).[27] This means that there is a series of brief respites, breaks when the patient thinks that the operation might be over, and then, appallingly, it is resumed. This is the climax of the series:

> Dr Larry rested but his own hand, & – Oh Heaven! – I then felt the Knife rackling against the breast bone – scraping it! – This performed, while I yet remained in utterly speechless torture, I heard the Voice of Mr Larry, – (all others guarded a dead silence) in a tone nearly tragic, desire every one present to pronounce if any thing more remained to be done; The general voice was Yes, – but the finger of Mr. Dubois – which I literally *felt* elevated over the wound, though I saw nothing, & though he touched nothing, so indescribably sensitive was the spot – pointed to some further requisition – & again began the scraping! – and, after this, Dr Moreau thought he discerned a peccant attom – and still, & still, M. Dubois demanded attom after attom. (JL VI, 612–613)

The effect of this staggering of the procedure is to inculcate in the reader the unconscious and irrational feeling that Burney is being deliberately tortured. She does use the term 'torture' in this passage. The reader is confronted, repeatedly, with details that prompt him or her to a defensive reaction, most commonly with hatred of the surgeons, less commonly to turn against Burney herself, inflicting such pain on a reader, who might ascribe her motive as 'a desire to shock'.[28]

If one can detach oneself enough from Burney's account – where it is apparent that the lingering hostility directed at Dubois earlier in the narrative has indeed turned into something like hatred, and consider the surgeons' practice impartially, it becomes evident that they are bent on doing their utmost to prevent a recurrence of the tumour. Writers on this surgery insisted that 'no half measures will answer', that it was mistaken kindness to leave any sign of cancer remaining in the breast area.[29] As Aronowitz writes, there was 'a long history of medical speculation that cancer had seeds, ferments, or roots, . . . that could sprout new disease'.[30] 'No glandular structure, nor any of the roots, should be allowed to remain,' the surgeon Astley Cooper was to advise in 1839. Later a physician at St Luke's Hospital in London insisted that '[m]ammary cancer requires the careful extirpation of the entire organ. Local recurrence after operations is due to the continuing growth of fragments of the principal tumour.'[31] This is why Burney's surgeons – progressive, experienced – are so determined to remove anything that might be a 'peccant atom'. What Burney inevitably experiences as cruelty is committed professionalism, carried through by the physicians despite their sympathetic feelings, their 'sensibilité.'

And in fact, this is recognised by Burney herself. After the passage just quoted, in which the horror of renewed 'scraping' is described, the dual time scheme, inherent in the calls to Esther throughout the narrative, is activated as Burney, now months after the operation, turns finally to address 'My dearest Esther' and underlines the time that has passed since. There is a stepping back, a formal summary:

> To conclude, the evil was so profound, the case so delicate, & the precau-
> tions necessary for preventing a return so numerous, that the operation,
> including the treatment & the dressing, lasted 20 minutes! . . . However,
> I bore it with all the courage I could exert, & never moved, nor stopt them,
> nor resisted, nor remonstrated, nor spoke – except once or twice, during the
> dressings, to say 'Ah Messieurs! que je vous plains! –' for indeed I was
> sensible to the feeling concern with which they all saw what I endured,
> though my speech was principally, – *very* principally, meant for Dr Larry.
> (JL VI, 613)

This speech, 'How I pity you, gentlemen!' is extraordinary in the circum-
stances and would be quite difficult to reconcile with a critical view that Burney felt oppressed or dominated by 'masculinist medicine'. It is clear, though, that here Burney manages to resurrect herself as a woman, a person, an identity. The phrase '*sensible* to the feeling concern' (my

italics: 'sensible', meaning 'alive to') fuses her feelings with theirs, the two,
patient and physicians, linked together by their participation in a terrible
but momentous experience. The link is reiterated after she opens her eyes
and sees 'My good Dr Larry, pale nearly as myself, his face streaked with
blood, & its expression depicting grief, apprehension & almost horrour'
(JL VI, 614). It seems as if he is feeling for her, as well as for himself, and she
is feeling for them both too.

   If the operation was a success, that was because the doctors, Dubois and
Larrey, forgetting their differences, acted in tandem, and because they did
not spare themselves or the patient. They extirpated the 'peccant attoms'
remorselessly. Susan Emlen was assured that 'the disease was completely
eradicated' and as her husband wrote, 'the diseased parts, both of the breast
and the arm-pit . . . extirely eradicated'.[32] She seems never to have entirely
recovered from the surgery, and died, possibly from cancer, five years later.
Madame d'Arblay lived for more than twenty-eight years with no further
symptoms. A report prepared by the pupil of Larrey who, with a nurse,
watched over the patient through the night, and sewn to Burney's document, is interesting. It includes the information that Burney got a little
sleep, that in the morning she was surprised how well she felt, and that
when Larrey visited his patient the next morning at ten, he found there was
almost no pain in the wound and that the dressings showed none of the
seepage of blood, which had been prevented by 'l'exacte ligature des artères'
(JL VI, 616). Since there was no sepsis following the surgery, one can
assume that doctors working at the highest levels of society had understood
the importance of cleanliness.[33] Larrey certainly knew of the dangers of
sepsis, which killed many men not fatally wounded on the battlefield, and
had immense experience in suturing wounds.[34]

   Larrey would have attended Burney regularly after the surgery, as
evidenced by a note made in January 1812, recording that he 'finished his
chiurugical [at]tendance' about that time. A little earlier she had written
that she was 'daily amending' (JL VI, 808). By the first of March the
same year Larrey was in Mainz en route to Berlin, where he gave a series of
lectures to the surgeons of the city.[35] He was to join the French troops
assembled for the campaign against Russia. That spring, Frances Burney,
accompanied by Larrey's wife, was well enough to visit the studio of the
famous painter Jean-Louis David, and there viewed and wrote critically
about his two portraits of Napoleon. Larrey remained loyal to Napoleon
and joined him at the battle of Waterloo in June 1815. While attending
wounded French soldiers he was attacked by Prussian lancers: his horse was
wounded, he fell to the ground and received two sabre cuts, which left him

unconscious.[36] But he was back in Paris by August 1815, where – as seen in the next chapter – he was consulted by Alexandre d'Arblay.

Even when one has read and studied Burney's account of her mastectomy many times, it remains a gruelling experience. It invites violent or simplifying reactions (and often enough, the impulse to skip a passage) and this is due, I believe, to its unimpeachable authenticity. There is very little trace of fictionality. Burney had trained herself to observe and to delineate these small, telling moments of human interaction, and even when she was under great duress, suffering intensely from fear and pain, this skill was retained and, moreover, could be operationalised in her writing. What other sufferers could or would not recall, she knew how to make present in precise and frightening detail.

The result is a dramatic portrayal, for the first time, of a whole medical scene, an *ensemble*, in which physicians and patient, gathered together, interact, and in which tensions between patient and doctors, as well as among doctors themselves, are inscribed through close and (strange though it is to use the word in these circumstances) empathetic attention. It is these partly implicit conflicts, as well as the dramatic tension generated by the recital of delays and impediments before the operation and the suspensions of the surgery itself, that create the document's uniquely frightening suspense. One further aspect of the narrative is that it evokes the fear and dread which still surround breast cancer and its surgery, however changed the medical circumstances, as seen when modern accounts of breast surgery are considered alongside Burney's in this book's eighth chapter. As a surgeon has written, 'her graphic details of the operation, "cutting against the grain," and the agonies of preanaesthetic surgery are fears shared in dreams and imagination by some modern-day patients.'[37] Few recent pathographies, though, have the dense, concentrated power of Frances Burney's account. It is indeed, as another surgeon suggests, 'one of the most remarkable in the history of medicine'.[38]

Notes

1. Epstein, J., *The Iron Pen*. Epstein's foundational and valuable chapter 2, 'Writing the Unspeakable' (pp. 53–83), stresses the recovery of agency that writing her account of her mastectomy enabled Burney to attain.

2. JL VI, 596–615. The letter to Esther is in an envelope marked 'Account from Paris of a Terrible Operation – 1812', evidently labelled when Burney was working towards publication of her manuscripts much later in the century (Epstein, J., *The Iron Pen*, p. 56). There is no indication that Burney gave the

document the title 'A Mastectomy', but the *Selected Letters and Journals*, edited by Joyce Hemlow, follows the 1975 precedent.

3. Garfinkel, S., '"This Trial Was Sent in Love and Mercy for My Refinement"', p. 19. Emlen's case history is fully discussed and briefly compared with Burney's in Robert A. Aronowitz's *Unnatural History*, pp. 21–50. I am indebted to Dr Aronowitz's wise and illuminating work.

4. Garfinkel, S., '"This Trial Was Sent in Love and Mercy for My Refinement"', p. 18.

5. Ibid., p. 18.

6. Ibid., p. 20.

7. Aronowitz, R. A., *Unnatural History*, p. 47.

8. Larrey became famous enough to be introduced into *War and Peace* (1864–1869), where after the Russian defeat at Austerlitz he pronounces that the wounded Prince Andrew is likely to die rather than to recover. '"C'est un sujet nerveux et bilieux," said Larrey, 'Il n'en rechappera pas."' These last lines in Volume I of the novel leave the reader to assume that the prince is dead for many subsequent chapters. Tolstoy, L., *War and Peace*, p. 294.

9. Larrey had spent 1811, a year of 'repose' in Paris, preparing his memoirs, covering a 'a war of twenty years duration' and 'thus rendering my labors profitable to younger military surgeons' which were published in three volumes at the end of the year. James, B., *Introductory Lecture*, p. 16.

10. 2 November 1810. Clark, L., ed., *Memoirs of the Court of George III*, p. 109. Amelia was the youngest of the king's children and his favourite. Amelia's illness and death greatly affected the king, who was already blind. Lucy Kennedy noted on 27 November that 'his Greif has seized upon his nerves . . . no occation, for, Coersion, quite different from his former Seizures, nervous Lamentation, for his Lost Child, and often Distray [*Distrait* or distraught]'. The king never recovered from this illness, which brought about the regency. Amelia had been attended by Rev. Charles Digby, the canon in residence at the court, who was Stephen Digby's son.

11. Garfinkel, S., '"This Trial Was Sent in Love and Mercy for My Refinement"', p. 18.

12. Cited in Welling, D. R., Burris, D. G., and Rich, N. M., 'The Influence of Dominique-Jean Larrey', p. 791.

13. JL VI, 610.

14. Foucault, M., *Birth of the Clinic*. Larrey is mentioned as one of a gathering of doctors in Paris which 'represented the opinions of the new medicine' (p. 74).

15. JL VI, 611.

16. Aronowitz, R. A., *Unnatural History*, p. 30.

17. Epstein, J., *The Iron Pen*, pp. 68, 73.

18. Mediratta, S., 'Beauty and the Breast', pp. 197, 198. Mediratta also argues that 'Burney's letter offers a critique of masculinist science or medicine.'

19. Chisholm, K., *Fanny Burney*, p. 21. Chisholm does add that 'their thoroughness saved her life.'

20. Précastaings, A., 'Frances Burney's Mastectomy and the Female Body Politic', p. 235.
21. Ibid., pp. 235, 239.
22. Garfinkel, S., '"This Trial Was Sent in Love and Mercy for My Refinement"', p. 21.
23. Susan Emlen preserved her faith in the midst of the whole experience of the illness: 'How inestimable is the comfort of believing ourselves under the protection of an infinitely wise and good father and friend, who afflicts his poor creatures not willingly, and knows how to extract a benefit out of every sorrow,' she wrote in the first weeks, and continued to take comfort in this belief (Garfinkel, S., '"This Trial Was Sent in Love and Mercy for My Refinement"', p. 26). It is striking that Burney, certainly a committed Christian, never expresses any such belief.
24. Ibid., p. 21.
25. Robinson, V., *Victory over Pain*, p. 211.
26. Dally, A., *Women under the Knife*, p. 107.
27. Larrey was reputed to have performed 200 surgeries in twenty-four hours at the battle of Borodino. Even allowing for exaggeration, this suggests that – taking perhaps ten minutes on average – they were much swifter and easier actions for the surgeon to perform than this.
28. Mediratta, for instance, declares that the 'army doctors . . . commandeer her body and butcher it' ('Beauty and the Breast', p. 201); 'Desire to shock' (Harman, C., *Fanny Burney*, p. 306).
29. JL VI, n. 34, citing Robert Liston, *Practical Surgery*, 1837. Liston adds that: 'The extirpation should be set about with a through determination to free the patient of the whole diseased structure.'
30. Aronowitz, R. A., *Unnatural History*, p. 26.
31. Cited in Mukherjee, S., *The Emperor of All Maladies*, p. 64.
32. Garfinkel, S., '"This Trial Was Sent in Love and Mercy for My Refinement"', p. 21.
33. Though they relate to surgery on the battlefield, Henry Dibble's comments make clear how aware Larrey was of the dangers of sepsis and the need for cleanliness: 'Larrey recognised that in favourable circumstances the wound resulting from an immediate amputation might heal if left untouched under its original dressings . . . in conditions in the field, with the knife being plentifully exposed to the antibacterial action of the blood and mechanically cleansed by repeated use, and with the full debridement which Larrey favoured, a wound could result . . . not ill placed for uncomplicated healing (Dibble, J. H., *Napoleon's Surgeon*, p. 135). Neither Dibble nor Robert Richardson, *Larrey*, makes mention of Burney's surgery.
34. Larrey was known for '[h]is superior method of dressing wounds on the field of battle, and thus protecting the soldier from the dangers attending undressed wounds [and for] [h]is invention of improved instruments for the taking up of arteries, and of many other improvements in the theory and practice of surgery' (James, B., *Introductory Lecture*, p. 16).

35. [no author], *Memoir of Baron Larrey*, p. 104. This is apparently a translation of *Larrey: chirugien en chef de la grade armée; étude par le docteur Leroy Dupré*, Paris, 1860.
36. Ibid., pp. 27–30.
37. Moore, A. R., 'Preanesthtetic Mastectomy'.
38. Dally, A., *Women under the Knife*, p. 104.

CHAPTER 6

Fighting for Life
The Last Illness and Death of General d'Arblay: *1818*

Like General Alexandre d'Arblay, Colonel Sir William De Lancey was an aristocratic career soldier, and both were called to take part in the last campaign against Napoleon after his escape from Elba on 1 March 1815. Magdalene De Lancey had been married for less than two months when her husband was ordered to join the Duke of Wellington in preparation for the battle that came to be known as Waterloo. The De Lanceys travelled to Brussels, where they arrived early in June 1815. About a fortnight later, anticipating that the fighting would start very soon, De Lancey arranged for Magdalene to go to Antwerp, about twenty-five miles away, where she would be safe. There, after a day, she received news that her husband had been killed, then that he had survived. In her memoir *A Week at Waterloo*, she recounts the very taxing time that followed, culminating in her nursing her husband during the last days of his life.[1] De Lancey's narrative is startling, moving, and dramatic, and is used in this chapter in counterpoint to a reading of Burney's 'Narrative of the Last Illness and Death of General d'Arblay', which like De Lancey's, but in a decidedly different mode, recounts her nursing of her own soldier husband until his death in May 1818.[2] Magdalene's short narrative has an artless art, but it is different from Burney's extended, extraordinary, wholly unconventional memoir.

Written in the first place to inform her brother, who had been a friend of her husband before their marriage, De Lancey's piece is now not widely known. Burney's 'Narrative', begun in November 1819 and completed four months later, has been neglected too, in contrast to 'A Mastectomy', but it is perhaps of even greater moment and certainly is the forerunner of many, many such pathographic memoirs concerning the final months of a loved partner or parent published since. It is a document that raises what are still important ethical issues concerning the treatment, both by family and by doctors, of a seriously and probably fatally ill patient.

Like Magdalene De Lancey, Frances Burney found herself in the vicinity of Waterloo while the battle was fought, about nine miles away. Much later, in 1823, she was to write an account of those harrowing days in her 'Waterloo journal'.[3] She had fled there with friends from Paris when the news of Napoleon's escape and march northwards had reached the capital. After a few days in Brussels her friends left again, fearing that Napoleon would conquer the city as he had Paris. She chose not to leave, because only there could she receive letters from General d'Arblay, who, resuming his old career, had joined the Royalist army against the insurgent. After the Allied victory, the d'Arblays decided to leave France and live in England again. They took up residence in Bath. This was a resort, as Jane Austen's *Persuasion* (1817) makes clear, which often provided a congenial and suitably genteel environment for retired admirals and military officers.

There in November 1815 the d'Arblays engaged Mr George Hay, 'an eminent Bath apothicary', as Burney called him, as their medical attendant, since the general was still recovering from an accident in which a horse had crushed his foot.[4] Though, like many such medical men, he was unlicensed, Hay became the d'Arblays' regular doctor, the 'gossiping physician',[5] who, frequently attending his patients, becomes a family friend. His attachment to his patient became an important element in the story of General d'Arblay's illness and treatment.

Though d'Arblay had not been well for some time, in June 1817 Mr Hay gave him permission to travel to France, where he hoped to recover his health, as well as some of the money he might be owed. After arriving in Paris, he consulted a Dr Esparron, who had been his physician in 1813. Esparron frightened him, d'Arblay wrote back to his wife, by telling him that his symptoms 'annonce une lesion dans la foie' – a problem in the liver, which might get worse (JL X, 475). He was to take care of himself, rest, take light exercise etc. Soon Fanny was asking him why he had not seen Larrey, since in England he 'languished daily to consult him'. She worried – and was to worry more – that he seemed no better than before he left for France. Dominique-Jean Larrey was back in Paris after having escaped being shot by enemy troops at Waterloo.[6]

Feeling himself very unwell, d'Arblay followed the erratic path taken by many seriously ill patients before and since – consultations with many different medical practitionrs, who prescribe different treatments, which don't work, and then in desperation trying unorthodox and quite possibly dangerous remedies. A gentleman whom he met out walking, seeing at once how jaundiced he looked, recommended a drug to him, boasting that he himself had had the same symptoms and was now completely cured. It led a day or two later to a collapse. Then d'Arblay did consult Larrey, who confirmed that he had an obstruction in the liver, and recommended avoidance of anxiety and cheerfulness, which, as he could only feel cheerful if he was with Fanny, he felt was not much use. Larrey seems to have also suggested that he might require surgery. Just what surgery is unclear, but by 20 August, Larrey and Ribes (who had assisted at his wife's mastectomy in 1811) 'avoir renoncé egalment à toute operation', both decided against any operation (JL X, 626). It's probable that d'Arblay's symptoms by this time included pain in the region of the rectum. The next day he talked with Larrey about *douches ascendants* recommended with success by one Dr Montagre, which Larrey thought he should try (JL X, 629).

Then, very surprisingly, d'Arblay bumped into Mr Hay in the Tuilleries garden. Hay, who seems to have been a bachelor and a free spirit, had got himself to France in the company of a duke. The general took the newly arrived visitor on a tour of Paris, sending back to Fanny a list of all the sights they had visited. It seems to have been quite a spree, and very possibly did him good. Hay, who 'loved and revered' d'Arblay, as Frances often declares, stayed on in Paris and consulted with Larrey and other doctors about his patient's condition. But it seems clear from a letter d'Arblay wrote to his wife in September that the French physicians had little respect for the English apothecary's opinions.[7] It must by October have been obvious to everyone that d'Arblay was very unwell. Hay encouraged him to go home, and then accompanied him, and on the seventeenth d'Arblay arrived in Bath, but, as Frances wrote to Mrs Waddingon, 'altered – thin – weak – depressed, full of pain' (JL X, 749).

Burney's *Narrative* opens about this time. At first she summarises the medical history I have related, with the improbable conclusion that it was in 'Paris he had first felt that deadly disorder, that carried him, in its effects, to the Grave!' Soon comes a detailed account of a royal *levée* at the Pump Room in Bath, just before Christmas, where Queen Charlotte singles General d'Arblay out for attention, which means that – 'suffering, emaciated, enfeebled' as he is – he has to stand up and make polite conversation with her until she decides to move on (JL X, 847). Burney says she relates this scene because it is the last one to take place other than under their own roof, but it is also the last occasion when she can display Alexandre as a happy man. 'Charmed' by the queen's seeking him out, he smiles 'winningly' – 'what sweetness beamed in every feature.' Thus the scene also allows her to celebrate how 'condescending' the queen still is to her and her French husband.

Soon, though, she sounds the note that is to echo through the whole ensuing narration:

Very soon after the opening of this fatal year 1818 expressions dropt from him of his belief of his approaching End that would have broken my heart on the very dawn of such a surmize, had not an incredulity – *NOW* my eternal wonder! – kept me in a constant persuasion that he was hypocondriac, & tormented with false apprehensions. Fortunate – benign – as wonderful was that Incredulity, which, blinding me to my coming woe enabled me to support my courage by my Hopes, – & helped me to sustain his own. (JL X, 853–854)

This is a retrospective account of a key matter about which Madame d'Arblay felt rather differently as the history she is to record unfolded. It introduces too a feature, common in pathographic narratives, as in her mastectomy letter, of a double time scheme: the time recalled and evoked, and the later time of writing. Throughout the memoir – epitomised in the exclamations of 'Alas!' that punctuate the narrative – the reader is reminded of the emotions Burney is experiencing as she remembers past events and commits them to writing. 'Alas!' sometimes expresses pity, sometimes sorrow or regret, perhaps sometimes even guilt. It is not clear whether Burney understands, even in looking back, that 'Hope' in such circumstances is not an unambiguous good.

In his *Unnatural History*, Robert Aronowitz, MD discusses some of the issues and challenges a consulting physician faces when dealing with a patient with almost certainly terminal cancer. In response to a medical ethics that emphasises respect for the patient's 'autonomy' or interrogates the expert's 'beneficence' he writes that 'such a *principled* approach glosses over the tragic conflict that often exists among competing goods, such as truthful communication, trust between doctor and patient, and hope for survival.' Furthermore, he argues, '[h]ope for survival and relief from suffering, trust that doctors and friends will not abandon you, and truth telling – a difficult matter given medical uncertainty and cancer progression – have been and continue to be competing goods to be balanced by cancer patients and the people who care for and support them.'[8] These three 'goods' – hope, trust and truth – are in a precarious and unstable relationship throughout the history that Burney's *Narrative* relates. Aronowitz writes of this difficult and delicate balance largely as a task of the cancer physician, but his argument applies to Madame d'Arblay, because in so many ways she, not the doctors or the patient, takes the executive role in her husband's treatment. In an important sense, her mandate is hope; the patient's is truth, and it may well be described as a 'tragic conflict'.

While Burney is writing the story of her husband's acquiescence in his death, she also tells the story of her own refusal to give up. If d'Arblay models acceptance of his 'approaching End', Burney exemplifies the more romantic or modern attitude of denial or defiance of death. Flying the flag of 'Hope' (her own capital letter) Madame d'Arblay commandeers the care of her husband. M. d'Arblay follows a traditional pathway, the *ars moriendi*; she defies it, acting (in two senses) with courage and outfacing friends, relatives, doctors and a priest, all of whom seek to tell her that the case is hopeless. She fends off or cuts short all ominous hints, even the patient's, conducting a campaign that seeks to banish the thought of death to the furthest reaches of probability. Her vigilance is extraordinary, since she believes that any hint of approaching death will hasten the end she is desperate to avoid. Thus one of the 'goods' that Aronowitz identifies is compromised, and even trust is tampered with. Burney complicates the conflict between the two attitudes by insisting, at the same time, on another romantic narrative – of her spiritual identity with her husband, of her courage inducing courage in him, of her hope transmitting hope to him, of their mutual admiration and love. At one point, for instance, she relates that her husband, marvelling, compares her to one of her own heroines, the indefatigable and devoted Cecilia (JL X, 864). She is still celebrating, at the time of writing, the union that, by implication, vindicates the illusion she has sustained.

But it is this conflict between the two moral attitudes that gives Burney's *Narrative* its dramatic and illuminating ethical tension. She refers to her husband's own diary and under the date of 14 February includes an extract that is reminiscent of Tolstoy's confronting tale of the last illness and death of Ivan Ilyich. 'Je n'ai pas eu depuis hier Matin un Moment de repos', d'Arblay writes, 'ni de relâche dans mes souffrances, très variés, et toutes horribles – mais surtout inquiétantes – Cependant point de fievre, ni mal de tête – et neanmois DEATH is always There! – & so near!' (JL X, 864). 'Since yesterday morning I haven't had a moment's peace, not a break in my sufferings, very varied, and all horrible – but most of all they make me frightened – no fever, and no headache – but all the same *DEATH is always There!– and so near!*').[9] D'Arblay confronts the absence of consolation, and like Tolstoy's fictional figure experiences his sufferings as having no other meaning than death. But if Tolstoy also presents Ilyich's sufferings as meaningless, and their meaninglessness as part of his suffering, he at the same time performs the feat of endowing his story with moral significance. This is much more difficult to do in a memoir, committed to the recital of inevitable uncertainty and mishaps, unpredictable and apparently arbitrary bodily events and crises, than in a novella. What gives Burney's *Narrative* its moral or ethical charge is precisely her determination never to give up

hope, the 'good' that challenges the reader to weigh its cost against trust as
well as truth.

Madame d'Arblay has put her trust in Mr Hay, and he earns it. But this
is not a straightforward matter. Back in December, under Hay's regime,
d'Arblay was 'indisposed almost to torture' by his wife's account (JL X,
847). In January '[h]is incessant & always augmenting malady' makes
Burney call in Mr Hay and express to him her anxiety that 'we were not
in the right path':

> He heard me with silent & grave attention, &, without venturing to
> pronounce a word, left me to mount to the Sick Room, which my poor
> Invalid had not yet quitted.
>   I waited – watching his return with unspeakable emotion. – It was not
> long deferred – & Oh God! what was my relief to see it easy & even gay!
> almost to mockery, as he cried 'I see no reason, Madam, for anxiety –'.
>   What words of extacy were these to my nameless – yet terrible fears! –
> I spent the day in thanksgiving. (JL X, 855–856)

Perhaps Hay's deep affection for his patient colours his judgement; perhaps
he, as much as the patient's wife, wants to believe General d'Arblay will
live. Perhaps her forceful and undoubtedly charismatic personality captures him in its aura. Perhaps he colludes with, rather than steadying, her.
It's just possible that he has invested too much faith in his own medications, though it is not clear what they were.

It is not long before d'Arblay declares that 'he felt an internal growing
ossification that menaced his life' (JL X, 858) (no one ever mentions the
word 'cancer') and asks that a physician be brought in. Hay recommends
Mr William Tudor, an army surgeon who had been in attendance on the
elderly queen during her Bath visit. When Mr Tudor first calls, on
24 January, his style is quite unlike Mr Hay's. 'When he came down,
after an interview & examination, his looks were even forbidding; they were
grave to austerity, & comfortless to rigour. – I sought to steel my struggling
alarm with an idea that he was a cold & hard Character; ... Mr. Hay had
lost his air of satisfaction & complacency' (JL X, 858). The next day Tudor
begins to treat the patient with *bouginage*, which entailed the insertion of an
instrument into the rectum, probably to expand the canal. It was certainly
excruciatingly painful, for the old soldier, as he confesses in his diary, cried
out loud (JL X, 860). During this time Burney records many examples of
her husband's loving words and extracts from his diary that praise her
courage: he writes, for instance that he could not bear the pain of his
treatment without the consolation of his *'Ange gardien'* (JL X, 860). On

29 March she records that 'Mr Tudor pronounced the joyful News that He was considerably Amended!' (JL X, 867). Tudor's words are probably carefully chosen to offer hope, but he does not say the patient will recover.

Up to this point the *Narrative* has drawn on both her husband's and Burney's own diary kept at the time. But from 19 April the only records she has are small pieces of paper, about the size of a post-it note, on which she had scribbled down some of her husband's words in moments snatched from attending to him through his last days.[10] The subsequent thirty or more pages cover only the last fortnight of her husband's life, and are preceded by a brief rededication and review of her purpose: 'To What End these piercing renovations! . . . to relieve the painful weight of eternal silent meditation, by a sort of Vent that seems like communication' (JL X, 872). As in her mastectomy narrative, Burney needs to imagine that she is addressing an understanding and beloved person, but she also expresses the common belief that such recall of the painful past might be cathartic, and indeed might soothe her on her own deathbed. She gathers her courage to proceed. This part of the narrative has a different character from the first; while drawing on Burney's memory, and probably written at a greater distance in time than the first in 1819, it has a more dramatic, more writerly character, as she recreates more intense and telling scenes. The situation itself has certainly become more fraught.

The second half of the narrative then opens with a scene that underscores the themes that organise the ensuing pages:

> ONCE, in This parting, yet not Last Month, April, while yet he daily came down to the Drawing Room, while I was chearfully, as usual, parrying his dread prognostications of his approaching departure, with gay incredulity, & assumed spirits, he so strongly – alas! so justly! pointed out reasons to prove his cure impossible, & his End advancing – that, suddenly struck with horrour, I lost all self-command of my *own* inward feelings at a blow, & exclaimed – with a scream rather than a Voice – 'Oh no! – no! no! – I do not believe it! – I will not believe it! – I cannot believe it! – But – if it were so – Oh God! – what a chasm! – what a Void! – What a non-entity for the rest of my life! ——
>
> Oh fatal sentence! how true has it proved! –
>
> I dropt upon my knees, & fell upon the sofa, in an agony almost convulsive. He was Walking out of the room at the time; – he preserved his composure – turned away from the sight of my distress, and walked on – He opened the door, slowly, but steadily; he spoke not; he looked not back; he was unwilling to trust himself to the view of my affliction, dreading his own sympathy; &, with an air of mournful self-possession, replete with pity

for his poor Wife, & regret for both, silent, too full for words, too sad for expression, he left the room. (JL X, 872–873)

This battle between hope and despair in the face of d'Arblay's decline is indeed to be enacted repeatedly in these last days. But in reopening the story with herself succumbing to her terrors, Burney the writer is more cunning than this, for her violent display informs the reader of the powerful emotions that the next two weeks are to show her, explicitly and valiantly, successfully controlling. Her writing here represents the two modes of response to crisis mimetically, in the incoherent, syntactically unformed outburst of the wife, as opposed to the firm and careful punctuation by which her husband's steady, purposeful, and self-controlled steps away from her are represented in words. But there is also a touching and convincing moment of insight into the probable complexion of his feelings. Cleft apart by the impact of their mutual disaster, husband and wife might be estranged, were it not for the countervailing sympathetic recognition (his of her grief; hers, retrospectively, of his courageous demeanour). In another sense, though, the contrast set up here, structured partly through gender stereotypes – he taciturn, courageous, controlled; she hysterical, gesturing, dramatic – is continued throughout the subsequent sequence.

But this means in effect that Burney comes to occupy the foreground of the narrative, and it is her active body, rather than d'Arblay's suffering one, that is continually being defined. Animated, resourceful, using 'every exertion', she flies across rooms, devising strategies to hide her tears and fears, constantly guarding her countenance and controlling her manner, able, energetic, determined, the skilful manager both of her husband's sickness and of her own self-presentation. While readers are asked to believe that she hid her forebodings and preserved an outward demeanour of invigorating calm and cheerfulness, the text continually represents her as full of violent conflict. She speaks of herself as 'repressing, even inwardly, all fearful foreboding', but it is this process of repression or suppression that proclaims her energies and makes her tension and its outward manifestations the active centre of the text. When she cries 'deluges of long restrained tears' (JL X, 879), these do not represent another breakthrough to acceptance of d'Arblay's view of his approaching dissolution, but rather the physiological cost of Burney's self-suppression, for soon she is reiterating, 'still I Nourished the dear belief that he would yet be restored to me! -!! (JL X, 880). As she looks back from the moment of writing, she is still wondering at this denial, as well as perceiving it as the source of the strength that enabled her to carry on.

In pursuit of her campaign of 'Hope', she must, in these last weeks, confront two potentially powerful enemies, which she occasionally suspects are in collusion: Medicine and the Church. These institutions, in the persons of the doctors and a priest, have their own ways of reading her husband's condition and structuring the dying process, and thus to make her own story, to live and to tell it her way, Burney must master and defeat their narratives. Burney's conflict with these institutions is conscious and conducted upon the plane of ideology, but there is a more vital, more personal urgency about it too. She fights off, like a mother defending her child, any attack on her hopes for a positive outcome, for to admit that their authority speaks from a world of rationality and experience is to violate the emotional-romantic dyad that is her lifeline. That there is an atavistic or unconscious charge to Burney's dealings with these others, the priest and the doctors, is revealed, finally, in her treatment of the other representative of medical agency, the nurse.

Interpenetrating or enacted through the psychological dynamics demonstrated in Burney's own conduct (as she narrates it) is a contest between an older and essentially Catholic tradition or ideology of death, and the newer ideology of sensibility. As Burney belatedly recognises as she reads her husband's diary, d'Arblay has accepted the fatal prognosis of his earlier French doctors: his entire effort has been to submit to his inevitable suffering and fate. By January 1818 d'Arblay knows he is dying, and seeks to prepare himself and his wife for that eventuality. 'Je voudrois que nous caussassions sur tout cela avec calme, doucement, – *chearfully*, même, as of a Future Voyage' ('I wish that we could talk on all that, calmly, gently'), he pleads, but Fanny is wholly unable to meet him on this: as she writes with an intensity that fuses her present and her past feelings, 'I could only attend his sick Couch, I could only *LIVE* by fostering hopes of his revival: & seeking to make them reciprocal' (JL X, 855). Beginning in early 1818 her husband performs a graded series of actions prescribed to him by ritual and tradition. Some, perhaps most, of these are not known to Burney at the time; she gives them weight only because, in the construction of her narrative, she consults the documents that describe them. D'Arblay is conducting himself according to received canons: he undertakes a series of ordered preparations, arranging his affairs, giving advice and instruction, saying last farewells, withdrawing himself, through conscious ceremonial acts, from the world. At one point towards the end, he forbids Fanny to speak to him, and retires from her in 'mute contemplation' for more than a day and a half (JL X, 894). (It seems likely that he found Fanny's insistent optimism getting on his nerves.) He makes a list of 'every sort of reclamation' of properties or debts in France and England that might be recovered after his death. He writes a long poem of advice to his son, Alexander, and a poetic address, 'à L'Inevitable!' (JL X, 884). Most significant, he agrees to see the priest, the elderly and scholarly Dr Elloi.

Burney, like other pious Christians, might have sought comfort from prayer and consultation with a minister, but she does not.[II] She is reluctant to admit the priest, and not only because she is a Protestant, though she makes a good deal of this. 'I had no faith in *Confession to Man*, & none in the pantomimic parade of their last & unaccountable shew of a Communion,' she declares (JL X, 875). She must be referring to the last confession, the viaticum and the administration of extreme unction, but especially to the viaticum, commonly brought to the dying person in procession through the streets, a ceremony in which all those who saw it participated. In effect, Dr Elloi stays upstairs with the patient for three hours, during which, as he afterwards tells Burney, 'added to the prayers he had been reading and making, & the Exhortations for renouncing This World, he had engaged the General to the duties, pious & Catholic, of a full Confession' (CJL 877). From then on, Burney depicts herself as besieged by the priest and his coreligionists 'with an energy disturbing to my studied tranquility', but at last she allows the priest another visit, in which he tells Madame d'Arblay that 'he had obtained the promise of the General that he should administer to him the last Sacrament' (JL X, 878). She attends the ceremony, but blames it for hastening her husband's death: he never recovers from the fatigue 'or its impression upon his Thoughts – Never! – alas! – never!' This done, the Catholics are still 'incessant in their demands for admission, & further ceremonies'. The priest must wish to administer extreme unction, a signal to the patient that his death is at hand, and in which the cross is given him to kiss, symbolising the relinquishment of all earthly loves. It is the ritual climax of a sequence designed to estrange the dying person from this world and to loosen the ties that bind him to his worldly affections. The pastor in *La Nouvelle Héloise* says '[a] dying Catholic' is 'surrounded by objects that make him afraid, and ceremonies that bury him alive'.[12] Burney calls it 'a Catholic rite that might impede all chance of restoration by its terrific & appalling solemnities' (JL X, 887).

These rituals are premised upon the sufferer's inevitable and imminent death, and that reading of d'Arblay's condition is the one Burney is giving all her energy to resisting. But her reluctance to have along the priest is not merely personal; it is also culturally conditioned. The d'Arblays are here implicated in the cult of sensibility, which increasingly, inspired by the work of the philosophes, saw the deathbed as a private place and the preparation for death as the opportunity for remaking family ties or righting family wrongs. John McManners compares the deathbed of Julie in *La Nouvelle Héloïse* with the deathbed of traditional Catholic practice: 'To Jean-Jacques [Rousseau], our last moments are left to us by God so that we can devote them to those we love. Julie will soon be concerned with God alone; in the meanwhile, her time is for her family – "c'est deux qu'il faut que je m'occupe, bientôt je m'occuperai de lui seul."' This is the direct opposite of the confessors' teaching, who urge their penitents to forget all earthly affections as the end approaches.[13] D'Arblay too, it seems clear, adheres to the new code of sensibility, making his deathbed an occasion to reaffirm his love for his family, advising Alexander, seeking to inspire his wife with the strength to survive him, though this purpose, of course, is premised upon that inevitability of his demise that she refuses to accept. For the d'Arblays, though pious, earthly affections and their sustainment matter as much as eternal salvation. Burney's drive to keep Alexandre d'Arblay to herself is here thus both a psychological necessity and the operation of the new ideologies of sensibility and the Enlightenment. But she seems unaware that her own attitude may be depriving her beloved husband of the consolation and peace his own religious faith might well supply.

Battling the priest and his coreligionist, Madame de Sommery, and their 'attacks', Frances must simultaneously defend herself against her husband's doctors, as is demonstrated in this remarkable scene:

> They were together in the Drawing room, in deep & low discourse when I was summoned to them. Mr Hay then went up to his Patient; I would have accompanied him; but he told me Mr Tudor would speak to me. I wished to fly out of the house! – but I had no resource; & therefore only resolved to urge their continued services by disclaiming all belief of danger. I thought it the most poignant way to secure their assiduity. When I was alone with Mr Tudor, I parried the subject with so much agitation, that I believe I frightened him from enforcing the dread sentence I saw menacing; & Mr Hay returned while yet nothing unusual had been pronounced. I saw them both disturbed & embarrassed: I would have taken the opportunity to escape: but they then

began both together to point out the encrease of weakness – the
thinness – the unabating pains – I felt to what this led, & could
endure no more: breaking in upon them with a tremulous eagerness
that startled them to silence, 'Well, Gentlemen,' I cried, 'the greater the
difficulty, the more honour will redound to your skill; – '
    Mr Hay hung his head, in undisguised depression, & Mr Tudor tried to
articulate some words of Cases incurable: but I interrupted him, with 'There
are NONE, sir! – no mortal man ought to pronounce such words!'
    They now looked at me, & at each other, with an aspect suddenly
changing from concern to resentment: I saw it, but would not – could not
heed it. (JL X, 881–882)

What to make of this extraordinary confrontation? The medical men, it
seems reasonable to suggest, interpret what today might be called their
'duty of care' as in the first place, now, to relieve not the patient, but his
wife, of the illusion that she has so strenuously maintained, and thereby
enable her to prepare herself for his death. This need not mean that they
abandon their patient. Madame d'Arblay resists their attempts to tell her
the truth. She knows it is the truth, but she fears to acknowledge what she
knows – not an uncommon psychological condition. She may have understood, like many patients and their relatives, that self-deception is necessary
in order to maintain hope. So she seeks to evade what she anticipates the
doctors are going to say – and this evasion is here made startlingly manifest
in bullying conversational tactics.
    She continues haranguing the two men:

'There is a Greater Physician, Gentlemen, than either of you above, & cures
the most miraculous have been worked where least expected. Hope is my
sheet Anchor! – It is the Anchor of England! – and it must be your's – !' I left
them, to still my poor shattered Nerves by the side of the precious Object for
whose peace I could yet keep them in subjection. (JL X, 882)

In her desperation to keep the truth at bay, Madame d'Arblay reaches
a height of patriotic fervour which is almost pathological in its absurdity,
and insults the doctors on whom she depends into the bargain. But is to
read it this way Burney's intention in recalling and recreating the exchange?
Does she think, looking back, that this was a valiant and honourable
moment? Or does she know, as she dramatises her thoughts, that when
she 'would not – could not' heed the doctors she was moved as much by
fear and self-protection as by determination and courage? She adds that '[t]
his HOPE, . . . this Anchor that rescued from positive Shipwreck my whole
Happiness . . . gave me nor peace, nor Confidence; it merely upheld me
from despair' (JL X, 882).[14]

Thus, while Burney gives very vividly a sense of the exigencies of her own emotions, she is also, as a narrator, able to present material that allows one to read beyond her immediate feelings and to construct rather different accounts of the situations she presents. She is capable of representing her conduct in such a way that it might be read as a continuous hysteria, as a pathological, maladaptive mode, appearing almost like an unreliable narrator who displays material that makes an attentive reader recognise that other interpretations than hers are more cogent. There is a moment towards the end which suggests the possibility that for all her pride in her own refusal to despair, this might have been maladaptive. A letter arrives that seems to suggest that Fanny has told her sister Esther that her husband is in a dangerous condition, and d'Arblay construes this as a call to her sister 'to hasten to Bath' to support her after his death. This would imply that she is in fact preparing for his death. 'Presently, in a voice tremulous with strong emotion, yet void of all anger, all resentment, he called out aloud "Oh Fanny, Fanny! – what is become of your veracity!"'(JL X, 893). It seems clear that this response, however void of anger, greatly exceeds the occasion, and is therefore readable as expressing d'Arblay's long pent-up feeling of protest against what he detects as her fiercely sustained masquerade. It suggests an alternative account of the impact upon him of the courageous act that she has spent so much energy sustaining.

Mistakenly, Burney seems to think her husband's loss of weight is due to a 'consumption', separate from his other painful disease. Two days before his decease, on 1 May, she relates:

> But Now, to keep down my own agony by any exertion that still saved from extinction the lambent flame of Hope, I flew to the Bed side, & would have pressed my lips upon the noble front of my adored Invalid, – he mildly waved me off, saying impressively: 'Plus de ça! – ' Oh God! Oh God! the perspiration that he felt he thought might injure me! – I durst not disobey – I could not speak – I only glued my lips on his loved hand! – But presently recovering, in my eagerness to combat my emotion, I earnestly besought him not to speak before the medical men of his own ill opinion of his case, which familiarized them to the idea, & lessened their responsibility.
>
> He smiled, in sweet compliance, & when Mr. Hay came on Friday afternoon, he urged himself, after asking some question, to say 'A n'est pas que je suis tout à fait sans quelque – faint hope – '
>
> This was scarcely pronounced audibly, & Mr. Hay made to it no sort of answer. (JL X, 901)

This vignette might seem designed to display d'Arblay's saintly mildness and magnanimity, but what it conveys, as if incidentally, is the overpowering drive, the flamboyant energy, and the implicit coerciveness of his wife. It is hard to believe that these were really congenial to the dying man. When Burney gets him to speak of hope, he speaks her language – as if she were speaking through him, and he the ventriloquist's puppet. A few moments after this incident, Mr Hay leaves the sickroom with the words: 'If there be any thing the General wishes for, let him have it.' Burney, 'aghast ... looked at him with a horrour that tried to look him to stone', but he stands his ground, only repeating this formula of abandonment, and then, as Burney writes, '[h]e left, with these words, a room he never more entered!' (JL X, 901–902).

Mr Hay's abrupt departure from the scene is interesting. It was certainly a violation of the contemporary protocols of dying. Medical ethicists exhorted their professional readers against the 'barbarous custom' of 'leaving your patients when their life is absolutely despaired of, and when it is no longer decent to take fees ... Even in cases where his skill as a physician can be of no further avail, his presence and assistance as a man and as a friend may be highly grateful and useful, both to the patient and to his nearest relations'.[15] 'Cruel – cruel Mr. Hay! – What false idea could guide this unnecessary, unuseful, & baneful blow!' Burney cries (JL X, 902). William Tudor does continue to call, and an explanation turning on Hay's psychology seems plausible. He may have been swept along by Burney's optimistic propaganda, forced perhaps not only to play up to her delusion, but even to share it himself. Now, when the signs are undeniable, he breaks etiquette and violates his friendship with d'Arblay in such a brutal gesture because he is breaking out of d'Arblay's wife's spell. There is only Burney's word for it, of course: the incident is one testimony to her power to make small incidents resonate with the psychological tensions of her own drama. She also declares her suspicion that Hay has been pressured to 'pronounce this sentence of Despair' so that 'no further obstacle would stand in the way of the dire ceremonies of the Catholic last Sacraments', which sounds slightly paranoid.

The other side of Madame d'Arblay's devotion is its possessiveness. Anyone else with claims, except their son, Alexander, is repudiated, and what underlies her attitude to the priest and the doctors comes out sharply in her treatment of the nurse. For most of the *Narrative*, Burney is her husband's sole attendant, his 'vigilant garde malade'. But nursing assistance becomes essential, and Mrs. Payne, recommended by Hay 'as a perfect Nurse for an Invalid', is taken on. Payne is a professional working-class woman who, as the text discloses, does her job efficiently and earns the appreciation of her patient. One might reasonably expect that she would thus earn the gratitude of his wife. But she becomes for Burney the object of a jealousy whose character as sexual rivalry is scarcely concealed. D'Arblay makes plain the high esteem in which he holds Mrs Payne. Prosecuting his agenda of preparation for death, he commits his wife to a promise to keep her on as companion and dressmaker after that event, but Fanny resists this, declaring 'she had evinced a total & even cruel want of interest & of feeling in her Master's situation, in many essential points, though her skill in Nursing – or rather aiding his removals, was such, that she frequently relieved his pains' (CJL X, 881). 'The next morning,' as she writes, 'he renewed his warm praises of Payne, with recommendations that I would keep her. I had much to offer against her, of cruel unfeelingness which she had manifested, in the midst of a plausibility that had deluded him' (JL X, 889). This might imply that Mrs Payne had been sensible and professional and offered no encouraging response to Madame d'Arblay's sentimental effusions. So by working on her husband, she succeeds in being allowed to retract her promise. Burney the writer and narrator again gives the information here that allows one to diagnose her motives, but does not rescind them.

Mrs Payne is thus not only a third person who comes between Burney and her beloved, she is also associated with ominous reality, the rational world that continually threatens the dream of identity and undying union. Like the priest and the doctor, the nurse is a functionary who takes away some of the exclusive right Burney claims to her husband's love. The fierce jealousy towards Payne suggests how unconscious, as well as conscious and ideological, motives are at work in Burney's prolonged contest with the priest and the doctors for the right to see it her way. (To use psychoanalytic terms, she is the marker of an Oedipal intrusion into the pre-Oedipal, or Imaginary, union between husband and wife.) Someone is brutally saying 'no' to the dream of fusion, but it is a dream the *Narrative* once again undermines. Burney fulsomely and thankfully declares how much spiritual sustenance she has been able to take from her husband's almost last pronouncement: 'Notre Reunion! –' But she also records as his actual last words an ironic, wry joke that displaces Burney in favour of Mrs Payne. While his wife and their son are attempting to make the bed, he murmurs 'Vous le faites – presque – aussi bien qu'elle!' ('you do it almost as well as her!') (JL X, 907).

The deathbed scene, when it arrives, is not therefore just the closure of d'Arblay's life, the inevitable terminus point to which the narrative has been travelling. It is the apotheosis of these narrative tensions that have circulated around the dynamic figure of his wife:

> The sleep was so calm, that an hour passed, in which I indulged the softest – though the least tranquil hope, that a favourable crisis was arriving – that a turn would take place, by which his vital powers would be restored, so as to enable him to endure some operation by which his dreadful malady might be overcome – but – when the hour was succeeded by another hour – when I saw a universal stillness in the whole frame such as seemed to stagnate – if I so can be understood – all around – I began to be strangely moved – 'Alex! I whispered, this sleep is critical! – a crisis arrives! – Pray God Almighty God! that it be p – –'[16]
> I could not proceed. He looked aghast – but firm – I sent him to call Payne. I intimated to her my opinion that this sleep was important but kept a composure astonishing – for when no one would give me encouragement, I compelled myself to appear not to want it, to deter them from giving me despair. (JL X, 907–908)

It is a moment of triumph, of exaltation, not a moment of grief or mourning; an awed retrospection on a momentous occasion, indeed, but a retrospection in which the awe is distributed equally between the finality of death and her own astonishing strength, self-control, and blindness. The scene climaxes Burney's psychological narrative. 'I have seen hopelessness of recovery some time – but now!' Burney had written to Alex on 22 April, a fortnight before, employing an opposite strategy to call him home: 'I see my approaching misery.' In the scene as she creates it in the *Narrative*, the magnificent delusion of her hope is still sustained, even at the point when despair is also admitted. Alone with the body, knowing and yet not believing that it is a corpse, simultaneously taking new flannel to wrap over and keep warm d'Arblay's feet and feeling his hands turning colder, she has her husband now undisputedly to herself.

A year later, in April 1819, some months before she began to write this narrative, a more composed Madame d'Arblay addressed a letter to George Hay:

> Your letter has extremely touched me, but the tears it has cost me, were soothing, not bitter. I never doubted your attachment, & General d'Arblay was always warmly convinced of it . . . it is therefore I will beg of you to spare an hour next Monday morning the anniversary of the fatal 3rd of May! to join the little congregation that will be collected at the Catholic Chapel to shew a last public mark of respect to his honoured sacred Memory.[17]

This suggests that when she sat down to write her reminiscences of her husband's last months, Burney was able to immerse herself in her memories so deeply as to dramatise with great vividness – so that they seem spontaneous – fierce, violent thoughts and emotions that in the process of mourning she had in actuality put behind her. She seems reconciled to the doctors and to the Catholic Church – her virtual enemies in the narrative. The extraordinary authenticity and raw self-exposure of that document may then be in effect an artefact. In 1823, three years after its completion, Burney found another dramatic and arresting subject, and composed the lengthy 'Waterloo journal'.[18]

In this document Burney recalls her own experiences eight years before when she found herself marooned and almost friendless in Brussels during the days before and after the decisive and bloody battle on Sunday, 18 June 1815. She gives a vivid account of the anxiety and terror she experienced, for if Napoleon should win the contest, Brussels would be captured and as an Englishwoman she feared for her life. There was no 'positive news' concerning the fighting to be had in Brussels, she writes. As a result, the streets of the city were thronged with terrified and panicking crowds. Reports came 'partially'; no one could trust them or 'build upon any permanency' of Allied success (JL VIII, 440). 'The fright, the horrour here cannot be depicted,' she told Princess Elizabeth in a letter. Even on the day of victory, there was panic: 'ONCE, on the Sunday, they shouted aloud with piercing outcries "Les Français arrivent ils sont à nos portes!"' (JL VIII, 221–222). Terrified at the news, Burney crammed letters, papers, and money into a basket and ran outside, 'crossing & crossed by an affrighted multitude' to take refuge with her friend Madame de Mauville. Safely there, she watched from the window 'continual, incessant arrivals of wounded, maimed, ill, or dying! on foot, on Horse, on Brancards; on carts, & in waggons! – a sight to break one's heart!' But there was no information to be had; it was not until the next day she learned that the besieging French were actually disarmed, but still uniformed, prisoners. An English officer 'just returned from the Field of Battle' told her that 'he *thought* all was going on well' (JL VIII, 223). For days there had been this uncertainty. It was Tuesday the twentieth before she was sure Napoleon had been defeated.[19] But as she writes, 'It is not near the scene of Battle that War, even with Victory, wears an aspect of Felicity!' (JL XIII, 447).

This chaos and misinformation surrounding the fighting is intrinsic to the story Magdalene De Lancey also has to tell. Brussels is the opening scene of *A Week at Waterloo*, as she recalls the few days of calm and happiness before the battle that her husband, as Wellington's agent and friend, knows will soon be fought. Magdalene, as she comments with quiet wit, 'enjoyed each hour as it passed with no more anxiety than was sufficient to render time precious'.[20] On Thursday, 15 June, her husband has to dine at the Spanish ambassador's. She watches from the window as he rides off, and has been there an hour, thinking how happy she is, when an aide-de-camp rides up and asks where her husband is and then gallops off to find him. 'I did not like this appearance, but I tried not to be afraid,' she writes. When she sees Sir William, he is keyed up for the coming battle and has arranged for her, as they have agreed, to take refuge in Antwerp. She must leave at six in the morning. He works more or less all night (the night of the famous ball) and in the morning they watch the assembled troops march off.

If accurate news of the battle was difficult to come by in Brussels, as Burney found, Antwerp, twenty-five miles further away, would have been worse. The events in De Lancey's narrative are in fact determined by the failures of communication incident to the chaos that followed the fighting. Antwerp 'was truly a scene of confusion' after the battle of Quatre Bras, fought on Friday, 16 June (W 48). De Lancey stays indoors, but her maid Emma listens to stories on the street and gets very frightened. She hears from her husband after this battle, but she has not expected him to be absent so long, and, as she writes, 'I began to find it difficult to keep up my spirits.' At this point the writer breaks away from herself and relates what happens to her husband. As throughout Burney's illness narrative, one is made aware of its retrospectivity, though there are none of the exclamatory heightenings so frequent in Burney's (there is only one 'alas', slipped, like a sigh, into an early sentence). Instead she writes as a historian, giving a sober recapitulation of the event that changed her life:

> Near three, when Sir William was riding beside the Duke, a cannon ball struck him on the back, at the right shoulder, and knocked him off his horse to several yards distance. The Duke at first imagined he was killed; for he said afterwards, he had never in all the fighting he had ever been in seen a man rise again after such a wound. Seeing he was alive (for he bounded up again and then sank down), he ran to him, and stooping down, took him by the hand.
>
> Sir William begged the Duke, as the last favour he could have it in his power to do him, to exert his authority to take away the crowd that gathered round him, and to let him have his last moments in peace to himself. The Duke bade him farewell, and endeavoured to draw away the Staff, who oppressed him; they wanted to take leave of him, and wondered at his calmness. He was left, as they imagined, to die. (W 50–51)

But De Lancey's cousin had seen him fall, and seeing that 'the ball had not entered', organised for him to be taken off the battlefield and eventually to a cottage in the village of Waterloo. There, after a night alone, he was found. The evening before the Duke of Wellington had listed him as killed, but changed this, apparently, when told that De Lancey had been carried off the field alive. Magdalene was told on authority by an officer who had seen the list that her husband was safe. 'I now found how much I had really feared', she writes, 'by the wild spirits I got into.' But late that night a Lady Hamilton confesses that she had written the list and out of mistaken kindness left De Lancey's name off to spare his wife the shock. Lady Hamilton then says he is alive, but seriously wounded, and not expected to live. Desperate to find her husband, Lady De Lancey sets out for Brussels, but it is a slow and terrifying journey, the carriage is 'entangled in a crowd of waggons, carts, horses, wounded men, deserters or runaways, and all a rabble and confusion, the consequence of several battles'; she draws the blinds of the carriage 'to avoid seeing the wretched objects we were passing' (W 8). ('Objects' as in Burney's account of her son's inoculation, might refer to foot soldiers, men of a lower class, but it might also convey a sense here of the inhuman degradation of the wounded.)

The carriage stops, and when she looks out she sees a Captain Hay who has been sent to verify the information. When he sees her, he turns his head away, but when she calls out, 'He hesitated and then said, "I fear I have very bad news for you." I said "Tell me at once, is he dead?" "It is all over."' (W 59). They turn back.

In Antwerp, she tries to find out more about her husband's death. All she wants is to be alone:

> I locked the outer door, and shut the inner one, so that no one could again intrude. They sent Emma to entreat I would be bled; but I was not reasonable enough for that, and would not comply. I wandered about the room incessantly, beseeching for mercy, though I felt that now, even Heaven could not be merciful. One is apt to fix on a situation a little less wretched than one's own, and to dwell upon the idea that one could bear that better. I repeated over and over that if I had seen him alive for five minutes I would not repine. (W 60–61)

The next day, Emma carries a message:

> 'I am desired to tell you cautiously' – I said, 'O Emma! Go away. Don't tell me anything, any more.' 'Nay, but I must tell you. I have good news for you.' 'How can you be so inhuman? What is good news for me now?' 'But – Sir William is not dead.' I started up, and asked what she was saying, for she would make me mad. (W 61)

General M'Kenzie, who was in command at Antwerp, assures her, through her disbelief, that what Emma has said is true, and that there

are even hopes for Sir William's recovery. 'I ran down to
General M'Kenzie, and began earnestly to persuade him it must be
impossible. I had suffered so much the day before, I durst not hope for
anything now. His voice faltered. And his eyes filled with tears. He said
"Can you believe any man would bring such intelligence unless it were
well founded?"' In fact, M'Kenzie is the last in a line of agents: a staff
officer has informed a man called Scovell who has informed him. She
must go back to the scene of the battle. This sequence of events might
drive anyone, as she implies several times, to near madness:

> I would not if I could, describe the state I was in for two hours more; then
> I lost all self-command. I would not allow Emma to put up my clothes, for
> fear of being detained. My agitation and anxiety increased. I had the
> dreadful idea haunting me that I should arrive perhaps half an hour too
> late. This got the better of me, and I paced backward and forward in the
> parlour very fast, and my breathing was like screaming. (W 63)

Like Frances Burney, Magdalene De Lancey recreates scenes and experiences that are so convincing the reader cannot doubt that they took place.
But where Burney is self-producing, De Lancey is self-effacing, not only as
an actor within the tale but as a writer. Her prose is simple, orderly,
transparent. She is forced to go through a roller-coaster of harrowing
emotions, as extreme as any of Madame d'Arblay's, but she records them
with an inflection of calm self-criticism. But it is on the ethical or moral
plane that the two narratives differ so markedly. In contrast to Burney's
compelling presentation of her own inner turbulence, De Lancey's writing
is conditioned by a kind of Christian stoicism. She seeks to control her
feelings as a matter of moral duty, but her prose gives no attention to this as
an occasion for struggle.

Circumstances have concurred to put De Lancey through emotional
torture, and she must be exhausted, but she says nothing about this. When
she finds her husband at last after another terrifying journey, lying in
a hovel in the village of Quatre Bras, she writes that she was so much
occupied with 'gathering comforts about him that I had not time to think
about the future':

> It was a dreadful but sufficient preparation, being told of his death; and then
> finding him alive, I was ready to bear whatever might ensue without
> a murmur. I was so grateful for seeing him once more, that I valued
> each hour as it passed, and as I had too much reason to fear that I should
> very soon have nothing left of happiness but what my reflections would
> afford me, I endeavoured, by suppressing feelings that would have made

him miserable, and myself unfit to serve him, to lay up no store of regret. (W 69)

The major difference from the circumstances in Burney's narrative is that De Lancey is fully prepared for her husband's death. She does not deceive herself, she says nothing about her hopes, and she soon discerns that the bleeding that's practised has not lowered Sir William's fever, and that means the 'water in the chest' will be fatal.[21] Army surgeons attend, and at first she asks them after every visit what they think, but she recognises that they will probably treat her, a woman, like any other nurse, and tell her what they think she wants to hear. She learns to recognise the symptoms herself and to observe the surgeons' expressions. But there is a moment that a little resembles Burney's confrontation with Hay and Tudor:

> On Friday evening Sir William was very feverish, and the appearance of the blood was very inflammatory. I had learnt to judge for myself, as Mr Powell, seeing how anxious I was, sometimes had the kindness to give me a little instruction. At about ten at night Mr Powell and Mr Woolriche came. While I told them how Sir William had been since their last visit, and mentioned several circumstances that had occurred, I watched them and saw they looked at each other. I guessed their thoughts. I turned away to the window and wept. They remained a little time, and I recovered myself enough to speak to them as they went out. They lingered, and seemed to wish to speak to me, but I was well aware of what they had to say. I felt unable to bear it then and shut the door instead of going out. (W 83)

In contrast to the passionate self-exposure of Burney's pathographic narrative, it is the reticence of De Lancey's style that gives it poignancy. That night Powell asked Emma what her mistress thought: Emma assured him that she 'had entirely given up hope for some time'.

During the last hours, the surgeon and a doctor disagree about treatment, and the usual unavailing measures are renewed. Sir William jokes that his wife has become adept at 'tormenting him with those little animals', the leeches used to draw blood. No priest or minister is mentioned, but Magdalene now feels it her duty to tell her husband that the surgeons think he has not long to live:

> I knew he was far above being the worse of such a communication, and I wished to know if he had anything to say. I sat thinking about it, when he awoke, and held out his hand for me to take my usual station by his bedside. I went and told him. We talked some time on the subject. He was not agitated, but his voice faltered a little, and he said it was sudden. This was the first day he felt well enough to hope he should recover! (W 87–88)

She speaks the truth to her husband. Trust between them is not in question. Both of them now understand that there is no hope. In these exceptional circumstances the tension between hope, trust, and truth that Aronowitz detected as moral imperatives in the care of the dying and that is so powerfully present in Burney's narrative is quite absent. When night comes De Lancey says he wishes he could come upon 'some device to shorten the weary long night'. Magdalene is at a loss, but he says if she could lie down beside him, it would help to pass the time. His bed is a primitive structure, fastened to the wall of the hut. She is afraid to hurt him, there is so little room, but '[h]is mind seemed quite bent on it. Therefore I stood upon a chair and stepped over him, for he could not move an inch, and he lay at the outer edge. He was delighted; and it shortened the night indeed, for we both fell asleep' (W 96–97). This loving proximity makes one realise that it is only when her husband is dead that Madame d'Arblay records touching his body.

Earlier William De Lancey had remembered how he felt when, on the battlefield, he thought he was dying. Magdalene writes '[h]e felt at peace with all the world. He knew he was going to a better one, etc, etc.' This casual dismissal, or perhaps taken-for-granted treatment of religious consolation, is telling: the ethics of the narrative and of both the protagonists are the stoical, courageous ethics of duty. His death after this night comes suddenly, soon after he has asked her to let him smell lavender water, which she also sprinkles around him. The doctor present simply says, 'Ah poor De Lancey! He is gone.' Magdalene is left alone with the body for some time, and writes '[a]s I bent over him, I felt as if violent grief would disturb his tranquil rest' (W 99).

The manuscript of Lady De Lancey's story was read by, among others, Dickens, who compared her straightforward factual style to Defoe, and urged that it be published. It was never published in fact until 1906. Its appeal was partly that it is a patriotic romance: a young heroine who exemplifies courage but also inhabits the traditional female role of the devoted wife and nurse; a young soldier husband, equally heroic, dying from his wounds in the great battle that brought final victory to the British troops. It also has a romantic apotheosis, with the calm death of the soldier in his loving wife's presence, still ministering to him. It is more substantial than this, though, because it is so direct, so honest, and so obviously not romantic in feeling. Each time De Lancey gives way to extremities of emotion, she censures herself and she defines, critically, some of the mental strategies or deceits that she and others play upon themselves in such situations as those that confront her. She never imagines she is writing as an artist: her task is to record what she remembers, and she does this with a fidelity to duty that sometimes, in its utter lack of rhetorical ornament or self-importance, can reach across two centuries as an impersonal, grave tenderness.

It would be possible – if one were a medical ethicist – to abstract from these two pathographic narratives a useful contrast between two attitudes towards the dying loved one, a contrast that becomes more striking as medical procedures become increasingly sophisticated and the population in the West lives longer. Madame d'Arblay would then exemplify the perhaps rather common attitude of 'denial'; she might model the patient, or rather the patient's family or spouse, who insist that all medical treatments available must be tried, that the 'battle', to use the common term, against the disease must be joined to the end. Magdalene De Lancey might stand for the alternative, in which death is resigned to or accepted and only measures to ensure the patient's comfort are taken. But to view these narratives merely through this ethical lens would be to simplify egregiously.

Burney depicts not just a woman refusing to accept or to know that her husband will inevitably die. Rather, her narrative exposes the complications inherent in the concept of a witness 'knowing'. She knows and does not know. Madame d'Arblay expresses in her body, and Burney through her writing, the fervency and energy of one who is determined not to give up: but she also sees, and not only retrospectively, that she deceives herself. Magdalene De Lancey's circumstances are very different; she has already gone through violent suffering at the news her husband is dead, and this, as she says, prepares her for what she will find, so that she can nurse him with calm and devotion. Her mode of 'knowing' is quite different from Burney's, since she has had this very unusual initiation. One of these narratives is written by a novelist skilled at seizing on dramatic situations and writing them up; the other is an un-self-conscious and in some ways naïve account. Thus, like all such illness narratives with actors in similar roles – the dying patient and the spouse as witness and narrator – these documents situate the problematics of illness experience within particular and unreproducible circumstances. This makes them resistant to bioethical appropriation.

Both of these narratives, so different, but relating so fully the experiences of the spouse as nurse or carer, and relating them with such emotional candour, are certainly extraordinary achievements for their time. In the past half century, however, many books telling such stories have been published, and the medical, ethical, and narrative issues raised here, especially in regard to Burney's memoir, have arisen, though in the various forms dictated by different historical circumstances, in the works discussed in the next chapter. It is certain that Frances Burney's decision to write a full, detailed account of her husband's decline and death, as well as her conflicted relationship with medical authority, makes her a pioneering pathographer.

Notes

1. Ward, B. R., ed., *A Week at Waterloo*. I have used the pdf at weekatwater looinoodelauoft.pdf (accessed 2018).
2. Derry, W., ed., *Journals and Letters, Vol. X*, pp. 842–910. Further references are to JL X, followed by the page number.
3. Hughes, P., *Journals and Letters, Vol. VIII*, pp. 339–456. Further references are to JL VIII, followed by the page number.
4. Derry, W., ed., *Journals and Letters, Vol. IX*, p. 73, Fanny Burney, Letter 939 to H.R.H. the Princess Elizabeth (pre 29 November 1815).
5. Trotter, T., *A View of the Nervous Temperament*, p. 246.
6. [no author], *Memoir of Baron Larrey*, pp. 229, 232.
7. '[S]on opinion sur ce sujet [the cause of his symptoms] est ici tournée en ridicule SOIT DIT *entre nous!*' d'Arblay had written to Burney from Paris on 27 September (JL X, 726).
8. Aronowitz, R. A., *Unnatural History*, pp. 17, 209.
9. Tolstoy, L., *The Death of Ivan Ilyich*, p. 57: '*It* kept coming back, facing him and looking at him, while he sat there rigid, the fire went out of his eyes and he began to wonder whether *It* was the only truth.' Like Ivan, d'Arblay conceives of death as a confronting, haunting presence.
10. These are held in the British Library, Barrett Collection (Egerton 3696 ff. 89–97).
11. One example, given by Anne Laurence in *Death, Ritual, and Bereavement*, edited by Ralph Houlbrooke, is of the wife of a Scottish minister who cannot submit to 'a final parting' with her husband, until with prayer and the aid of another minister she is able to be 'perfectly composed' (p. 73).
12. Jean-Jacques Rousseau, *Julie, ou la Nouvelle Héloïse* in *Oeuvres*, Paris: Pleiade, n. d. 2, 718, quoted in McManners, J., *Death and the Enlightenment*, p. 257.
13. Ibid., p. 256.
14. At moments she acknowledges her own self-deception: as in 'a sentiment I then permitted not myself to see, even while, latently, I felt it' (CJL X, 876). This is about her being won over by Dr Elloi, though.
15. John Gregory, *Observations on the Duties and Offices of a Physician* (London, 1790), cited by Roy Porter in 'Death and the Doctors in Georgian England', in Houlbrooke, R., ed., *Death, Ritual, and Bereavement*, p. 219, n. 61. Porter quotes similar sentiments from John Ferrier (1792) and Thomas Percival (1803).

16. In the version in the British Library (Egerton 6964) this is transcribed alternatively as 'Pray God – Almighty God! that it be fav–.'
17. Hemlow, J. and Douglas, A., eds, *Journals and Letters, Vol XI*, p. 97. Burney also asks Mr Tudor to attend. It is not known whether either of the two medical men did so.
18. Hughes, P. ed., *Journals and Letters, Vol. VIII*, pp. 339–456.
19. JL VIII, p. 446.
20. Ward, B. R., ed., *A Week at Waterloo*, p. 42. Further references are given in the text as for example (W 42).
21. In fact the autopsy revealed that one of De Lancey's broken ribs had pierced a lung.

CHAPTER 7

Between Hope, Trust, and Truth: 1965–2015

'Since yesterday morning I haven't had a moment's peace, not a break in my sufferings, very varied, and all horrible – but most of all they make me frightened – no fever, and no headache – but all the same *DEATH is always There! – and so near!*' (JL X, 864). By including this extract from d'Arblay's diary in her narrative Burney allows the reader to gain momentary direct access to the suffering patient's private thoughts – thoughts at complete odds with her own conception of his condition, defiantly flying the flag of hope. As I mentioned in the previous chapter, it recalls Tolstoy's fictional depiction (access being no problem) of Ivan Ilych's thoughts, or perhaps rather of his deepest fears: '*It* kept coming back, facing him and looking at him, while he sat there rigid, the fire went out of his eyes and he began to wonder whether *It* was the only truth' ('It' being death itself).[1] This is not the only moment in Burney's narrative when a reader might recall Tolstoy, even though encapsulated in the brief, fleeting moment of reproach when d'Arblay cries, '"Oh Fanny, Fanny!– what is become of your veracity!"'(JL X, 893): 'Ivan Ilych's worst torment was the lying – the lie, which was somehow maintained by them all, that he wasn't dying, he was only ill . . . Whereas he knew that, whatever was done to him, nothing would emerge but more and more agony, suffering and death. And this lie was torture for him.'[2]

In the past half-century multitudes of narratives like Burney's *The Last Illness and Death of General d'Arblay* have been published by close relatives about the last days of loved ones, so many in fact that they form an important subgenre of the modern pathography. They tend to focus, like Burney's, as much or more on their own psychological strategies and sufferings as on the patient and to raise, implicitly or otherwise, many unresolved or irresolvable ethical issues. They are written often by professional writers who have attended to husbands, mothers, lovers, and friends in the last years or months of their lives. These books are composed, like Burney's, partly to honour the dead and to assuage their own grief, but also because they are writers by instinct who have felt the dramatic qualities of events witnessed and shared. And, like Philip Roth, who confesses in *Patrimony*, a memoir that ends with his father's decline and death, 'in keeping with the unseemliness of my profession, I had been writing all the while he was ill and dying,' they would probably have kept a diary, or like Burney, memoranda.[3] What makes the events dramatic is not just their momentous nature, but the tensions between medical personnel and the patient as well as within the writers themselves. They recall tending the ill person while wrestling with their own varied distresses, mundane or complex. But what feeling for or access to the thoughts and feelings of the dying do they have while dealing with their own experience?

To frame my discussion of Burney's narrative, I draw on Robert Aronowitz's formulation of the difficulties a consulting physician faces when attending a patient with almost certain terminal illness. In his introduction to *Unnatural History*, Aronowitz briefly discusses a case in which the patient has been told by her doctor that her cancer was 'sub-optimal', implying that her chances of survival were slim. 'A contemporary bioethicist might find this a straightforward case,' he writes. 'Was the patient's "autonomy" respected? Was the expert "beneficent"?' He goes on to argue that 'such a *principled* approach glosses over the tragic conflict that often exists between competing goods, such as truthful communication, trust between doctor and patient, and hope for survival.'[4] Later in his book he writes that 'hope has often remained in an unavoidable tension with the limits of biological life, clinical realities, and truth, however defined and constructed.'[5]

Aronowitz writes from the physician's point of view: in this chapter I adopt his terms, but seek rather to illuminate their intertwining complexity by attending to these narratives by carers, the third actors in the drama of serious illness. How does the task or duty of balancing those goods play out within their inner life, where the issues that occur are to be seen as they really exist, in the experience of the person – friend or family – who cares for and watches over the dying patient?[6] As Aronowitz suggests, the 'goods' of hope, trust, and truth whose demands must be reconciled are in practice deeply problematic and complicated by another 'good' which is in play for the caregiver: the good of love which seems necessary to evoke the drive that lies behind the dual roles of carer and narrator. 'The word of all work Love', as the novelist George Eliot once called it, 'will no more express the myriad modes of mutual attraction than the word Thought can inform you what is passing through your neighbour's mind'.[7] This sentence applies just as much to trust, truth, and hope. We might imagine these terms as cells, whose immense complexity of inner processes their outward designation as a 'cell' gives no hint of. Thus Burney's undoubted love for her husband was expressed as a romantic faith in their 'union'; it was also a driving possessiveness and need that put truth in jeopardy. Hope undergoes transformations as a disease progresses, and the hopes of the patient and the caregiver scarcely mutate in tandem.

The five books considered here then are a selection from many other illness narratives published by carers in the past half-century, from the Stinsons' *The Long Dying of Baby Andrew* in 1969 to, for instance, Gerda Lerner's *A Death of One's Own* (1978, republished in 2006), Michael Dorris's *The Broken Cord* (1989) and Deborah Wearing's *Forever Today* (2005). They do not include any of the hundreds of memoirs relating the writers' history of care for a wife, husband, or parent slipping away into dementia, or the many books, of which John Foster's *Take Me to Paris, Johnny* (1993) is likely one of the more distinguished, telling the story of a partner dying of AIDS.[8] The works I have selected are Simone de Beauvoir's *A Very Easy Death* (1965), Martha Weinman Lear's *Heartsounds* (1989), *Swimming in a Sea of Death*, by David Rieff (2008), Helen Garner's *The Spare Room* (2008) and Marion Coutts's *The Iceberg* (2014). None of these books is merely a chronicle – relating this happened and then that happened – even though they follow the quotidian course of a patient's illness as it occurred. They have been selected firstly, because they are shaped by urgent moral purposes, and in them hope, trust, truth, and love are manifestly, though differently, in play, and secondly, because each in its different way has affinities with Burney's narrative.

A Very Easy Death (*Une Mort Très Douce*, 1964) was first published in English in 1966. A contributor to the journal *Medical Humanities* wrote in 2004 that it remains 'a document of great richness' since it 'raises many points for reflection' for medical readers, and this is still the case.[9] Besides taking us to the bedside of a woman dying progressively over six weeks, it defines and confronts one moral conflict that might face an attendee or caregiver of the dying in its most acute form. Times have changed and medical practices have altered greatly, but the relevance of this text has not. It might be noted that the English translation by Patrick O'Brian tends to soften the raw edge of de Beauvoir's prose.

Francois de Beauvoir is seventy-seven when she is rushed to a Paris 'clinic', or private hospital, after suffering a fall that has left her struggling across the floor of her apartment for two hours to reach the telephone. Simone has had a difficult relationship with her mother, but she immediately flies in from Rome. She is violently distressed by her first sight of the old lady's exposed body, helpless in the hospital bed. 'Voir le sexe de ma mere,' she writes: the statement is less confronting when it is rendered in English as 'the sight of my mother's nakedness had jarred me.'[10] She struggles to understand her reaction; the sight is 'both repugnant and holy – a taboo'. It opens up old wounds and conflicts and it leads later to the writer's accounting of her mother's life and character, and the treatment of her daughter that estranged the two of them. Thus this pathography has a depth that few others have, a revisiting and eventual revision of the fraught relationship between sufferer and carer. The unflinching attention to the mother's body throughout the text – to the material facts of physical suffering – might recall nothing more strongly than Burney's account of her own body's agony during the mastectomy. Neither writer spares her reader in her attention to these particulars.

It appears to de Beauvoir that 'Maman's doctors condescend' to the elderly woman. Because, as it seems, they suspect something serious, X-rays are ordered, which the nurses, frightened, say they can't interpret. Then one of the doctors, 'Professor B', calls Simone in the evening: after some preliminary patter, he informs her that there is 'a tumour blocking the small intestine', or, as de Beauvoir more bluntly states, 'Maman had cancer.'[11] Another man, Dr P the surgeon, appears as the 'good doctor' figure in this pathography; Dr N, the 'resuscitation expert' who carries out procedures that hurt their mother despite the daughter's protests, is the bad, virtually evil one. P talks to Simone's mother as 'though she were a human being' while for N, 'she was the subject of an interesting experiment and not a person.' He seems 'infatuated with technique', or professional expertise. This ancient duality discernible in Burney's account of her mastectomy (the cruel, authoritarian Dubois opposed to the sensitive, kindly Larrey) reappears in many illness narratives.

Simone and her sister Poupette reluctantly consent to a drastic operation: the surgeon finds 'four pints of pus in the abdomen, the peritoneum burst, and a huge tumour, a cancer of the worst kind'.[12] Poupette has apparently begged: 'Operate on Maman. But if it is cancer, promise me you will not let her suffer.' (This seems extraordinary: in more modern terms, she is asking the doctors to perform 'medically assisted death'.) Simone writes that: 'He had promised. What was his word worth?' 'Sans aucune doute, il avait réusit un superbe exploit technique; les conséquences, sans aucune doute il s'en lavait les mains.'[13] When Maman is back in bed, she is led to believe that she has peritonitis, a severe condition in the elderly, but without the aura of terror around 'cancer'. Dr P tells Poupette that even if the cancer appears in another place, '[w]e shall find something to say. We always do. And the patient always believes it.'[14] Truth will be forfeited and trust will be violated in order to preserve the dubious third 'good', hope.

De Beauvoir now writes, '[t]he betrayal was beginning.' It is not just the doctors' or her own betrayal of her mother. It is the betrayal of her own beliefs. She has become an accomplice in the deception, and tormented self-hatred follows. This woman, a figure famous in France for her frankness and honesty, is made to play a false part. She rationalises her remorse; she should have insisted that her mother not be operated on, or if a cancer was found, to let her die: 'At the first trial I had given in: beaten by the ethics of society I had abjured my own.' But this rational account of a contest between ethical systems that she formulates after a conference with Sartre does not reach to the heart of the matter, which ultimately resides in the very different referential vocabulary de Beauvoir is driven to use, as when her mother's frail voice speaks to her with the 'mystery' of an 'oracle'.[15]

As throughout Burney's narrative, the emotional states of the carer and the patient now radically diverge. Burney seeks to defy death and invests everything in hope; her husband accepts the imminence of his death and prepares for it through the rituals of his religious faith. No longer in pain, Maman is revived by the operation: she is cheerful and the colour returns to her cheek; she seems to believe she is cured. 'It was as though, at the age of seventy-eight, she were waking afresh to the miracle of living.' She becomes a person Simone can admire, amused and amusing, accepting herself. But her daughter is on another trajectory entirely, now tortured by the falsity she finds herself trapped in: her mother will die, probably in pain. They renew their feeling for each other, but this is, as she writes retrospectively, 'six weeks of an intimacy rotted by betrayal'.[16] So this pathography is remarkable for the presence it gives to Maman, the authority it gives to her courage, while it tracks simultaneously Simone's despair and emotional suffering, a suffering she can only express through a vocabulary belonging to a realm of thought that, as it gradually appears, her mother has found no further use for.

As the days go on and Francois de Beauvoir's condition palpably worsens (though she apparently still imagines she will get better), Simone is no longer so rattled, but when she helps the nurse to lift her mother to a different position in the bed, she is 'frightened by the horrible mystery that I sensed . . . under the dressings . . . that skeleton clothed in damp blue skin'. But at the same time she admires the suffering patient's will to live. 'She seemed so exhausted that Mademoiselle Lebron hesitated' to give a painful injection, but Maman consents, saying, 'since it is good for me'. In one simple paragraph that follows this there is an extraordinarily visceral glimpse of the anguish that is transmitted from the dying woman to her daughter and that seeks refuge in something uncannily like a prayer. Here the tender attentiveness to her mother is so kindly that it seems as if the two of them blend for a moment into one – a moment that swiftly and tragically relapses into Simone's own desolation.

> Once more we turned her over on to her side; I held her and I watched her face, which showed a mixture of confused distress, courage, hope and anguish. 'Since it is good for me.' In order to get well. In order to die. I should have liked to beg someone to forgive me.

A page or so later, more herself, Simone expands on this: 'Maman thought we were with her, next to her; but we were already placing ourselves on the far side of her history. An evil all-knowing spirit, I could see behind the scene, while she was struggling, far, far away, in human loneliness.' And again, 'Despairingly, I suffered a transgression that was mine without my being responsible for it and one that I could never expiate.' 'She rested and dreamed, infinitely far removed from her rotting flesh, her ears filled with the sound of our lies.'[17] The very prose enacts a tug-of-war between spirituality and self-disgust.

Madame d'Arblay fights off as long as she can any concession to her husband's Catholic faith. Maman too is a devout Catholic, and it is not long before a priest makes his appearance. Just as Burney attempts to shield her husband from visits she feels may interfere with what she thinks is the need to keep death from his mind, the sisters shield their mother from her coreligionists and turn the priest and others curtly away. What surprises them is that Francois de Beauvoir herself declines to see these visitors. It seems that quite unlike Alexandre d'Arblay, she herself is turning away from her religious inheritance, perhaps renouncing it. The words her daughter finds and needs, though, reverberate with the religious education she has herself forsworn. It's as if the realm of ethics, the discourse of abstraction outside of human consciousness, fails in the face of actual moral suffering. So de Beauvoir has recourse to words like 'holy', 'transgression' and 'expiate', loaded with meaning in some other moral universe, to edge towards her anguish. Her mother's body is a 'mystery'. She herself is an evil spirit. She is in a condition for which modernity has no language. Is 'I should have liked to beg someone to forgive me' anything other than a pitiful paraphrase of a thought she cannot entertain: 'I wish I still believed in the Lord'?

In David Rieff's *Swimming in a Sea of Death*, as in *A Very Easy Death*, a child finds himself accompanying his mother through to her extinction. The crucial difference of Rieff's narrative from de Beauvoir's is suggested by the contrast in their titles: Rieff's is a book in which the writer struggles with his feelings, buffeted this way and that by contending thoughts and impulses, gasping for his own emotional survival. De Beauvoir's crisp ironic title tells us she knows exactly what she has felt and feels. Nevertheless, the tension between truth and hope that takes such a toll on her is replayed, though in a different key, a different emotional and ethical domain, in this book. There is moreover a crucial affinity between Rieff's story and Burney's *Last Illness*, because the virtual protagonist, here the patient, as the carer is in hers, is a powerful, strong-willed, proud, and articulate woman who refuses to accept the certainty of imminent death.

Susan Sontag had gone through two treatments for cancer before she was diagnosed with myelodysplastic syndrome (MDS), a particularly lethal form of blood cancer, at the age of seventy-one in 2004. She had already survived two attacks of cancer: breast cancer in 1975, for which she submitted to the drastic, dreadful radical mastectomy commonly recommended at that time in the United States, known as the Halstead procedure, and a uterine sarcoma in 1998. Her recovery from both seems to have fuelled her conviction that she would come through triumphantly again. Sontag was a force: a famous writer. The power of her personality was so great that she virtually compelled those around her, including most importantly her only child, to support her in her driving optimism, which steadily became more and more factitious, forced and unreal.

This summary does not capture the troubled quality of Rieff's narrative, which returns again and again to the dilemma that Aronowitz's triad of 'goods' outlined. To put this bluntly, is it right to offer hope when you know you are lying, and when you also suffer in your own conscience for your weakness, your incapacity, to make a convincing job of the lies? He finds himself acquiescing, or becoming an 'accomplice' in his mother's fantasy goal of survival, as for example, searching the Web or newspapers for reports that might offer her a scintilla of hope, although he doubts them himself. But whereas Simone de Beauvoir is brutally frank about the 'lies' she comforted her mother with, compelled by the fact that she has been in effect trapped by the misrepresentations of her doctors, Rieff is not trapped by anything but his love or attachment (or is it his duty?) to his mother, and he acquiesces in her desperate need for hope reluctantly and to his shame and guilt. And yet he sees how easily his mother saw through the encouraging remarks or hopeful prognoses of her friends. 'What she wanted from me was an adamant refusal to accept that it was even *possible* that she might not survive.' To do this, he writes, 'I had to not think.'

The bad news about the blood cancer had been given roughly and tactlessly by a 'Doctor A', who speaks to Sontag and her son as if they were children, and with no feeling for the dread his information is creating. He is another of the bad guys of pathography, but much later, when Sontag has opted for the last resort – a bone marrow transplant in Seattle – appears a doctor who exemplifies the successful reconciliation of the apparently contending obligations of his practice. 'When pressed', Rieff observes, the surgeon 'would be very frank with my mother about just how terrible her MDS was'.

> It is true that he never allowed himself to be drawn out on whether he personally thought my mother would survive or not (though she repeatedly tried to get him to do so, and asked me to ask him on a number of occasions as well). Instead, he would reframe the question, and in doing so, or so it seemed to me, let the hope back in. My mother would almost always take a deep breath, shake her head, hair flying, and ask questions concerning the next step Nimer wanted to take in her treatment. They would go on from there, with my mother growing visibly calmer with the passing minutes.[18]

The doctor has what might be called a skilled ameliorative strategy, though that suggests something akin to a technique. It is a pity that Rieff does not or cannot recall what words of his achieved the reframing of Sontag's demands. Perhaps underlying the success of Nimer's approach is his respect for this patient, who – as in the rare glimpse her son offers here – still has presence and style. Rieff goes on to wonder whether doctors like this are 'less physician-scientists than shaman-scientists, with the power to somehow mitigate the unthinkable'.

> And it is all very well to deride that aspect of the relationship between doctor and patient, to speak of how patronizing or objectifying it is, but I am by no means sure there is a way out of the dilemma or even that more candor from the doctors would have been any sort of improvement. For the sad reality is that without the doctors' power to infantilize, which in this context meant to lull and reassure, not condescend to or lord it over her, my mother would have gone mad months before she died.[19]

This doctor is there, holding her hand, when Sontag dies some days later. Towards the end of his pained meditation, Rieff concludes that the issues boil down 'to hope or truth', and 'if that' (opting for hope) 'meant making myself an accomplice in an illusion, it was not a steep price to pay for any measure of solace.'[20] Ultimately – and this is what makes his book so unusual – it is not clear what measure of solace he found for himself.

Though he strives towards it, it seems as if the emotional wounds, the buffeting of the waves, of this experience and of this relationship, remain unhealed.[21]

Heartsounds is quite different – not a troubled meditation, but a dramatic narrative, this time by a wife about her husband's five heart surgeries and his rocky road towards death over three years. I have chosen to discuss this problematic and taxing book because in so many respects Martha Weinman Lear is a reincarnation of Madame d'Arblay. This may sound absurd: Lear is a twentieth-century New Yorker; Burney was a genteel woman in the early nineteenth century. But the Lears, like the d'Arblays, were elite: Dr Lear was a respected, even famous, professional man; Madame d'Arblay was a famous novelist, her husband an aristocrat. Both couples carry a sense of entitlement. Both women campaign, Burney over many months, Martha Lear over three years, to keep their own hopes and their husbands' alive. Like Burney, Martha is militant, aggressively challenging Hal Lear's doctors, fighting off any hint that her husband is going to die. She too will not give in. Her will is as ferocious as Burney's. This being the world of modern medicine, she does battle not with visiting apothecaries, but with the hospital system, with doctors and nurses, interns, residents, and specialists. She confronts her husband's colleagues, men who with remarkable tolerance continue to support her husband for many months, until they tire of her pestering telephone calls and rude insinuations. She is absolutely intransigent in her possessiveness and protection of her husband. She is so like Burney too in her mixture of self-knowledge and passionate, self-displaying – and self-defeating – energy.

Heartsounds, again rather like Burney's *Last Illness*, offers itself as a love story. It's about the identity of the partners, an identity in this case problematically realised in the text itself, for much of the record of Hal Lear's experience is told from his point of view, and apparently it's a transcription of his own words. This is the case with an account of his angiogram cited in the next chapter. Lear will have collaborated with his wife, supplied her with his experience and memories, but it is impossible to resist the suspicion that, in the process of writing, the drama has been heightened, or sometimes even invented. And this narrative, quite unlike Burney's, jolts from one viewpoint to another, the present to past experience, the prose from dramatised dialogues to private commentary. Unlike Burney too, Martha's inner conflicts or debates with herself sometimes are openly explored.

But the crucial difference in the situation is that while d'Arblay accepts death and conscientiously prepares for it over the will of his wife, this husband, though he must know, as a professional, that his death is inevitable, does not, and fights with all his might against the thought. This is New York in the 1970s, and you do not give in: your rage is good, it will keep you alive. The Lears are Jewish, but there is not a whisper of any religious resource, hope, or consolation; rather aggression than depression – as Martha declares in so many words. She has a career as a freelance journalist, they are both apparently fit, strong-willed, educated people. Dr Lear may be famous, but has suffered from humiliating professional treatment; either because of this or not, he suffers a massive heart attack. Rushed into the hospital where he is on staff, he is operated on and as he recovers, finds out, as Martha Lear writes, what being a patient is like. Growing stronger, for instance, he realises he doesn't need the 'shots' that kept him out of pain:

> So he said to one of the residents, 'I am having only low-grade discomfort. But whenever I report any pain at all, I get a shot. It makes me dizzy and disoriented. Could I have something milder?'
> The resident got angry. He said, 'There is medication ordered for you. If you want it, you can have it. If not, you'll get nothing.' And walked out, leaving him lying there, helpless.
> So he went through the evening with this pressure in his chest.[22]

The shift changes and the next resident says, 'sure', and gives him aspirin.

This is only one of many instances which convince Dr Lear that patients are 'neglected, or infantilized or patronized or otherwise abused'. Patients, he says, did not complain: 'there was a reciprocal acceptance of the ground rules, and the ground rules stank.'[23] This critique of hospital medicine, which his wife takes up with great energy, runs like a furious current through the book. 'I put it to you', she later writes, 'all you nurses who race like mice from one nocturnal crisis to another, and you doctors who lumber like sleepy bears' that she is 'not your standard hospital hysteric', though on the next page she writes of 'the most hideous night of mistakes, bad judgments, oversights, fatigue, neglect, institutional paralysis, the very worst of institutional medicine'.[24] Lear has another, milder heart attack and then undergoes the angiogram, then an operation for a heart bypass. This leaves him left 'teetering on the very edge' because the 'massive' operation (as one of his surgeon friends calls it) had resulted in another heart attack, a fact which seems to have been kept from him for some time. Consequently he is unable to read, unable to orient himself, terribly weakened, a 'cardiac cripple'. The saga continues, with apparent improvements, followed by crushing setbacks and increasing strain on the marriage.

Late in the narrative, Martha chances to read an entry in a notebook in which Hal writes, '[p]robably I will die quite soon,' adding, '[w]hatever Drs say I know it means a progressive myocardial degeneration'. Honesty between them being a priority, Martha tells him she has read his entry:

> He sank into a chair. 'Oh, God, that is terrible. I am so sorry you read that. You had no right.'
> We talked across chasms. I begged him to talk straight and would not let him talk straight, which was the way I boxed him in all the time. Please share your thoughts with me. And he would open up a bit. And: Oh, I would say, you *must not* think such dreadful thoughts. I can see *clearly* that you are getting better. Locking him in like that, which I did not understand until long after.[25]

'Boxing in' is probably as good a way as any to describe Burney's strategy with her dying husband. Here, though, a number of ethical issues or rather ethical quandaries are meshed together. Martha wants to give her husband hope, but because she loves him, she is herself seeking comfort. She will not allow herself to access her own fear. Lear too, who apparently is strong enough to face the truth, wants to keep it from her. She does not want him to suffer the thought of his coming death alone, but actually she is also suffering from her own dread of losing him. They are sparing each other the truth out of love, but at the cost of pretending to each other, hence damaging the trust and honesty they value. Later Martha Lear sees their doctor, now a friend, who evades her questions: she guesses that her husband must have told him to conceal the truth. The saga trundles on.

After Sontag's death, David Rieff interviews a palliative care specialist who offers a 'despairing' comment on the approach some doctors take towards a dying patient. She speaks of

> the denial, the kind of winking that goes on, where, yeah, we all know the patient's going to die but we're all going to pretend there's hope, so we're all going through these rituals because that's what we believe the patient wants. In the meantime the patient is watching the doctor, who is offering the treatment, and clearly thinking to himself, if the doctor didn't think it would work, he or she wouldn't offer it, but what the doctor's not saying is that the odds are minute and that he is trying to respond to the needs of the patient for hope. It's like a minuet. It's surreal.[26]

'This very wearing kind of cognitive dissonance', a phrase this doctor also uses, is, as in *Heartsounds*, often the plight of the watching carer as much or more than it is of doctors. In Helen Garner's *The Spare Room*, a woman who takes in an old friend experiences it acutely, and the book explores the consequences for someone who, like de Beauvoir, closely attends on the patient, not briefly like a consulting physician, but for many days – in this case three weeks of physically as well as morally exhausting days. I have earlier used the phrase 'fictionality in non-fiction' to describe the effect of many accounts of illness experience (as occasionally in *Heartsounds*). It would be more appropriate to say of *The Spare Room* that it is 'non-fiction in the guise of fiction'. The book is published as a novel, but its effect is of authentic experience, which is not only conveyed by the fact that the main character bears the same first name as the author – the rule of thumb (the 'autobiographical pact') long established to distinguish autobiography from fiction.[27] So I treat it here as a pathography.

Early in *In Shock*, a remarkable work discussed in the next chapter, a physician, Dr Rana Awdish, is told that nothing can be done to drain fluid from her lung, which means that she will always be dependent on oxygen to survive. She writes:

> I felt the kind of panicked desperation and disbelief I had seen in the faces of my patients with terminal conditions. I recognized it as the same feeling that drove people to embrace unproven alternative treatments. It felt distinctly as though I had nothing to lose. I thought of my patients who had spent their final days away from their children, traveling for experimental therapy only offered at distant cancer treatment centers. The patients who had spent their life savings on vitamin infusions, purified herbs and tonics.[28]

Nicola, the cancer patient in *The Spare Room*, is one of these people. She flies from Sydney, where she has been cared for by a niece, to stay with Helen in Melbourne so that she can be near the clinic she wants to attend regularly for the next three weeks. There she will be given treatment for her cancer, consisting each week of vitamin C infusions in very large doses, and for which she will pay very large sums of money. Nicola has absolute faith in 'The Theodore Institute' and in its practitioners. Helen, who has done some research, is sceptical.

But Nicola is dreadfully ill, as Helen sees as soon as she meets her friend at the airport. She is bent over, 'stripped of flesh' and shuddering. Nicola is from a squatters family, in Australia the equivalent of blue blood; her style is aristocratic and elegant, unconsciously condescending. Garner presents her entirely dramatically, in verbal exchanges with Helen, so that the reader is left to assume that behind her forced smiles, effusive gestures, and confidence lie anxiety and fear. Her smile challenges everyone to share her apparent optimism. She has wrapped a carapace about herself, just as she throws her stylish red cape around her shoulders. That first night, Helen has to undress her like a child and put her to bed: she lies close to Nicola to keep her from shuddering.

They visit the Institute next day. After waiting more than four hours, they see a Dr Tuckey, to whom Nicola gives her history – bowel cancer which has spread to other parts of her body. In Sydney she's had chemotherapy and radiation. Tuckey tells her he thinks she will respond to their treatment – she's 'the perfect person' for their approach. On their next visit, Nicola is taken into another room for an 'ozone sauna'. While this goes on, Helen idly picks up Nicola's file. The heading *Prognosis* leaps out at her, and underneath is written 'Terminal 1–3 years'. There follows a passage in which the ethical issues germane to this work clearly emerge:

> My legs were quivering. I took a few deep breaths. What was going on? Hadn't Dr Tuckey, the night before, assured Nicola that she would respond 'very well' to the clinic's treatment? Surely he should have said, 'Would you like me to tell you what I think your future is?' And if she said yes, wouldn't it be more honourable to tell her the truth, and then say, 'But we can offer you certain treatments that may shrink the cancer, slow it down, make it possible for you to live more comfortably in the time you have left?'[29]

Each time Nicola gets back from the vitamin infusions, she is a wreck and in severe pain. She sweats terribly. Helen has to change Nicola's sheets several times a night, wash them, over and over, and lug her mattress out into the sunshine. She gets very little sleep. The book makes the toil and exhaustion involved in the mundane daily tasks of nursing manifest, a major factor in the increasing tension between the friends. Nicola believes that her sweating and increased pain are signs that the vitamin C is driving out the cancer.

Helen suggests she should see a general practitioner and get a script for a stronger painkiller; Nicola refutes the idea in her best condescending manner: 'Helen, I have to trust the vitamin C . . . I need you to believe in it too.' 'Till this minute', Garner writes, 'I had dodged the question by concentrating on simple tasks. Now I took my first real breath of it, the sick air of falsehood. I forced myself to nod.'[30] Like de Beauvoir, but momentarily, she has fallen into a moral trap; it's what might have been the betrayal beginning. But things are different, and later Helen finds she can open the issue. When Nicola, for the first time, gives her that opening, by offering sympathy for Helen's exhaustion, and asks, 'What's the worst part? Is it the sweating?', she responds with the existentialist term that de Beauvoir does not use: 'No – it's feeling we're in bad faith with each other.'

Nicola's niece arrives. Encouraged by her, and exhausted, frustrated, and maddened, Helen tries again one morning to force Nicola to see the truth of the situation. Nicola heads her off:

> Her eyebrows formed an inverted V of patronising concern. 'I'm so sorry, darling. I had no idea I'd offended you.'
> She tilted her head, stretched her lips, and there it was again, plastered across her face like latex – the smile.
> The last of my self-control gave way.
> 'Get that grin off your face. Get it off, or I'll wipe it off for you.'[31]

She tears into her friend, who offers pitiful, childish defences. If the scene which ensues is almost unbearable it is because of Helen's hatred of what she finds herself doing. 'Where was this rage stored in me? It gushed up like nausea,' she thinks. 'Shame choked me.' 'Like an old, tired dog', Nicola tries to defend herself, begging Helen not to go on. She launches into a full-scale attack on Nicola's defences, telling her that they hate her smiling, upbeat mask. 'We want to smash it. We want to find you.' They force her to see that the Institute's treatments are phony and causing her increased pain. So they strip her of hope in the name of truth. Helen wants her 'to live in the truth'.

If hope is a 'good' then to strip someone of it, as Helen and her niece set out to do, is a moral failure, born of their own exhaustion and impatience. They certainly have rational grounds – solid evidence – that Nicola is being deceived. But hope doesn't work like that: hope is that which exists precisely in the absence of hard evidence. But it is here that the other 'good', love, comes into play. This is not wanton cruelty: it may be born of frustration, but it is born also, as Garner makes the reader understand, of real affection for and admiration of Nicola. Helen is acting partly out of her pity for the terrible, increasing pain that she sees Nicola enduring from the vitamin treatment, and partly because, like the reader, she intuits that Nicola's smile is a means of hiding her own misery, disbelief, and fear.

So Nicola is persuaded to see an oncologist. Garner describes the interview with Dr Molony:

> He faced us pleasantly across his desk. Behind him a window gave on to a cold grey courtyard fringed by a low hedge of box. He kept his gaze strictly on Nicola's face while she spoke at length about her illness and its treatments: not once did he betray her by glancing at me. I sat beside her,

exasperated, fascinated, watching the river of her trust re-direct itself and flood towards him.[32]

This passage illustrates what Paul Komesaroff has identified as the 'micro-ethics' of the clinical encounter.[33] 'The doctor within the clinical interaction', he contends, 'is constantly faced with the ethical decision about what she should do. How for example, should she ask this difficult or potentially intrusive question? How should she palpate the abdomen of this man in pain? How should she express the diagnosis of lung cancer to this elderly woman?' The doctor's response to these questions may be intuitive, but it will be embodied in 'a particular choice of words, or manner of delivering those words, or it may be embodied in the pitch of the voice, the length of the pause or the softness of the touch'. And, as he comments, the patient will respond to these 'micro-ethical' signals, and this 'is of crucial importance with respect to the clinical outcomes'.[34] Thus the demeanour of the physician, his or her apparently innate or casual gestures, facial expressions, and tones of voice are laden with serious significance for the patient, whose attention may well be heightened by the apprehension that is almost inseparable from a clinical encounter. They are not dismissible as casual concomitants of the interview, but deliver meanings that can contribute to its success or otherwise. Not letting his eyes stray from Nicola's face as she carries on at length about her case history and her faith in her recent treatments (as the narrator implies) and then offers her his diagnosis in a quiet, tentative voice, Dr Molony succeeds in persuading Nicola to have an MRI and a bone scan. In the car as they leave, Nicola says 'I like him. He cares about me. He's clever.' She cancels her appointment with the Institute.

James Wood has described *The Spare Room* in the *New Yorker* as a 'powerful re-writing of *The Death of Ivan Illych*'.[35] The difference is that the novella is told from the suffering patient's point of view while *The Spare Room* is told from the perspective of the anguished carer. In *Ivan Ilyich* it is the falsity around him that increases his suffering; in *The Spare Room* it is the falsity of the patient Nicola's refusal to face the truth that unbalances Helen. What certainly links the two texts is the unsparing starkness with which they confront the two distinct psychological states: Ilyich's pain and terror, Helen's anger and cruelty.

It is important to acknowledge that a carer will sometimes feel, besides love and compassion for the patient, hatred and anger. A passing example can be found in John Bayley's memoir of his wife, the novelist Iris Murdoch, *Iris* (1998), as her dementia becomes more and more marked.

On a bus travelling to Oxford at night Iris, in the endless fidgeting that is one sign of her illness, takes another passenger's bag; its contents spill onto the gangway. The woman is distraught and desperately tries to regain her handbag and other possessions. Bayley writes, 'Iris says, "So sorry", and gives the woman her beautiful smile. I get Iris into a seat and give her a violent surreptitious punch on the arm by which I am holding her.'[36] Here, as in *The Spare Room*, the carer's rage, which Bayley then discusses, is tinctured with pity for its victim.

The case in Marion Coutts's *The Iceberg* is more complex and expanded upon. Coutts's husband, Tom, an art critic who writes regularly for the *Observer* newspaper, is diagnosed with a brain tumour in the region of the brain that governs speech and language. Over two and a half years, he loses the ability to recognise words, then to put sentences together, until ultimately he can only make noises intended to be speech. After the removal of the tumour he suffers seizures, and soon it is evident that his capacity to find the words he wants – this in a man whose fluency was his gift – is ebbing away. But Marion develops techniques to aid him, which ultimately become almost telepathic. Eventually Tom can only make blunt, confused sounds, but his wife is able intuitively to grasp what they mean and to write their meaning down. He is able, very slowly and with her help, to continue to compose.

In this diary-like narrative there is neither hope nor hopelessness. Instead, there is a calm anticipation of what must happen in the future and shifting plans to deal with it. Neither husband nor wife denies the truth – which is in any case manifest in Tom's steadily deteriorating speech. At one point Coutts writes that she is 'trying to arrive at an intellectual accommodation with death.'[37] Early in *The Iceberg*, she describes a charge nurse, whom, she comments, would not be noticed outside the ward: 'He carries his authority carefully and ever so gently separate from himself, as you would a bowl of water.' Something of the same quality is present in her own prose: however violent the feelings she owns and depicts, they are presented with an authority and dispassion that rids them of the taint of complaint.

Coutts's book is, at the same time, un-self-sparing in its relation of the stressful life of the carer. But that other 'word-of-all work', 'stress', does not capture anything of the various, sometimes bizarre emotional states that, normality having left a vacuum, rush in to occupy the psychic space. The situation is extreme: besides her husband, she has a child, Ev, to care for, eighteen months old when Tom is diagnosed, and with all the demandingness of a three-year-old while his father is dying. Marion offers an inner soliloquy to the child to explain her bursts of anger:

> What I feel as I watch you a living/living being and he a dying/living being seems supernatural. I don't know why I am not mad, or blind. But I am not. Still, we have this life and we float about in it and many things continue to happen to us for very good and very ill. I am not dissolved. I do not moan or despair. I do not panic. But I am über-naturally tired. The edges of my vision are distorted. The fibre of my muscles is weak. My tongue lacks spring. My hands do not rest. Pressure can cause me to lose my shape under tension and when this happens I lose my temper. I regret this.[38]

The physical symptoms Coutts mentions here become worse as the pressures on her intensify and she becomes nearly desperate: 'My flesh is morbid. The epidermis jangles with static in a continual electric burn, a low fire on the tundra of my arms and shoulders.' Her desperation deepens as she searches for suitable accommodation for Tom when he needs twenty-four-hour care, and the system seems to be failing them. But the anger in this book is rarely directed at the patient or medical personnel. There are nurses Marion distrusts, but more whose tact and kindness she admires: there is one obtuse doctor in a country hospital with whom she quarrels (and ridicules) but both Mr K, the neurosurgeon, and Dr B, the oncologist who treats Tom, are presented as exemplary medical figures in their fields, though she comments on their first meeting that K's 'manner and words are functional, and in no way sweet as the high art of his knife'.

Marion Coutts is an artist by profession, and *The Iceberg* is threaded through with delicately observed and vividly described details. She attends carefully to Mr K on their first interview:

> If the conversation strays from the visual or the factual, his lack of interest is ever so faintly and minutely signalled. I try to work out how the signal goes: a slight breath, a shift, a nostril flares, his mouth marginally puckers, a muscle in his leg adjusts itself. This occurs when we introduce narrative. Narrative means symptoms. Symptoms mean the description of how this thing affects us in daily life. Tom finds this comforting. On the scale of things, his expertise outweighs our anecdote.[39]

Coutts's reading of the faint signals given by the surgeon's face and body is an unusual, almost preternaturally attentive instance of the micro-realm. Patients can receive information like this without necessarily being aware of their impact or meaning. The ubiquity of such signs – a constantly recurring one being a doctor who talks to the patient without looking in their eyes – gives substantial support to Komesaroff's hypothesis. Microethics inheres in such minute particulars. The momentous effect of apparently insignificant aspects of a doctor or a nurse's demeanour and address on the patient's well-being is explored in the next chapter.

The works I have selected and discussed here all centre around an intensely difficult moral problem or ethical dilemma.[40] It is a challenging circumstance that another genre, also concerned with the moral issues that arise in medicine, emerged at more or less the same historical moment as the pathography's ascendency – bioethics.[41] Like the pathography, bioethics tells stories and features characters, or at least personages, and deals with conflicting views, though these are presented quite differently from the dramatic interplay between patients and medical staff that I have emphasised as a key aspect of the pathographic form. The essential difference is that bioethics is a realm of medical discourse: its many journals and monographs are addressed to medical professionals. In the case histories it represents, patients and their families (whose identity is disguised for legal and other reasons) are only individualised insofar as they present issues, apparent dilemmas, options for courses of action or treatment. Devoted to the formulation of principles as a guidance for action, its project, like its partner 'the ethics of care', is undermined by its failure to attend to the complexity of human relationships that inhere, and can only be understood as actualised, in specific and real-life examples. The site of ethical anxiety is not the patient or carer, but the doctor or nurse. Nevertheless, as the next chapter demonstrates, there is an emerging interplay between bioethical discourse and personal narrative in autobiographical pathographies by doctors.[42]

Robert and Peggy Stinson write in their preface to *The Long Dying of Baby Andrew* that: 'We present the ethical problems which concern us as part of an unfolding personal story, not because we welcome the abandonment of our own privacy, but that is where the ethical dilemmas occur: inextricably embedded in the lives of real people.'[43] Not only in their lives but in their consciousness and conscience are ethical issues 'inextricably embedded', and, as in their narrative, these matters often involve contesting the priorities of contemporary medicine. Like microethics, many pathographic narratives, in exploring the moral issues that lie in the interstices of life and relationships, in tones, looks, gestures, as well as actions, and rendering them with specificity and honesty, make a serious contribution to our medical culture.

Notes

1. Tolstoy, L., *The Death of Ivan Ilyich*, p. 57.
2. Ibid., p. 64.
3. Roth, P., *Patrimony*, p. 237.
4. Aronowitz, R. A., *Unnatural History*, p. 17.
5. Ibid., p. 283.
6. This chapter does not engage with the philosophical discourse around 'the ethics of care'. See for example, Virginia Held, *The Ethics of Care*. The term 'carer' is now taken to designate a professional or semi-professional role, so I use it because of its concision, though with some reluctance. The carer in this sense is someone who is powerfully attached to the ill person and witness to their last days, or as David Rieff names it, the 'accompany-er' of their loved one in their travails.
7. Hadley, G., ed., Eliot, G., *Daniel Deronda*, chapter 27, p. 279. The previous sentence is: 'The subtly varied drama between man and woman is often such as can hardly be rendered in words put together like dominoes, according to obvious fixed marks.'
8. Foster, J., *Take Me to Paris, Johnny*. In this book the issue of trust has a special poignancy and heft, since the narrator regards the relationship as a marriage, only to realise that his partner, fatally, does not.
9. Brennan, F., 'As Vast As the World'. 'The insights it gives us as health professionals are fascinating – here we have one of the great minds of 20th Century Europe struggling through, and recording with aching honesty, the terminal phase of her own mother's life' (p. 85).
10. de Beauvoir, S., *A Very Easy Death*, p. 18; de Beauvoir, S., *Une Mort Très Douce*, p. 28. 'Nakedness' as an euphemism for the exposure of the genitals has a long history. See Genesis, chapter 9, verse 22, where Ham 'saw the naked-ness of his father', and his brothers are horrified. The words 'holy' and 'taboo' reach back into that realm of atavistic thought which has a significant role in this pathography.
11. de Beauvoir, S., *Une Mort Très Douce*, p. 23.
12. Ibid., p. 27.
13. Ibid., p. 46. The pungency is lost in translation: 'There was no sort of doubt that he entirely washed his hands of the consequences of that feat' (p. 27). There is some confusion in the text as to who actually performs the operation.
14. Quotations in this paragraph are from de Beauvoir, S., *A Very Easy Death*, pp. 27, 40.
15. Quotations in this paragraph are from ibid., pp. 40, 50, 41.
16. Quotations in this paragraph are from ibid., pp. 44, 84.
17. Ibid., pp. 48, 51, 68.
18. Rieff, D., *Swimming in a Sea of Death*, p. 111.
19. Ibid., p. 136.
20. Ibid., p. 151.

21. Ann Jurecic gives a harsher reading of Rieff's narrative, writing that 'Rieff is trapped in his sense of personal failure. His writing does not lead to forgiveness or understanding' (*Illness As Narrative*, pp. 86–91, 90).
22. Weinman Lear, M., *Heartsounds*, p. 41.
23. Ibid., p. 44.
24. Ibid., pp. 22, 323.
25. Ibid., p. 284.
26. Rieff, D., *Swimming in a Sea of Death*, p. 113.
27. This precept was first suggested by Philippe Lejeune in *On Autobiography*, pp. 3–30. (My thanks to Dick Freadman and Paul John Eakin for this reference.) The house in Melbourne in which events take place is clearly identifiable as Garner's own, and as in the text, this is next to her daughter's house and her grandchildren, as in the text, live next door.
28. Awdish, R., *In Shock*, p. 74.
29. Garner, H., *The Spare Room*, p. 45.
30. Ibid., p. 59.
31. Ibid., p. 137.
32. Ibid, p. 170.
33. Komesaroff, P. A., 'From Bioethics to Microethics', pp. 62–86.
34. Komesaroff, P. A., *Experiments in Love and Death*, p. 5.
35. *New Yorker*, 9 December 2009.
36. Bayley, J., *Iris*, p. 176.
37. Coutts, M., *The Iceberg*, p. 72.
38. Ibid., p. 133.
39. Ibid., p. 95.
40. One would be Lerner's *A Death of One's Own*. This book is the record of a pact between a dying husband and his wife that in practice is impossible to carry out. When he is diagnosed with inoperable brain cancer, they vow that illness will not separate them. But they are already divided: 'We battled on separate battlefields, very much alone. Mine: to prepare myself for his death, to help him die a good death. His: to live' (p. 49). Like de Beauvoir and Garner, she feels drawn into a compact that burdens her, forcing her to act against what she believes to be right. The book contains a moving meditation on the different 'knowledges' of death held by the dying and the carer (p. 145).
41. This paragraph draws on my chapter 'The Patient Writes Back', in *Renegotiating Ethics in Literature, Theory, Philosophy*, edited by Richard Freadman, Jane Adamson, and David Parker.
42. Another example is Rodney Syme, *A Good Death*. Despite its subtitle, this book is an autobiographical narrative by a doctor, relating his experiences with patients and the law. The authentic 'cases' are described in detail and with understanding.
43. Stinson, R. W. and Stinson, P., *The Long Dying of Baby Andrew*, p. xiii.

CHAPTER 8

Patienthood across Two Centuries

The medical occasions in Frances Burney's life that are the focus of this book took place at widely separated times over thirty years, and in widely different locales: in the embattled residences of the royal court, in a small house in rural Hampshire, in the drawing room of a house on a busy Parisian street, where straw had been laid to deaden the sound of the carriage horses passing, and in rented premises in Bath. They obviously concern quite different medical conditions too.

But one thing they have in common is that they all take place in domestic settings. Even the king's illness was managed in his own apartments, and Burney's own psychological and physical decline was treated, if it were treated at all, largely within Windsor Castle, whether in grand or in confined rooms. Alex's immunisation was performed at home, with a nursemaid assisting his mother; Madame d'Arblay negotiated with her surgeons at home on the Rue de Miroménil, and – her husband dying upstairs – with the apothecaries in Bath. Susan Emlen was surrounded by family while she endured her mastectomy. This domestic site of medical practice – absolutely usual and expected – is what makes the intrusion into the private realm of the d'Arblays' home in Paris by 'seven men in black' so disturbing. Burney finds herself surrounded in her own 'salon' by men who seem to wear the uniform of a professional cohort – and we can read them, as perhaps she felt them, as crow-like messengers of a fundamentally altered relationship between medical practice and the patient.

For between Burney's experiences of doctors and the modern pathography stands, both monumental and complicated, the hospital. Many of the dramas of medicine now take place in consulting rooms, in emergency rooms, in operating theatres, intensive care units (ICUs), wards, waiting rooms, even sometimes in hospital corridors or in liminal spaces like staircases and vestibules, where, it seems, 'news, great and terrible, is imparted' to patients, as well as occasionally in a room at home.[1] If Burney is the unconscious pioneer of a radically new genre of writing, and a pioneer principally because she describes negotiations, confrontations – in a word, interactions – between doctors and the patient, it is the same dramatic feature that is at the core of the modern pathography, and its bearer of the emotional, ethical, and political issues that lie at the heart of the genre's importance.

By 'the hospital', I intend something like what Foucault must have meant by 'the clinic': 'both clinical medicine and the teaching hospital'.[2] It was during Burney's lifetime that the public hospital in England – now key to the vast unsystematic system that is the health care operation in Western democracies – began to develop.[3] As the lingering use of the term 'ward' implies, the hospital originated in the Middle Ages as a hospice, a charitable refuge for the sick poor. The transformation into 'an all-purpose medical institution', though beginning in the later years of Burney's life, took a century or more.[4] In the process, as Paul Komesaroff writes, 'health care . . . took the form of a technological system, bureaucratically organised and linked to social structures of power.'[5]

So a great chasm seems to lie between the medical culture and physical surroundings of Burney's experiences and those of contemporary patients. (The ambulance, that essential component of the modern medical system, originates from Larrey's prototype, first designed for battlefield use in 1792 – as its French name indicates.) The large modern hospital, with its multiple functions and departments, is staffed by people in a great range of different specialties. One effect of the development of hospitals in eighteenth-century England was that, as in France, they facilitated the progress of medical knowledge, and with that the need for professional nurses who had clinical training, as well as an increasing range of so-called allied professionals and technicians.

Nurses play a vital role in hospitals, as everyone knows, and are important presences in almost all modern patient narratives. Nurses and nursing, though, are barely detectable in the episodes of Burney's life I have discussed. Betty, a maid, helped Madame d'Arblay manage her child during his inoculation; a nurse ('my nurse') was present at the mastectomy in Paris, and one in Pennsylvania at Susan Emlen's surgery, but you have to look hard for them; a nurse had to be employed during Alexandre d'Arblay's last days in Bath, but was treated with obvious mistrust. Much informal nursing was carried out by genteel women (in *Cecilia*, for instance, the heroine takes on the role of gentlewoman nurse to Mrs Delvile, watched over by the 'good Dr Lister'). During the king's confinement, the necessary nursing functions were carried out by a team of pages, only one of whom ever broke silence. This invisibility is, of course, a form of censorship, since nurses, like pages, were employed in menial tasks that no lady or equerry would perform or care to know about. Magdalene De Lancey did nurse her husband on the battlefield outside Waterloo, but hers was a brief and exceptional act of love. Jane Austen's *Persuasion* (1817) seems to have been for a long time the only notable novel to depict and to treat with respect a professional domestic nurse.[6]

The nurse today may be considered as a kind of ligature between modern and premodern medical care: she or he takes on some of the tasks previously carried out by menials, and at the same time has duties, such as giving injections, that only medical men would have been responsible for in Burney's time. In broad terms, nursing staff have a dual function now: to operationalise doctors' orders, and at the same time to provide care and comfort to the patient. The tension between these roles is apparent in many contemporary patient narratives.

It is often doctors who have found themselves in the position of patient, though, who provide the most acute and penetrating insights into modern hospital life and the 'patienthood', in Sacks's word, it entails. Oliver Sacks did more than anyone else to bring the medical narrative to public consciousness in the later twentieth century. His own pathography, *A Leg to Stand On*, first published as a book in 1984, tells the story of a terrifying accident while climbing a mountain in Norway that resulted in serious injury to his left leg. His second chapter, called 'Becoming a Patient', recounts his initial encounters with the staff at a small 'cottage hospital': first, a nurse, unaccommodating and unkind, as it happens, then an X-ray technician, whose kindness compensates for the nurse's rough handling, then the doctor in charge, a local general practitioner, 'a nice motherly woman' covering the hospital that night, and next a young surgeon, whose lithe, healthy body and comradely manner the patient, whose mother was a surgeon, finds inspiring. In the next chapter, Dr Sacks, flown to a famous (but unnamed) London hospital for the necessary operation, confronts his surgeon there, an experienced man, 'Mr Swan', efficient, cold and brusque, who offers very little in the way of reassuring human contact:

> 'Well', he said loudly. 'How are we doing today?'
> 'Bearing up,' I replied, and my voice sounded muzzy.
> 'Nothing to worry about,' he continued briskly. 'You've torn
>   a tendon. We reconnect it. Restore continuity. That's all there
>   is to it . . . nothing at all!'
> 'But . . . ' I said slowly – but he had already gone from the room.[7]

Later in a longer sequence Mr Swan is offered as the archetype of the uncaring surgeon, not listening to or even looking at the patient. Non-recognition by medical staff is a frequently resented event in modern patient narratives, a salient and in some ways symbolic occurrence: in the broadest sense non-recognition is the motivating force behind the writing of many of these. But perhaps the hard-pressed Swan is simply treating Dr Sacks as colleague and peer. He might have spent the night standing up in an operating theatre.

Other perspectives on hospital life by doctors who have themselves become patients feature later in this chapter. As the previous chapter has shown, there are many descendants of *The Last Illness and Death of General d'Arblay*, written by Burney in the first place for her son, but ultimately meant for posterity. As in that discussion, the organising premise here is to illustrate modern variations on the medical experiences Burney wrote about. Though there are few modern hospital narratives about operations without anaesthesia, they do exist, if not in the extended and excruciating form of Burney's mastectomy; 'madness' and break-down are written about and confronted. (I revisit the medical circum-stances of George III in the context of contemporary works that circulate around the notion of madness.) Modern pathographies dramatise, within a quite different culture and intellectual context, some similar, if not the same, conflicts, tensions, emotions, and crises. 'Looking at the history of doctor-patient interactions,' Robert Aronowitz writes, 'one sees more continuities than discontinuities.'[8] One crucial discontinuity will, how-ever, be uncovered.

I have already summoned Eula Biss's *On Immunity* (2014), a book in which pathographic autobiography is dovetailed into a compelling argu-ment in defence of immunisation, to suggest the continuing fears and superstitions that still hover around the practice – fears that were real enough when Burney undertook to inoculate her two-year-old son cen-turies ago. Intrusion into the flesh of the living body, whether by knife, lancet, scalpel, or a needle, injecting some foreign substance, can still arouse terror, still be a radically disturbing experience. And a major opera-tion, even under general anaesthetic is, to use Arthur Frank's potent understatement, 'no small thing'.[9] For example, Biss describes her experi-ence when, having delivered her first child, her uterus inverted, 'bursting capillaries and spilling blood':

> I was rushed to surgery and put under general anesthesia. I woke up
> disoriented, shivering violently under a pile of heated blankets. 'That

happens to everyone who comes down here,' my midwife observed from
a bright and hazy place above me, inadvertently reinforcing my sense that
I had, indeed, gone down to the banks of the River Styx. *Where is down here?*
I kept wondering. I was too weak to move much, but when I tried
I discovered my body was lashed with tubes and wires – I had an IV in
each arm, a catheter down my leg, monitors on my chest, and an oxygen
mask on my face.[10]

The verb 'lashed' here turns ordinary therapeutic devices into cruel weap-
ons and captures how for the frightened and still partly drugged patient
experience is distorted. This successful medical event leads to what seems
to Biss in the weeks afterwards an unaccountable fearfulness. Invoking the
river Styx here, Biss communicates her condition by recourse to an image
from an ancient culture, a memory of something deep and fearful in the
human psyche, the dark mythical realm of the newly dead. Like de
Beauvoir's recourse to a vocabulary that belongs to an older, mysterious
world (the frail voice of her mother coming from some strange and fearful
place, like an oracle) momentary references like these to the mystical,
archaic unknown tend to occur, as if incidentally, in many pathographic
texts. Roy Porter cites an early seventeenth-century patient who in his
madness 'turned the mundane realities of his friends restraining, yet help-
ing, him' into a 'spiritual world of torturing demons'.[11] In the hours after
an operation remarkably sane modern patients can briefly enter the same or
a similar world.

Anaesthesia, though a crucial and benign advance in medicine, is also an
accomplice, if an indirect way, to a division in the sensibilities of hospital
staff and patients, a matter addressed later in this chapter. The absence of
anything like an anaesthetic to help Burney during her mastectomy is of
course the most striking difference that contemporary accounts of breast
surgery record. But this does not mean that the circumstances prefacing
and surrounding an operation and its aftermath are eventless. The first
discovery of a strange lump in the breast, the fear and anxiety that
inevitably follows – 'At work at my desk, then to the hospital for a test.
Finally, the terrible hours at night when I'm in bed but awake, soaked in
sweat',[12] – the desperate wish to believe it's not malignant, the sequence of
tests and interviews with specialists and surgeons, sympathetic or brusque,
who finally condemn you to the operation as the only course, the waiting
and delays: all these can be paralleled in Frances Burney's narrative. She
'felt no courage' for the mastectomy, she told her sister, from 'a thousand
reasons *besides* the pain'.[13] A woman in the twentieth or twenty-first
century will feel no pain during the actual operation, but she will suffer

before and after: there is the prospect of chemotherapy and radiation treatment and their consequences; the horror of mutilation, then the decision of what prosthesis to purchase, if any; the reaction of her partner or husband to the disappearance of his favourite object of desire,[14] – a thousand anxieties *without* the pain.

Readers of Burney's 'A Mastectomy', some of whom I quoted in Chapter 5, have felt that her account of the operation conjures up the sort of uncanny horror in them that Biss felt after her operation.

> I saw the hand of M. Dubois held up, while his fore finger first described a straight line from the top to bottom of the breast, secondly a Cross, & thirdly a Circle ... again I saw the fatal finger describe the Cross – & the circle. Hopeless, then, desperate, & self-given up, I closed once more my eyes.[15]

When Burney looked over the manuscript narrative of her experience much later in life she added the words 'the Magician' before Dubois's name, giving him a role that intensifies the superstitious aura.[16] Together with the dead silence of the seven men congregated around her bedstead, these movements in the air above the patient suggest to some modern critics a male conspiracy against this supine and exposed woman, in Julia Epstein's phrase 'the sacrosanct female body here to be defiled', something primitive, eerie, and terrifying.[17] ('Sacrosanct' is another of those words that reach into the mystical darkness.) It is not only female readers who feel this. In his *The Greatest Benefit to Mankind* (1997) Porter wrote that Burney was 'evoking the ghastly, gothic and macabre ritual (A woman in the hands of a male executioner?)' of a surgical procedure (or torture) that nevertheless saved her life.[18]

The black feminist poet Audre Lorde's account of her experience in *The Cancer Diaries* (1980) can be compared:

> Then through the dope of tranquilizers and grass I remember Frances' hand on mine, and the last sight of her dear face like a great sunflower in the sky. There is the horror of those flashing lights passing over my face, and the clanging of disemboweled noises that have no context nor relationship to me except they assault me. There is the dispatch with which I have ceased being a person who is myself and become a thing upon a Guerney cart to be delivered to Moloch, a dark living sacrifice in the white place.
> I remember screaming and cursing with pain in the recovery room, and a disgusted nurse giving me a shot.[19]

This succinctly echoes many aspects of Burney's 'A Mastectomy': the alienation, the loss of agency and above all the horror of the woman who feels a helpless victim of some primitive ritual sacrifice. One element, though, is different, for unlike Burney's 'seven men in black' it is 'the white place' (and a little later the 'white surgical bandages') that register the fearful alienation of her surroundings for this black woman. The white gown that was a symbol of purity in Burney's novel *Camilla* now connotes sterility instead, a mechanistic rather than human environment. This reversal demonstrates how far from rational are the patient's fears, but equally how irrational it might be to deny their depth. As the paediatrician and psychoanalyst D. W. Winnicott wrote in a letter responding to a friend's question: 'All women having a mastectomy must be disturbed; somewhere in every one of them is a tremendous reaction ... in my opinion nothing can really do away with their anger, hate and sense of insult which is inherent in any mutilation, even if it saves life.'[20] Men can also feel that they have been 'raped' after drastic surgery, and a surgeon can feel that he has 'mutilated' his patient.[21] After a few days the institution offers Lorde consolation: 'The very bland whiteness of the hospital which I railed against and hated so, was also a kind of protection, a welcome insulation in which I could continue to non-feel. It was an erotically blank environment within whose undifferentiated and undemanding and infantilizing walls I could continue to be emotionally vacant.'[22]

Rebecca Solnit's more recent account of breast surgery in a chapter of *The Faraway Nearby* (2013) is written with an eye to the similarities between her own 'medical adventure' and the tortures endured by patients in the past. In the modern hospital, she suggests, you are still a victim, this time of advanced technology: 'You may ... see X-rays and be reminded of death's skeleton under the flesh of life, you may be invaded, have parts of yourself removed, or tubes, shunts, devices, plates, and more added, your chemistry and hormones may be tinkered with, drugs administered,' she writes. 'The system has been opened up and so has your awareness of it.'[23] The notion that one's body has been taken over, that in preparation for the surgery she inhabits 'that other world where people weighted and measured and sampled me and wrote reports as though I was a newly discovered island or a crime' is reiterated when after the operation she discovers 'a disk' stuck to her back 'like a leech', an allusion to the treatment armoury of a previous medicine.[24] Yet this attempt to suggest that the experience of surgery in the modern hospital replicates the sufferings of patients in the past is unconvincing. Solnit fails to tap into the fear and horror that Lorde communicates in a few words, and the medical personnel might as well not be there. Though probably influenced by Burney's now famous account of her surgery, this absence of interaction between patient and surgeon makes this 'adventure' read quite unlike hers.

Frances Burney had only a 'wine cordial' to help her through the agonising experience. The nearest thing to a recent account of breast surgery with less than total anaesthesia can be found in Joyce Wadler's *My Breast* (1992). 'This is a modern story,' Wadler announces at the beginning of her book, and so it is: she does her own research, and she herself draws a line on her breast with a ballpoint pen 'making a mark', as she writes, 'that says, Cut me'.[25] Her surgeon, 'Luke', is companionable:

> They paint my left breast with a red ointment that smells like iodine and cover the rest of my chest with sterile cloth. I can't see the surgery itself, because Luke has asked me to turn my face to the right; but as he has promised, he tells me what I will feel, and what he is doing as he moves along. The painkiller is Xylocaine. He injects it at various points around my breast, waiting for the area to numb; then he makes a cut. I have a feeling of warmth and wetness. Then there are strong sensations of tugging, as he pulls back tissue and starts tunneling up from the incision to the lump, in the inner upper quadrant of my breast. Sometimes I feel a bit of pain, almost a burning sensation, and he gives me more Xylocaine. The tunneling seems to go on for twenty minutes, and while it is not as uncomfortable as a dentist's drilling, the more tissue that is being pulled apart and clamped, the more uncomfortable I become. I am having second thoughts now about being so concerned about looking good in a low cut dress.[26]

Xylocaine is a trade name for lidocaine, first used as an effective and safe numbing agent in 1948. Like Burney's surgeons, the friendly Luke is determined to go 'a little beyond' the lump 'to make sure they've got it all by getting a good margin of healthy tissue from all sides'. Then she feels 'some final tugging and the thing is out'. She asks to see it: 'It was the size of a robin's egg, with the gray brain-like matter which gives its name, medullary cancer. It rested in the middle of a larger ball of pink and white breast tissue, sliced down the center like a hard-boiled egg.'[27] Luke tells her that for medullary cancer the 'overall cure rate' is more than 80 per cent. Four years later Wadler was diagnosed with advanced ovarian cancer, from which she also recovered.

Men, as well as women, sometimes need surgery for cancer in intimate sites of their body. Frank's *At the Will of the Body* (1991) is a rare example of a male relating and discussing this experience:

> When drying myself off after showering, I began to notice a persistent soreness in one testicle ... As the discomfort increased I began to do what all men should do regularly: examine my testicles. I could feel a sharp ridge

that had formed around the lower third of the left one. It felt as if the normal oval shape was turning into a figure eight.[28]

'Panicked but not totally irrational', he sees his doctor, who misdiagnoses his condition as chlamydia, but he begins to experience severe back pain, which this doctor declares is unrelated to the testicular soreness. The pain gets intolerable, so he is taken to hospital and given routine tests, which appear to show nothing abnormal. Then he is sent to a sports medicine specialist, who 'actually probed my abdomen with his hands, locating what felt like a mass', and mentions the possibility of cancer:

> I had been in too much pain for too long, and I was relieved, at least momentarily, to be told that, yes, he believed that something was wrong with me. Being told that you may have cancer does not have to be devastating. Even though my worst fears were realized in what he said, the physician showed, just by the way he looked at me and a couple of phrases he used, that he shared in the seriousness of my situation. The vitality of his support was as personal as it was professional. Physicians I encountered later were optimistic about my diagnosis and prognosis; he was almost alone in expressing optimism about me, not as case, but as a person.[29]

Much later in his book, the subtitle of which is 'Reflections on Illness', Frank develops this into a more general and militant commentary on the tendency of the medical professions to 'deny the ill person' and their suffering. 'Nurses and physicians cue patients to deny their own experience,' he writes:

> Continuing suffering threatens them, so they deny it exists. What they cannot treat the patient is not allowed to experience. Physicians and nurses often forget that when treatment runs out, there can still be care. Simply recognizing suffering for what it is, regardless of whether it can be treated, is care . . . Professionals can and do care, but when they do they are acting a bit unprofessional.[30]

The question whether there need be opposition between 'professional' and 'care', as in this patient's angry analysis, arises later in this chapter.

Dr Hal Lear's anger at the way he and other patients are treated has been illustrated in the previous chapter. His is an intemperate attack partly fuelled by self-blame: he feels he has been a part of the same negligent medical culture. Soon he finds himself undergoing an extraordinary event, a dangerous surgery without anaesthetic – in the late twentieth century. Lear suffers a severe heart attack, followed by weeks of crippling pain, and his colleagues urge an angiogram: 'X-ray of the heart. Pictures to show whether the heart is a candidate for surgery' in Martha Lear's explication.

Dr Lear, who has performed similar, though not the same, operations in the past, is well aware that, as his wife puts it, 'in that blisteringly cool way of medical language, surreal as military language . . . the major complication of coronary angiography was death.'[31] As this makes evident, Lear's experience is mediated through his wife's forceful commentary. Martha glosses: 'when you stick a tube [or catheter] up into the heart, and fill an artery of the heart with dye, you are depriving that artery of oxygen . . . Functionally, it is the same as having a heart attack.' The anaesthetist fails to appear, but the operation goes ahead. Chapter 14 of the book relates the doctor's thoughts as, completely conscious, he watches the operation on a screen above him:

> Now, he thought, 'They've pulled out the stylette and my blood is spurting out at them . . . Now I will see the catheter entering me.'
> He looked up at the screen. There he was. Live on TV. He saw his pelvis, his bones, his spinal column. And then, in a corner of the screen, he saw this thing, this intrusion, this snakelike tube beginning to creep into his pelvis.
> He was sweating harder. His body was rigid. His heart was pounding.
> Someone yelled out. 'Tell that anesthetist to get in here, we've started.'
> He closed his eyes. He said to himself:
> You are too tense. You are getting very frightened. It is not good to get this frightened. Your heart is racing and it's a weak heart, it can't afford to race. You must relax. Keep your eyes closed. Shut out what frightens you. Don't watch.[32]

He succeeds in calming himself, and even takes pleasure in detecting one of his coronary arteries on the screen. 'He felt astonishment at this thing which was happening to him. And yet, even now, a kind of detachment. Detached astonishment. And then, all at once, he felt it: that flush, that tremendous flush, as though his whole body had been thrust into an oven. It wasn't scary. There was an almost amused recognition: right on, the flush.' (A nurse has warned him earlier that this 'flush' might be terrifying.) Then:

> Suddenly a massive pain in his chest, a life-sucking pain, as though the life were being squeezed out of him. He felt on the verge of a fatal heart attack. And that sudden loss of strength, that dread, that foreboding. Terror.
> 'I am having pain', he said aloud.
> No answer.[33]

One is very aware that, though the patient's experience itself must be authentic, it is being relayed to the reader through the prose of a journalist, who, shifting back and forth between the first and third person points of view, is wringing every ounce of drama out of this remarkable event. Lear lies, fully conscious, waiting to see whether he will live or die. It is only when the operation is almost over that he sees a masked figure approach and he is given anaesthesia. Such mistakes or miscommunications may be one of the penalties of the size and complexity of the modern hospital system, though they can rarely have been exposed like this.

Any similarities between the treatments of George III's mental illness and those recorded by modern patients may well be thought tenuous, linked only by the still current use of the word 'mad', but they can be found. The king's illness was a remarkable event in the history of medicine (or psychiatry) because two conflicting, contradictory techniques to deal with his illness were more or less copresent. Those two approaches, broadly characterised, are still copresent, it can be argued, in the treatment of mentally ill patients today.

In the latter half of the eighteenth century there were, again broadly speaking, two schools of thought about insanity among medical practitioners: the first, now known commonly as iatromechanist, and the second which may be called psychological. The case of the king shows those two approaches at a historic moment of simultaneity and conflict. His official doctors, though arguing among themselves, adopted what were basically physical remedies – vomits, blistering, bloodletting, purging etc, designed to assault the body and provoke the brain into normal functioning. These treatments, which seem to us cruel and bizarre, were used because 'madness' such as the king's was conceived by them as a bodily condition. William Battie, who was chief physician at St Luke's Hospital for Lunatics in London, founded in 1751, published a widely read and influential *Treatise on Madness* in 1758, which presents the iatromechanist theory that lay behind their practice.[34] Battie argued that the nerves were akin to the other vessels of the body in that they might get hardened or distended, and this would produce symptoms of 'madness' like the king's. It followed that when, for instance, 'gentle evacuants' fail to relieve the patient, 'it becomes absolutely necessary to shake with violence the head and hypochondria by convulsing the muscular fibres with emetics, rougher purges and errhines.'

When Francis Willis, the famous 'mad doctor', was summoned to deal with the king's condition in December 1788 he brought a quite different conception of treatment for the king's symptoms. As the record by Robert Greville cited in Chapter 2 shows, Willis's first encounter with his patient was devoted to assuring his ascendency over the king, and as part of this he threatened the king with the straight waistcoat. More significant, as

Greville noticed, he used his voice to gain control. James Boswell reports Samuel Johnson as saying that '[a] madman loves to be with people whom he fears; not as a dog fears the lash; but of whom he stands in awe,'[35] the crucial point being that physical methods are not needed if a patient can be calmed by other means. Willis's project was to inspire the patient with 'awe'.[36]

There was intense hostility between the attending physicians (who tried to get rid of him) and Francis Willis. For his treatment to have any chance of working, it was essential that the other medical men, with their competing theories and treatments, be excluded from the room. The tensions between these royal doctors, desperate to find something that would cure the king or at least moderate his behaviour, would have created the worst possible environment for their patient, who mad or not, must have picked up their anxiety and desperation, if not their mutual jealousy and ill will. Willis's unflagging belief, often voiced, that his tactics would work and that the king would surely recover, seemed to Robert Greville close to deceitful, but the same confidence, as well as the generosity of spirit that Frances Burney captured when he visited her after her collapse, might well have had a therapeutic effect on his patient. It was not long before Willis allowed the king to look out of the window to see his daughters (which the previous doctors had forbidden), let him shave himself, and allowed a visit by the queen. The eventual cure of the king's illness apparently brought about by Willis, and widely celebrated (he had 'restored a beloved monarch to his people'), gave an impetus to the movement towards non-mechanistic and more psychological modes of treatment.

Willis had established a hospital for the insane in Lincoln, where the mother of Lady Harcourt, a woman close to the queen, had been cured. The establishment of such hospitals for the insane became an important eighteenth-century development, with results that were not altogether benign. Willis's privately run hospital was one of many, such as Nathaniel Cotton's at St Alban's, where one of the grateful patients was William Cowper. In what is usually understood as a significant moment, William Tuke, a Quaker, purpose-built and established the York Retreat in 1792. Patients were allowed to wander the grounds of the house freely and not restrained except as a last resort. This was called 'moral management' and though railed at later by Foucault, is widely thought to be a great step forward in the treatment of the mentally ill, and a model for institutions around the world.[37] Publicly funded mental hospitals were established after the passing of the County Asylums Act in 1808, and by the middle of the century so-called lunatic asylums had been built in most English counties.

Though the term was replaced in England by 'mental hospital' in 1933, it seems to have lingered on in the colonies. The most widely known account of 'madness' in the twentieth century is by Janet Frame, who was confined to Seacliff Lunatic Asylum in the South Island of New Zealand, several times from the 1940s onwards. A glimpse of the atmosphere at this notorious place is given when, after praising junior staff and some nurses, she writes that:

> The attitude of those in charge who unfortunately wrote the reports and influenced the treatment was that of reprimand and punishment, with certain forms of medical treatment being threatened as punishment for failure to 'co-operate' where 'not co-operate' might mean a refusal to obey an order, say, to go to the doorless lavatories with six others and urinate in public while suffering verbal abuse by the nurse for being unwilling. 'Too fussy are we? Well, Miss Educated, you'll learn a thing or two here.'[38]

Frame was scheduled for a leucotomy, later to become notorious as lobotomy, in 1951, but was rescued at the last minute when a new doctor at the asylum learned about her having just won a literary prize. She was diagnosed as a 'schizophrenic', and when she was eventually discharged from Seacliff she had received, she writes, 'over two hundred applications of unmodified E.C.T., each the equivalent in degree of fear to an execution'.[39] When years later she eventually found her way to the Maudsley Hospital in London and was given diagnostic tests, she was told categorically that she was not suffering and had never suffered from schizophrenia. As a step towards her orientation back into the world of work, she was given the task of cataloguing papers and, as she wrote, learned from studying the journals there that 'ECT Electric Shock or Convulsive Therapy' was commended as a means of provoking *fear* in the patient, the fear being as it were a *bonus* – for the psychiatrist no doubt and not for the patient!'[40] Johnson's idea that 'madmen love to be with those with whom they stand in awe' is thus distorted into a process that – though addressing the brain rather than the body – belongs to an iatro-mechanist culture.

A not dissimilar experience to Janet Frame's is reported by another important writer, Hilary Mantel, in *Giving Up the Ghost* (2003). In the early 1970s Mantel was studying law at Sheffield University and suffering continual pain. In a tutorial, she writes, 'a pain sliced through me, diagonal, from my right ribs to my left loin.' She seeks medical help, but 'the more I said I had a physical illness, the more they said I had a mental illness.' 'Dr G.', the psychiatrist in the university clinic, prescribes minor tranquillisers, but when they didn't work 'the possibility arose that you were not simply neurotic, hypochondriacal and a bloody nuisance, but heading for a psychotic breakdown, for the badlands of schizophrenia, a career on a back ward.' (As this shows, Mantel is scathing about her doctors and the medicines she was prescribed):

> The first drug I was given was Fentazine. That would do the job, Dr G thought.
> Do you know about akathisia? It is a condition that develops as a side-effect of anti-psychotic medication, and the cunning thing about it is that it looks, and it feels, exactly like madness. The patient paces. She is unable to stay still. She wears a look of agitation and terror. She wrings her hands; she says she is in hell.
> And from the inside, how does it feel? ... No physical pain has ever matched that morning's uprush of killing fear, the hammering heart ... You choke; pressure rises inside your skull. Your hands pull at your clothing and tear at your arms. Your breathing becomes ragged. Your voice is like a bird's cry and your hands flutter like wings. You want to hurl yourself against the windows and the walls. Every fibre of your being is possessed by panic. A desperate feeling of urgency – a need to act – but to do what, and how? – throbs through your whole body, like the pulses of an electric shock.[41]

The narrative jumps to Christmas week 1979. She is in St George's Hospital in London, in great pain, but without a diagnosis. She thinks it might be endometriosis, possibly cancer.[42] The operation that follows removes her womb and ovaries, her whole 'reproductive apparatus'. The bitterness, hardly contained by wit, is caused by the fact that at twenty-seven bearing the child she has dreamed of has been made impossible, apparently without warning. (I assume that the title of her memoir alludes to this 'ghost', the lingering wish for a child she can never bear.) Then a decade or so later the endometriosis came back. Her illness narrative exemplifies Eric Cassell's 'paradox ... that suffering is often caused by the treatment of the sick' which was all too obviously the case in George III's 'madness'. And like Mantel's 'mad' symptoms his may have been due to what at the time was an undiagnosable disease.[43] If chemical treatments can be subsumed under the general heading of the physiological they can be seen as a later variation of the iatromechanist practices carried out by George III's doctors, and were perhaps just as destructive when they were used without psychological help.

William Styron's *Darkness Visible* (1992) is subtitled 'A Memoir of Madness', and within its text Styron states categorically that it should never be doubted that 'depression, in its extreme form, is madness', later adding the caveat that 'the madness of depression is, generally speaking, the antithesis of violence.'[44] This may illustrate just how far the word 'mad' can be stretched. What he describes vividly in this book is the onslaught of a depression so deep that a 'gray drizzle of horror' 'takes on the quality of physical pain' which leads him to plan his suicide.[45] He seeks help from a psychotherapist who offers him no solace but 'an antidepressant medication called Ludiomil' that brings about a violent reaction. When he complains, this doctor tells him he must wait ten days before trying another drug – 'ten days to someone stretched on such a torture rack is like ten centuries'. 'Dr Gold' becomes the epitome of the bad doctor, uncomprehending, even fatuous, as when he decides to substitute another antidepressant, Nardil:

> Dr Gold said with a straight face, the pill at optimum dosage could have the side effect of impotence. Until that moment, although I'd had some trouble with his personality, I had not thought him totally lacking in perspicacity; now I was not at all sure. Putting myself in Dr Gold's shoes, I wondered if he seriously thought that this juiceless and ravaged semi-invalid with the shuffle and the ancient wheeze woke up each morning from his Halcion sleep eager for carnal fun.[46]

In a moment of relief from his suffering, Styron decides he must go into a hospital (apparently a clinic specialising in care of the mentally ill) which despite its 'stupefying dreariness' he finds a sanctuary, and after nearly seven weeks of calm and care leaves, apparently cured. He contends, perhaps not without reason, that many psychiatrists 'maintain their stubborn allegiance to pharmaceuticals', and simply fail 'to comprehend the nature and depth of the anguish their patients are undergoing'.[47]

A more recent pathography, Jay Griffith's *Tristimania* (2016), subtitled 'A Diary of Manic Depression', is also interesting on several counts. Her description of her 'hypomania', recurrently referred to as 'madness', is extensive and elaborated, but without much dramatic power and narrative progression. 'Madness forces you to concentrate on it. It is attention-seeking because it wants an audience. Madness wants to paint its vision of the world so the world can see what the human mind is capable of,' she writes, possibly accurately.[48] She has a general practitioner whom she has consulted since girlhood, and who is presented as the ideal friend and listener: in effect he is her psychotherapist. She is aware of the idealisation, writing '[p]eople in a crisis of manic depression are said to be prone to idealizing people or demonizing them,' the testimony of many pathographies.[49] Griffiths is also plainly conscious of the solipsism of her manic state, but her writing can itself seem solipsistic. She quotes frequently from others who have suffered similarly, but these read like fragments pulled into the whirlpool of her own manic distress.

Jay Griffiths refers several times, for instance, to Kay Redfield Jamison's *An Unquiet Mind*, first published in 1996 and reprinted in 2015. I have suggested that some of the most searching and self-aware accounts of patienthood are written by medical personnel who find themselves with the roles reversed, and Jamison's book certainly is one of these, except that she went into medicine knowing already she was ill. She suffers from manic-depressive psychosis and has become nevertheless and simultaneously a renowned medical authority on the condition. Her writing in *An Unquiet Mind* fuses the vivid recall of her own wildly see-sawing episodes with a dispassion that may be the fruit of her medical training. She is a powerful advocate for the naturally occurring chemical lithium as a treatment for manic depression. She relates without qualms or apology her initial refusal to take the substance, and when she was finally persuaded to try lithium, which does not 'cure' manic depression but evens out the highs and lows, she describes her refusal to continue with it (even though, or perhaps because, it was working) – a mistake that led to the most terrible, savage and destructive episode of 'depressive' behaviour.[50]

One of the most powerful episodes in her book concerns a patient who, like Jamison herself in the past, leaves off his lithium once he feels it's been effective. It gives both a quick insight into the emergencies that hourly confront hospital personnel, and into a special doctor–patient relationship. Dr Jamison is called down to the emergency room, a busy place 'alive with residents, interns, and medical students':

> I found myself unavoidably caught up in the exhilarating pace and chaotic rhythm. Then came an absolutely blood-curdling scream from one of the examining rooms – a scream of terror and undeniable madness – and I ran down the corridor: past the nurses, past a medical resident dictating notes for a patient's chart, and past a surgical resident poring over the *PDR* with a cup of coffee in one hand, a thermostat clamped and dangling from the short sleeve of his green scrub suit, and a stethoscope draped around his neck.
>
> I opened the door to the room where the screams had begun, and my heart sank. The first person I saw was the psychiatry resident on call, whom I knew; he smiled sympathetically. Then I saw my patient, strapped down on a gurney, in four-point leather restraints. He was lying spread-eagle on his back, each wrist and ankle bound in a leather cuff, with an additional leather restraining strap across his chest. I felt sick to my stomach. Despite

the restraints, I also felt scared. A year before this same patient had held
a knife to my throat during a psychotherapy session in my office . . .
    He screamed again. It was a truly primitive and frightening sound, in part
because he himself was so frightened, and in part because he was very tall,
very big, and completely psychotic. I put my hand on his shoulder and could
feel his whole body shaking out of control. I had never seen such fear in
anyone's eyes, nor such visceral agitation and psychological pain. Delirious
mania is many things, and all of them are awful beyond description. The
resident had given him a massive injection of an antipsychotic medication,
but the drug had not yet taken hold. He was delusional, paranoid, largely
incoherent, and experiencing both visual and auditory hallucinations.[51]

It is impossible not to be taken into George III's apartment by this picture:
by the 'delirious mania', the animal violence that has to be controlled by
'coercion', the strapping down that makes you sick to see or read about.
(The king's calling his pillow 'Prince Octavius' would qualify as an
hallucination.) Jamison continues with a tactic that has a family resemblance to Francis Willis's technique: 'I tightened my hold on his shoulder,
shook him gently, and said, "It's Dr Jamison. You've been given some
Haldol. We're going to take you up to the ward. You're going to be all
right." I caught his eye for a moment.' The patient screams again and she
repeats her assurances.
    A little later, after the calming medication has taken effect, he says 'in
a slowed and slurred voice, "Don't leave me, Dr Jamison. Please don't leave
me,"' and she promises, knowing that she has been 'his psychotherapist for
years'. This is very interesting. Though I think Jamison here uses the term
'psychotherapist' loosely, it does not seem an over-interpretation of this
passage to suggest that Jamison can feel for and treat this patient because,
like him, she herself has needed to see and is dependent on seeing
a psychotherapist. Her own experience may be enabling her to manage
this situation, not by empathising or feeling with the patient, but by
recognising his projected anxieties and employing techniques to calm
them. This terrible episode is far from a gratuitous intervention into her
story; it plays a significant role in two aspects of her underlying purpose –
to persuade readers that lithium works in the treatment of manic depression if it is taken regularly and consistently, and that the medication cannot
act alone, but must be supplemented by counselling, consistent, kindly, if
not loving, attention given by a physician, as in this case, or by an official
psychiatrist.
    Dr Jamison also relates the many times when she feels forced to confess
to colleagues that she has the illness – confessions, because on each

occasion she was risking her career as a psychiatrist. Almost all of them were encouraging (she was obviously an outstanding clinician and medical researcher) but one, who features in her memoir as the dramatically necessary 'bad' doctor, was not, and is rewarded with the sobriquet of 'Mouseheart'. A similar incident occurs when she sees a physician to discuss having children. She tells him that she plans to stay on lithium during pregnancy:

> Before I finished, however, he broke in to ask me if I knew that manic-depressive illness was a genetic disease. Stifling for the moment an urge to remind him that I had spent my entire professional life studying manic-depressive illness, and that in any event, I wasn't entirely stupid, I said 'Yes, of course.' At that point in an icy and imperious voice that I can hear to this day, he stated – as though it were God's truth, which he no doubt felt that it was – 'You shouldn't have children. You have manic depressive illness.'
>
> I felt sick, unbelievably and utterly sick, and deeply humiliated. Determined to resist being provoked into what would without question be interpreted as irrational behavior, I asked him if his concerns about my having children stemmed from the fact that, because of my illness, he thought I would be an inadequate mother or simply that he thought it was best to avoid bringing another manic-depressive into the world. Ignoring or missing my sarcasm, he replied 'Both'.[52]

The doctor-patient leaves, telling this doctor 'to go to hell'. But his words did 'the kind of lasting damage that only something that cuts so quick and deep into the heart can do'.

Like Jamison, Rana Awdish can write almost simultaneously as physician and patient. *In Shock* (2017) is both a powerful autobiographical narrative and a compelling critique of medical culture within the environment of a large and famous modern hospital. She relates how, when the child she was carrying was at twenty-seven weeks, she suddenly experienced intense and crippling pain, a breath-taking wave that intensified so much that she is rushed into the hospital where she is a physician in the intensive care unit. There the violence of her pain goes unrecognised; clumsy delays, as she knows, may well be fatal. She is given morphine and tests are run, but the concentration of the doctors is on saving her baby, which because she can read the ultrasound images, she knows is already dead. The resident surgeon is another man who will not meet the patient's gaze. Finally she is wheeled into the operating theatre:

> As they began sedating me, I heard the anesthesiologist's voice: 'We're losing
> her ... her systolic is 60.'
> I was drawn back into myself, from failing consciousness, by these words.
> *Are they losing me?* I attempted to survey the situation. *Focus*, I told myself.
> Words echoed, or were they repeated this time?
> 'Guys! She's circling the drain here!'
> '*You know I can hear you,*' I thought.[53]

She passes into unconsciousness. That overheard phrase 'She's circling the
drain' (meaning that she is losing blood at a great rate) is referred back to
several times in the narrative as the epitome of the cruel carelessness that
she begins to detect in many nurses' and doctors' casual words in the
ensuing months. However, treating staff have their own anxieties about
death, which might be enhanced through identification with a 'doctor'
patient. In this case shifting responsibility onto her as patient relieves them
of their own fear of failure, bolsters their need for omnipotence (perhaps
necessary in such a desperate situation) but in turn leaves her feeling all
alone. Dr Awdish is saved and returns home, but it is several months
before, very bravely and still not pain free, she returns to work as the
attending physician in the ICU. 'Standing outside the unit', she writes in
the chapter called 'Shifting Frames', 'I silently hoped for the strength and
clarity of thought to unite my experiences as patient and a physician into
a cohesive whole, in a way that would honor all that I had been through.'[54]

She relates another incident when the words 'She's trying to die on us'
are said above her, and thinks, as the patient, '[i]f my care team didn't
believe in me, what possible hope did I have? I felt the ice I was balancing
on begin to detach and fall away.' Then she shifts into her medical persona:
'I had used that phrase, often and thoughtlessly, in my training: he "was
trying to die on me"':

> Oh, my God, we said it all the time. And inherent in that phrase is the reality
> that we attribute intention to patients, rudely hurling them towards
> death ... We unconsciously construct a narrative in which the doctor-
> patient relationship is somehow antagonistic. I recalled the relief I would
> feel in the ICU after a night of being alone on call, when the day team would
> walk in.[55]

These movements from one role to another, at one moment the drugged
and nearly dying patient, the next to recognise herself in the words being so
carelessly said, and then back into identification with the doctor's feelings,
typify this pathography. She needs to work calmly and efficiently, intelli-
gently and thoughtfully, at the same time struggling to integrate what she

has learned and continues to experience as a patient. At one point she speaks of herself as 'hybrid', at another as 'amalgamated', but actually there is more tension and difficulty involved than these words convey. There are many instances in which, alerted by her own experience, she detects hurtful or condescending overtones in her colleagues' speech to patients (for example, the cardiologist who tells a patient's wife, 'I found the blockage in his artery. We call it the widow-maker.'[56]) These cumulatively lend a *bildungsroman*-like quality to the narrative, as this woman who has trained intensively for fourteen years to reach her professional status undergoes what she speaks of as a real education.

Her book gradually broadens from an account of what she has learned from her experience as a patient into a critique of modern medical training and culture. She traces this back to the influence of the 'father of modern medicine', William Osler, the pioneer of the teaching hospital. The difficulty was this: at the same moment as he was inaugurating a great and positive change, teaching at the bedside rather than the lecture hall, he was inculcating in medical students a culture of detachment, epitomised in his famous lecture 'Aequanimitas' in which he wrote: 'Even under the most serious circumstances, the physician or surgeon who allows "his outward action to demonstrate the native act and figure of his heart in complement extern," who shows in his face the slightest alteration, expressive of anxiety or fear, has not his medullary centres under the highest control, and is liable to disaster at any moment.' He insisted too that '[k]een sensibility is doubtless a virtue of high order, when it does not interfere with steadiness of hand or coolness of nerve; but for the practitioner in his working-day world, a callousness which thinks only of the good to be effected, and goes ahead regardless of smaller considerations, is the preferable quality.'[57] In practice this cultivation of detachment, Awdish argues, has become destructive not only to the relationship of hospital doctors to patients, but to the physicians and surgeons themselves. In the chapter called 'Censors of Light' she recalls her own training: 'We were told that the goal was to conquer, suppress and internalize our emotions . . . We took their instructions and wrapped ourselves in them like bandages, leaving our true selves to suffocate beneath.'[58] The cultivation of these 'illusory selves' leads not only to the casual unkindnesses of a medical culture in which, as patients complain, they are treated as 'cases', and perhaps to an unconsciously antagonistic relation to patients, but to intolerable, because suppressed, internal suffering – including fear of their own death – and self-blame by doctors. 'It made no sense', she writes, 'we belonged to a profession that should have anticipated failure at every turn. The complexity of the medical system made failure an inevitability. The human body itself is designed to fail. Senescence is embedded in our genetic code. Our patients would die; it was an unavoidable reality. So if we knew this, then why hadn't we built resiliency into the system?'[59] Here 'the complexity of the medical system' might be better expressed, perhaps, as the bureaucratic and hierarchical culture of the vast and complex modern hospital, which would include nursing staff and technicians. Not only have technological advances increased the need for a range of specialists they have also vastly increased hospital budgets. The pressure from administrations, no longer controlled by medical doctors, to achieve successful results and shorter patient stays cannot be disregarded as influences on the private circumstances of doctor–patient interactions.

Awdish's accounts of her own experiences as a patient over several hospital admissions are harrowing, and her pathography is, in addition, a serious contribution to medical ethics. If contemporary, or near-contemporary patients, as demonstrated in this chapter, so often feel that they are treated as 'cases', not as people, and so often remember bitterly the careless demeanour or maladroit words of a doctor, as she herself recalls being labelled a 'difficult' patient, it may well be, as she says, that doctors had been taught to neglect their own emotions: 'to establish clinical distance, to don white coats ... an intentional declaration of ourselves as separate, and therefore safe'.[60] But the question of context, of the social, economic, and political circumstances of the modern world in which doctors and nurses act, must surely have a role as significant as medical education.

A year before Awdish's *In Shock* appeared, another remarkable pathography, by a neurosurgeon who was tragically not separate nor safe was published: Paul Kalanithi's *When Breath Becomes Air* (2016). Like Awdish, Kalanithi held a responsible position in a major hospital; also like her, he became seriously ill, and was treated as a patient in the same hospital. As she does in her book, he deals sometimes with medical failures and the ensuing desperate guilt that doctors can feel for fatal mistakes and wrong decisions. He also conveys the frenetic atmosphere of the contemporary hospital and the incessant demands on its staff, as in this account of a 'twenty-year old male' rushed into surgery following a motorcycle accident:

> We pumped him full of mannitol to reduce brain swelling and rushed him to the scanner: a shattered skull, heavy diffuse bleeding. In my mind I was already planning the scalp incision, how I'd drill the bone, evacuate the

blood. His blood pressure suddenly dropped. We rushed him back to the trauma bay, and just as the trauma team arrived, his heart stopped. A whirlwind of activity surrounded him: catheters were slipped into his femoral arteries, tubes shoved deep into his chest, drugs pushed into his IVs, and all the while fists pounded on his heart to keep the blood flowing. After thirty minutes, we let him finish dying. With that kind of head injury, we all murmured in agreement, death was to be preferred.[61]

Kalanithi regards it as a privilege to be present at the most dramatic events that a patient and their relatives have ever faced, and in which 'questions intersecting life, death and meaning' are shared with them. 'Because the brain mediates our experience of the world, any neurological problem forces a patient and family, ideally with a doctor as a guide, to answer this question: what makes life meaningful enough to go on living?' Like so many other authors of pathography, contra Osler, he stresses the need for the surgeon to respond to the patient and to give recognition to the anxiety, grief, and suffering that attends all serious or final illness. He gives illustrations of doctors who achieve this 'human relationality' which forms 'the bedrock of meaning', and is unsparing of himself when he has failed.[62] Discovering at the age of thirty-six that he has the lung cancer that killed him a year later, he even manages a rueful irony: 'Shouldn't terminal illness ... be the perfect gift to that young man who had wanted to understand death?'[63]

In the Introduction to *In Shock*, Rana Awdish recalls an incident in the ICU unit when she was head of the team as their attending physician. The patient had been on the list for a lung transplant and had been waiting there for months, her condition steadily worsening. The ICU nurse reports that she had had a bad night, and was on 'high-flow oxygen ... fifteen liters', adding, '[s]he's different today. If you ask me I think she's really scared.' The woman has asked the resident doctor to write a message of hope to join many other cards on her wall, cards with messages like 'I have hope that I will see you on the other side of this, when you can breathe freely and be well.' The doctor says he feels uncomfortable about this request because 'Transplant says she has a lot of antibodies and it's going to be hard to find a matching donor.' After a pause he says, '[i]t seems like I'd be lying.' Dr Awdish, who knows the patient is days away from death, but who in this preface to her own narrative is demonstrating the distinction between medical attention and caring, asks her team what the patient is 'telling us in this moment'. One person responds: 'she needs us to see her, even as sick as she is, not just to see her as sick, but as being healed ... Those cards make the hope visible.' A nurse remarks, '[t]hat would be a success', but a doctor demurs, 'with an edge of apathy', 'Well, that and she gets a transplant.' The others there 'laughed quickly, like childish conspirators'.[64]

Here the interplay within the medical group (as well as with the patient) that Frances Burney could capture is brilliantly reiterated in a passage that simultaneously raises several issues. 'It was so hard to palpate the borders of authentic hope, to know where falseness began,' Awdish also writes. In the previous chapter of this book I pursued the difficult question she mentions: put simply, the conflicting pulls of hope and truth – not from the perspective of the medical attendants, but from the viewpoint of the often neglected third figure in the medical triad, the attending relative or carer. Here that dilemma takes on a different cast – to be 'with' the patient, but at the same time to behave as responsibly as their clinical knowledge and experience commands them.

Another important matter is touched on in Awdish's vignette. 'She needs us to see her,' says one of the team, and this ordinary phrase has immense resonance and meaning in the reports of modern hospital patients. They want to be *seen* – that is to be recognised as people, not as cases. When a patient is alone in a hospital bed, away from their family, and being treated, however efficiently, by a retinue of different professionals with different approaches, skills and techniques, they become acutely alive to the human aspects of their treatment. By 'human' I mean not just their awareness, for example, of the care or clumsiness of the nurse who gives them an injection, but their hypersensitivity to the presence of the man or woman, the stranger, who is engaged in the clinical treatment, often the handling, of their own human body. 'I needed him to see me,' Awdish herself writes when as a desperately ill patient she encounters a resident for whom 'I was abdominal pain and Fetal Demise', not an individual or equal, but 'an interesting case'.[65] Over and over, the patient will complain that the doctor or surgeon does not look at them, does not make eye contact, and understands this as the abolition of their equality as a person. 'For Dr N', de Beauvoir states, her mother 'was the subject of an interesting experiment and not a person'.[66] 'The night before surgery, I was visited by an anesthesiologist . . . he refused to look at me,' writes Arthur Frank. 'I wanted him to recognize that the operation I was having and the disease it was part of were no small thing.'[67] Oliver Sacks angrily reports that after his operation:

> Swan neither looked at me nor greeted me, but took the chart which hung at the foot of my bed and looked at it closely.
> 'Well, Sister,' he said, 'and how is the patient now?'

'No fever, now Sir,' she answered. 'We took the catheter out on Wednesday. He is taking food by mouth. There is no swelling of the foot.' 'Sounds fine,' said Mr Swan, and then turned to me, or, rather to the cast before me. He rapped it sharply with his knuckles.[68]

The crucial aspect here is not the formality of this ritual, which Sacks satirises with his phrase 'ceremonial tools', but the lack of contact: 'I looked at sister', he writes a moment later, 'but her face was stony.' What has happened is a suspension during this ceremony of normal human relations, and this is encapsulated most keenly in the failure of both the surgeon and the nurse to look at the patient. The implication is that the professional structure of the hospital deters the nurse from showing any sign of dissent from the surgeon. This is some time ago, but similar instances might certainly be found in contemporary narratives.

In Frances Burney's world of domestic medicine the doctor's visual engagement with the patient is assumed. After all, the doctor is attending his client at home. One simply understands that when Mr Ansell performs Alex d'Arblay's inoculation, besides giving the child some barley sugar, enlisting his mother's help, and asking her leave to inoculate Alex's other arm, he exchanges looks with the child, the mother, and the nursemaid. Nearly thirty years later, Mr Hay and Mr Tudor certainly had conversations with their employers: if they didn't look at them this would be gross discourtesy.[69] But when in Burney's account of her mastectomy the officiating surgeon places a muslin handkerchief over her eyes this has immense premonitory significance. Perhaps kindly meant, this gesture removes – or seeks to remove – the patient as a person, and it may register for the first time an attempt at that 'professional' detachment which was to become, as Awdish argues, a feature of modern medical culture.

Looking or not looking at the patient – seeing or avoiding seeing them as a person – is one of those microethical moments that Komesaroff so perceptively identifies as critical to the 'clinical encounter'. Looking at the patient, being with them, may be therapeutic in itself. Called to attend her terrifyingly mad patient Kay Jamison writes: 'I had never seen such fear in anyone's eyes, nor such visceral agitation and psychological pain.' In the middle of the frenetic circumstances of a major hospital she nevertheless looks in the patient's eyes; she sees him. And this helps him. The hectic conditions that she so dexterously captures certainly might mitigate against such opportunities. The social structures, the complexity, the often necessary haste of the major hospital, may, in addition to the ethos that Awdish invokes, create conditions that lead to the patient not being in this way 'seen'.

William Blake's line 'He who would do good to another must do it in Minute Particulars' has added both a phrase and an injunction to the language.[70] Why is this apparently 'minute particular' of looking at the patient so recurrent a feature of the pathographical narrative? One clear answer is that eye contact is a fundamental part of human interaction. This is because eye contact between baby and nursing parent is critical for the child's development of attachment, and babies become distressed if mothers fail to look at them. Lack of eye contact occurs in modern pathographies because it is keenly remembered, and is remembered because it is hurtful and because the patient's state, often anxious and fearful, can well lead to a degree of regression.[71] Already depersonalised by the hospital gown, already alone, in surroundings of alienating blankness, in pain, he or she feels this carelessness as an insult – in the medical sense of an injury or trauma within the body. In their memoirs they record such moments, not wholly out of revenge, but to restore themselves as actual living beings, with their own identity. 'How vain, alas, my representation!' Frances Burney writes of her attempt to make the encircling doctors listen to her and thus take heed of her as a person (JL V, 612). Representation in the broadest sense was the project of her narrative: the written account recreates, or represents the episode so that it can be read, but in doing so it makes her a representative, someone who is now an active presence to her reader, and who certainly has her own contribution to make.

If one were to define the role of the modern pathography in a sentence it would be this: to return the patient to visibility. The writer who is a patient is recognised as a living unique and suffering being, not as an instance, a case, interesting or otherwise. The need for recognition that is jeopardised in the circumstances of the modern hospital is fulfilled. When you read one you cannot fail to recognise that it is an individual's experience of suffering, or of caring, that you are reading. The denial of visual engagement is so important a signifier because it reverberates with and metonymically represents the whole experience that Sacks called patienthood. Such moments do not occur in earlier accounts of medical experience; they are concurrent with the vastly expanded and complex operation that is the modern hospital, the not inevitable downside of very much better and effective health care.

In this book I have sought to give the pathography a pedigree in Frances Burney's writings and to present pathography as a significant and richly suggestive literary genre. I argue too that questions of ethics and microethics are uniquely explored in these texts and can be explored through them. These ethical questions, intrinsic to the practices of medicine, whether by nurse, physician, or surgeon, are invisibly present, hovering over every medical interaction. Thanks to the drama, vividness, and candour of her writing, we can see that they were also present in the encounters between Frances Burney and her doctors.

Notes

1. Coutts, M., *The Iceberg*, p. 26.
2. 'Translator's Note' prefacing Foucault, M., *The Birth of the Clinic*.
3. In 1785 for example, the London Hospital became the first hospital in England to house its own medical school and at St Barts, also in London, comprehensive courses for medical students were developed and formally approved in 1822.
4. Porter, R., *The Greatest Benefit to Mankind*, p. 380.
5. Komesaroff, P. A., *Experiments in Love and Death*, p. 166.
6. See Pamboukian, S., 'Entertaining and Profitable'.
7. Sacks, O., *A Leg to Stand On*, p. 30.
8. Aronowitz, R. A., *Unnatural History*, p. 17.
9. Frank, A., *At the Will of the Body*, p. 55.
10. Biss, E., *On Immunity*, p. 84.
11. Porter, R., *Mind Forg'd Manacles*, p. 264.
12. Batt, S., *Patient No More*, p. 7.
13. JL VI, 600.
14. See Lyman, J. S., *Diary of a Breast Cancer Husband*.
15. JL VI, 364–365.
16. This item is in a list of small changes or additions that Burney apparently made to her manuscript late in life, given in Epstein, J., *The Iron Pen*, p. 60.
17. Ibid., p. 68.
18. Porter, R., *Mind Forg'd Manacles*, pp. 364–365.
19. Lorde, A., *The Cancer Journals*, p. 36.
20. Rodman, F. R., ed., *The Spontaneous Gesture*, p. 167 (September 1967).
21. After his own open heart surgery the surgeon feels 'I have been anatomically raped.' (Weinman Lear, M., *Heartsounds*, p. 143).
22. Lorde, *My Breast*, p. 46.
23. Solnit, R., *The Faraway Nearby*, pp. 119, 129.
24. Ibid., p. 120.
25. Wadler, J., *My Breast*, p. 29.
26. Ibid., pp. 32–33.
27. Ibid., p. 1.
28. Frank, A., *At the Will of the Body*, p. 22. Lance Armstrong's *It's Not about the Bike* presents another account of surgery for testicular cancer (pp. 9–15), as well as follow-up treatment (chapters 4 and 5).

29. Frank, A., *At the Will of the Body*, p. 26.
30. Ibid., pp. 100–101.
31. Weinman Lear, M., *Heartsounds*, p. 103.
32. Ibid., p. 115.
33. Ibid., p. 116.
34. After Herman Boerhaave, Battie conceived of the body as a system of pipes and vessels, through which liquid substances passed, sometimes distending or obstructing them. The notion of the 'nerves' as similar in constitution and operation to other parts of the body, like the veins, was critical. Madness, being a disorder of sensation and perception, must, Battie argued, be due to some interference with the nerves, which must be caused by pressure from adjacent vessels in the body. It was brought about by 'the sudden intrusion of improper fluids into smaller canals'. Most significant for the king's treatment, Battie believed that '[t]he same sanguinary or serous obstructions are capable in any other part of the body of exciting false ideas as well as in the brain.' 'Serous' means 'watery'. An errhine, according to Samuel Johnson's *Dictionary*, is a substance stuffed into the nose to draw phlegm from the head. The hypochondria were the viscera that lie under the ribs, such as the liver, gall-bladder, and spleen.
35. Hill, G. B., ed., Boswell, J., *Life of Johnson*, III, 176.
36. It is important to notice that the king's suffering was greatly exacerbated by the continuing use of the blisters advocated by Pepys on his leg, a perfectly orthodox iatromechanist procedure that, according to the records kept by John Willis, Francis's son, 'burnt and tortured him' so much that he could not walk and, in his distress, he obviously raged so much that he had to be 'confined'. If, as Frances Burney wrote on 17 December, the surgeon's report was 'most afflictive', and 'cruelly subversive of all our rising hopes', it is as well to recognise that it was not the straightjacket alone that was cruelly subversive (CJL IV, 662).
37. Foucault, M., *Madness and Civilization*, pp. 243–255. Foucault's original book, of which this is a redaction, was published in 1961. He argued that 'moral management' deprived the inmates of the freedom of their condition.
38. Frame, J., *An Autobiography, Vol. III*, p. 229.
39. Frame, J., *An Autobiography*, p. 224.
40. Frame, J., *An Autobiography, Vol. III*, p. 376.
41. Mantel, H., *Giving Up the Ghost*, pp. 175–176.
42. 'Mantel describes endometriosis: 'The endometrium is the lining of the womb. It is made of special cells, which shed each month by bleeding. In endometriosis, these cells are found in other parts of the body ... Typically, they are found in the pelvis, in the bladder, the bowel ... Wherever they are found, they obey their essential nature and bleed. Scar tissue is formed, in the body's inner spaces and small cavities. It presses on nerves and causes pain, sometimes at distant sites (etc.)' (pp. 185–186).
43. Cassell, E. J., *The Nature of Suffering and the Goals of Medicine*, p. 30.
44. Styron, W., *Darkness Visible*, pp. 46–47.

45. Ibid., p. 50.
46. Ibid., p. 60.
47. Ibid., p. 68.
48. Griffiths, J., *Tristimania*, p. 64.
49. Ibid., p. 54.
50. Jamison, K. R., *An Unquiet Mind*. 'Within three months of becoming a professor, I was ravingly psychotic' (p. 63). The episode is recounted in detail in part two of the book, 'A Not So Fine Madness' (pp. 67–83). 'Lithium' or lithium salts is a naturally occurring chemical first found to be useful in controlling the symptoms of manic depression in 1948–1949 by Dr John Cade, a Melbourne psychiatrist, who tested it out on patients in the psychiatric hospitals close to his home. It could not be patented because it was a natural substance, and this led to long delays in its adoption. It was not used in the United States until 1970. Cade, J., 'Lithium Salts in the Treatment of Psychotic Excitement'.
51. Jamison, K. R., *An Unquiet Mind*, pp. 105–107.
52. Ibid., p. 191.
53. Awdish, R., *In Shock*, p. 29.
54. Ibid., p. 117.
55. Ibid., p. 41.
56. Ibid., p. 249. This is actually a remark reported to her, and occurs in a collection of unfortunate and unkind remarks by medical staff at the conclusion of the book.
57. Osler, W., 'Aequanimitas', p. 165. Cited here from *Celebrating the Contributions of William Osler* at www.medicalarchives.jhmi.edu/osler/aeques say.htm accessed 15 March 2018. The quotation is from *Othello*, act 1, scene 1. Curiously enough, Osler is suggesting that physicians be like Iago.
58. Awdish, R., *In Shock*, p. 169.
59. Ibid., p. 171.
60. Ibid., p. 152.
61. Kalanithi, P. *When Breath Becomes Air*, p. 83.
62. Ibid., pp. 80, 70, 71, 142.
63. Ibid., p. 147.
64. Awdish, R., *In Shock*, pp. 5–9.
65. Ibid., p. 27.
66. de Beauvoir, S. *A Very Easy Death*, p. 46.
67. Frank, A., *At the Will of the Body*, pp. 11, 45.
68. Sacks, O., *A Leg to Stand On*, p. 72.
69. In Burney's novels the case is different, and the doctor's visual engagement with the patient is accorded significance. In *The Wanderer*, Mr Naird, the surgeon, faced with Elinor Jodrell's renewed attempts at self-harm, 'steadfastly, yet quietly fix[ed] his eyes upon his patient' as a means 'to use his authority for checking this dangerous violence' (p. 376). (Though this is reminiscent of Dr Francis Willis's approach to the violence of George III, Frances Burney may not have known about that.) In the earlier *Cecilia*,

Dr Lyster seems to feel he might be exceeding his brief when he says to the heroine as he leaves Mrs Devile 'in her care': 'But, my good young lady, in your care of her, don't neglect yourself; I am not quite pleased with your looks, though it is but an old-fashioned speech to tell you so' (p. 687).
70. Sampson, J., ed., *The Poetical Works of William Blake, Jerusalem*, line 60, p. 399.
71. I owe these thoughts to Dr David Mushin, MB.BS, FRANZCP, Dip. Child Psychiatry (Toronto).

Bibliography

Primary Texts

Madame d'Arblay, *Memoirs of Dr Burney*, 3 vols, London: Moxon, 1832.

Barrett, Charlotte, *Diary and Letters of Madame D'Arblay*, edited by her niece, a new edition, 7 vols, London: Henry Colburn, 1854.

Balderston, Katherine C., ed., *Thraliana, the Diary of Mrs Hester Lynch Thrale*, 2 vols, second edition, Oxford: Clarendon Press, 1951.

Bladon, F. McKno, ed., *The Diaries of Colonel the Hon. Robert Fulke Greville*, London: Bodley Head, 1930.

Bloom, Edward A. and Bloom, Lillian, D., eds, Frances Burney, *Camilla or A Picture of Youth*, London: Oxford University Press, 1972.

Clark, Lorna J., ed., *The Court Journals and Letters of Frances Burney, Vol. III, 1788*, Oxford: Clarendon Press, 2014.

Clark, Lorna J., ed., *The Court Journals and Letters of Frances Burney, Vol. IV, 1788*, Oxford: Clarendon Press, 2014.

Cooke, Stewart, ed., *The Court Journals and Letters of Frances Burney, Vol. II, 1797*, Oxford: Clarendon Press, 2011.

Cronin, Richard and McMillan, Dorothy, eds, Jane Austen, *Emma*, Cambridge: Cambridge University Press, 2005.

Derry, Warren, ed., *The Journals and Letters of Fanny Burney, Vol. IX, Bath, 1815–1817*, Oxford: Clarendon Press, 1982.

Derry, Warren, ed., *The Journals and Letters of Fanny Burney, Vol. X*, Oxford: Clarendon Press, 1982.

Dobson, Austin, ed., *Diary and Letters of Madame D'Arblay*, 6 vols, London: Macmillan, 1904, 1905.

Doody, Margaret Anne, Mack, Robert L., and Sabor, Peter, eds, Frances Burney, *The Wanderer; or Female Difficulties*, Oxford: Oxford University Press, 1991.

Hadley, Graham, ed., George Eliot, *Daniel Deronda* [1876], Oxford: Clarendon Press, 1984.

Hemlow, Joyce, ed., *The Journals and Letters of Fanny Burney, Vol. III, Great Bookham, 1793–1797*, Oxford: Clarendon Press, 1973.

Hemlow, Joyce, ed., *The Journals and Letters of Fanny Burney, Vol. VI, France 1803–1812*, Oxford: Clarendon Press, 1975.

Hughes, Peter, ed., *The Journals and Letters of Fanny Burney, Vol. VII, 1815*, Oxford: Clarendon Press, 1980.

Johnson, Nancy E., ed., *The Court Journals and Letters of Frances Burney, Vol. VI, 1789*, Oxford: Clarendon Press, 2019.

Redford, Bruce, ed., *The Letters of Samuel Johnson*, 5 vols, Oxford: Clarendon Press, 1992.

Ribiero, Alvaro, ed., *The Letters of Dr Charles Burney, Vol. I*, Oxford: Clarendon Press, 1991.

Sabor, Peter, *The Subscription List to Frances Burney's Camilla*, with an introduction by Peter Sabor, Montreal: The Burney Centre and the Burney Society, 2003.

Sabor, Peter, ed., *The Court Journals and Letters of Frances Burney, Vol. I, 1786*, Oxford: Clarendon Press, 2011.

Sabor, Peter and Doody, Margaret Anne, eds, Frances Burney, *Cecilia, or Memoirs of an Heiress*, Oxford: Oxford University Press, 1988.

Sill, Geoffrey, ed., *The Court Journals and Letters of Frances Burney, Vol. V, 1789*, Oxford: Clarendon Press, 2016.

Secondary Texts

[no author], *Memoir of Baron Larrey, Surgeon-in-Chief of the Grande Armée, from the French*, London: Henry Renshaw, 1861.

Armstrong, Lance, *It's Not about the Bike*, London: Allen and Unwin, 2002.

Aronowitz, Robert A., MD, *Unnatural History: Breast Cancer and American Society*, New York, NY: Cambridge University Press, 2007.

Awdish, Rana, *In Shock*, London: Bantam Press, 2018.

Bateson, Gregory, Jackson, Don D., Haley, Jay, and Weakland, John, 'Towards a Theory of Schizophrenia', *Behavioral Science*, 1, 1956, 251–264.

Batt, Sharon, *Patient No More: The Politics of Breast Cancer*, North Geelong, Australia: Spinifex Press, 1996.

Baxby, Derrick, *Jenner's Smallpox Vaccine*, London: Heinemann, 1981.

Bayley, John, *Iris: A Memoir of Iris Murdoch*, London: Duckworth, 1998.

Biss, Eula, *On Immunity: An Inoculation*, Greywolf Press, [2014], London: Fitzcaraldo Editions, 2016.

Black, Jeremy, *George III, America's Last King*, New Haven, CT: Yale University Press, 2006.

Brennan, Frank, 'As Vast As the World – Reflections on *A Very Easy Death* by Simone de Beauvoir', *Medical Humanities*, 30:2, 2004, 85–90.

Brooke, John, *King George III*, London: Constable, 1972.

Burney, Charles, *A General History of Music*, 4 vols, London: Payne and Son, 1776–1789.

Burney, Frances [as 'Madame d'Arblay] *Memoirs of Dr Burney*, 3 Vols, 1832.

Burton, Robert, as Democritus Junior, *Anatomy of Melancholy*, 1638 (1641).

Cade, John F. J., 'Lithium Salts in the Treatment of Psychotic Excitement', *Medical Journal of Australia*, 2:36, 1949, 349–352.

Carel, Havi, *Illness, the Cry of the Flesh*, Durham: Acumen, 2008, Routledge, 2013.

Cassell, Eric J., *The Nature of Suffering and the Goals of Medicine*, second edition, Oxford: Oxford University Press, 2004.

Chisholm, Kate, *Fanny Burney:Her Life 1752–1840*, London: Chatto and Windus, 1998.

Chisholm, Kate, *Hungry Hell*, London: Short Books, 2002.

Clark, Lorna J., 'The Afterlife and Further Reading', in Peter Sabor, ed., *The Cambridge Companion to Frances Burney*, Cambridge: Cambridge University Press, 2007, pp. 163–179.

Clark, Lorna J., 'Epistolarity in Frances Burney', *The Age of Johnson*, 20, 2010, 193–217.

Clark, Lorna J., ed., *Memoirs of the Court of George III, Volume II: The Diary of Lucy Kennedy*, London: Pickering and Chatto, 2015.

Couser, G. Thomas, 'Autopathography: Women, Illness, and Lifewriting', *a/b: Auto/Biography Studies*, 6:1, 1991.

Coutts, Marion, *The Iceberg, a Memoir*, London: Atlantic Books, 2014.

Cowper, William, *Memoir of the Early Life of William Cowper Esq., Written by Himself*, second edition, London: R. Edwards, 1816.

Dally, Ann, *Women under the Knife: A History of Surgery*, London: Hutchison Radius, 1991.

Davenport, Hester, *Faithful Handmaid: Fanny Burney at the Court of King George III*, Stroud, UK: Sutton, 2000.

De Beauvoir, Simone, *Une Mort Très Douce*, Paris: Editions Gallimard, 1964.

De Beauvoir, Simone, *A Very Easy Death*, trans. O'Brian, Patrick, Penguin, 1969.

Dibble, J. Henry, *Napoleon's Surgeon*, London: Heinemann Medical Books, 1970.

Doody, Margaret, *Frances Burney:The Life in the Works*, Cambridge: Cambridge University Press, 1988.

Doody, Margaret, Mack, Robert L., and Sabor, Peter. *The Wanderer, or, Female Difficulties*. Oxford: Oxford University Press, 1991.

Dorris, Michael, *The Broken Cord*, New York, NY: Harper Perennial, 1989.

Elwin, Malcom, ed., Thomas De Quincey, *Confessions of an Opium Eater*, London: Macdonald, 1956.

Epstein, Julia, *The Iron Pen: Frances Burney and the Politics of Women's Writing*, Bristol: Bristol Classical Press, 1989.

Felski, Rita, *The Limits of Critique*, Chicago, IL: University of Chicago Press, 2015.

Fisher, Richard B. *Edward Jenner 1749–1823*, London: Andre Deutsch, 1991.

Foster, John, *Take Me to Paris, Johnny*, Melbourne: Text, 1994, second edition, 2004.

Floyer, Sir John, *The Physician's Pulse Watch or an Essay to explain the old Art of Feeling for the Pulse and to Improve it by the Help of a Pulse-watch*, 1707.

Foucault, Michel, *The Birth of the Clinic: An Archaeology of Medical Perception*, trans. Alan M. Sheridan, London: Tavistock Publications, 1973.

Foucault, Michel, *Madness and Civilization: A History of Madness in the Age of Reason*, trans. Richard Howard, London: Vintage, 1973.

Frame, Janet, *An Autobiography*, London: Women's Press, 1990.

Frame, Janet, *An Autobiography, Vol. III*, London: Women's Press, 1989.

Frank, Arthur W., *At the Will of the Body: Reflections on Illness*, Boston, MA: Houghton Mifflin, 1991.

Frank, Arthur W., *The Wounded Storyteller, Body, Illness and Ethics*, Chicago University Press, 1995, 2013.

Fraser, Flora, *Princesses, the Six Daughters of George III*, London: John Murray, 2004.

Garfinkel, Susan, '"This Trial Was Sent in Love and Mercy for My Refinement": A Quaker Woman's Experience of Breast Cancer Surgery in 1814', *New Jersey Folklife*, 15, 1990, 18–31.

Garner, Helen, *The Spare Room*, Melbourne: Text, 2008.

Gilbert, Sandra M., *Wrongful Death: A Memoir*, New York, NY, and London: Nortons, 1995.

Godwin, William, *Memoir of the Author of* A Vindication of the Rights of Woman (1798), London and New York, NY: Garland, 1974 reprint of 1779 edition.

Griffiths, Jay, *Tristimania*, London: Hamish Hamilton, 2016.

Grundy, Isabel, *Lady Mary Wortley Montagu*, Oxford: Oxford University Press, 1999.

Gurney, Michael S., 'Disease As Device: The Role of Smallpox in *Bleak House*', *Literature and Medicine*, 9, 1990, 79–92.

Guttmacher, Manfred S., MD, *America's Last King: An Interpretation of the Madness of George III*, New York, NY: Scribner's, 1941.

Hadlow, Janice, *The Strangest Family*, London: William Collins, 2014.

Harman, Claire, *Fanny Burney: A Biography*, London: HarperCollins, 2000.

Held, Virginia, *The Ethics of Care, Personal, Political and Global*, Oxford: Oxford University Press, 1992.

Hemlow, Joyce, *The History of Fanny Burney*, Oxford: Clarendon Press, 1958.

Henley, William Ernest, *A Book of Verses*, London, 1886.

Hill George B., ed., James Boswell, *Life of Johnson*, second edition, revised L. F. Powell [1934], Oxford: Clarendon Press, 1964, Vols III, IV, and V.

Hillary, Richard, *The Last Enemy*, London: Macmillan, 1942.

Houlbrooke, Ralph, ed., *Death, Ritual, and Bereavement*, London: Routledge, 1989.

Hyde, Mary, *The Thrales of Streatham Park*, Cambridge, MA: Harvard University Press, 1976.

James, Bryan, *Introductory Lecture . . . on the Life and Character of Barron Larrey*, Geneva, NY, 1848, p. 16.

James, Henry, '*The Lesson of the Master' and Other Stories*, London: John Lehmann, 1948.

Jamison, Kay Redfield, *An Unquiet Mind* (1995) London: Picador Classics, 2015.

Jurecic, Ann, *Illness As Narrative*, Pittsburgh, PA: University of Pittsburgh Press, 2017.

Kalanithi, Paul, *When Breath Becomes Air*, London: Bodley Head, 2016.

King, James, 'Cowper's *Adelphi* Restored: The Excisions to Cowper's Narrative', *Review of English Studies*, New Series, 30:119, August 1979.

Kleinman, Arthur, MD, *The Illness Narratives: Suffering, Healing and the Human Condition*, Basic Books, 1988.

Komesaroff, Paul A., 'From Bioethics to Microethics: Ethical Debate and Clinical Medicine', in *Troubled Bodies: Critical Perspectives on Postmodernism, Medical Ethics and the Body*, Ithaca, NY, 1985.

Komesaroff, Paul A., *Experiments in Love and Death: Medicine, Postmodernism, Microethics and the Body*, Melbourne: Melbourne University Press, 2008.

Komesaroff, Paul A., *Riding a Crocodile*, Austin, TX: River Grove Books, 2014.

Le Fanu, William, ed., *Betsy Sheridan's Journal*, Oxford, 1986.

Le Faye, Deirdre, ed., *Jane Austen's Letters*, third edition, Oxford: 1995.

Lear, Martha Weinman, *Heartsounds*, New York, NY: Simon and Shuster, 1980.

Laqueur, Thomas, 'Nothing Becomes Something: Pathography', *London Review of Books*, 38:8, 22 September 2016.

Lejeune, Philippe, *On Autobiography*, Minneapolis, MN: University of Minnesota Press, 1989.

Lerner, Gerda, *A Death of One's Own*, New York, NY: Simon and Shuster, 1978.

Lonsdale, Roger, *Dr Charles Burney, a Literary Biography*, Oxford: Clarendon Press, 1965.

Lorde, Audre, *The Cancer Journals*, New York, NY: Spinsters Ink, 1980.

Lyman, J. Scott, *Diary of a Breast Cancer Husband*, Aptos, CA: Times Publishing, 2002.

Macalpine, Ida and Richard Hunter, *George III and the Mad-Business*, London: Allen Lane, 1969.

Macdonald, Betty, *The Plague and I*, London: Hammond, 1948.

Macleod, Sheila, *The Art of Starvation*, London: Virago, 1981.

Mantel, Hilary, *Giving Up the Ghost*, London and New York, Fourth Estate, 2003.

McCrea, Brian, 'Frances Burney and Professional Men: From Dr Lyster to Mr Naird', in Lorna J. Clark, ed., *A Celebration of Frances Burney*, Cambridge Scholars Publishing, 2007, pp. 198–209.

McManners, John, *Death and the Enlightenment: Changing Attitudes to Death among Christians and Unbelievers in Eighteenth-Century France*, Oxford: Clarendon Press, 1981.

Mediratta, Sangeeta, 'Beauty and the Breast: The Poetics of Physical Absence and Narrative Presence in Frances Burney's *Mastectomy Letter* (1811)', *Women: A Cultural Review*, 19:2, 2008, 188–207.

Michell, Juliet, ed., *The Selected Melanie Klein*, London: Hogarth Press and Penguin Books, 1986.

Moore, Anthony R., FRACS, 'Preanesthetic Mastectomy: A Patient's Experience', Surgery, February 1978, 200–205.

Mukherjee, Siddhartha, *The Emperor of All Maladies: A Biography of Cancer*, London: Fourth Estate, 2011.

O'Brian, Patrick, trans., Simone de Beauvoir, *A Very Easy Death*, 1966, Penguin: 1966.

Osler, William, 'Aequanimitas', www.medicalarchives.jhmi.edu/osler/aequessay.htm.

Osler, William, *On Chorea and Choreiform Affections*, London: H. K. Lewis & Company, (1894) Houghton Mifflin, 1991.

Pamboukian, Sylvia, 'Entertaining and Profitable: Nursing in Persuasion', in Marcia McKlintock Folsom and John Wiltshire, eds, *Approaches to Teaching Jane Austen's* Persuasion, New York: MLA, forthcoming.

Pearce, J. M. S., 'A Brief History of the Clinical Thermometer', *JQM, An International Journal of Medicine*, 95:4, 2002, 251–252.

Peters, Timothy J. 'Fitzpatrick Lecture 2014: King George III and the Porphyria Myth: Causes, Consequences and Re-Evaluation of His Mental Illness with Computer Diagnostics', *Clinical Medicine* (2015), 15(2): 168–172.

Peters, Timothy J. and Beveridge, Allan, 'The Madness of King George III: A Psychiatric Re-assessment', *History of Psychiatry*, 21:1, 2010, 20–37.

Peters, Timothy J. and Wilkinson, D., 'King George III and Porphyria: A Clinical Re-examination of the Historical Evidence', *History of Psychiatry*, 21:1, 2010, 3–19.

Porter, Roy, *Mind Forg'd Manacles*, London: Athlone Press, 1987.

Porter, Roy, ed., *The Faber Book of Madness*, London: Faber, 1991.

Porter, Roy, ed., *George Cheyne: The English Malady (1733)*, London and New York, NY: Tavistock/Routledge, 1991.

Porter, Roy, *The Greatest Benefit to Mankind*, London: HarperCollins, 1997.

Préastaings, Annie, 'Frances Burney's Mastectomy and the Female Body Politic', *Prose Studies*, 33:3, December 2011, pp. 230–240.

Razzell, Peter, *The Conquest of Smallpox: The Impact of Inoculation on Smallpox Mortality in Eighteenth-Century Britain*, second edition, Firle: Caliban Books, 2003.

Richardson, Robert, *Larrey: Surgeon to Napoleon's Imperial Guard*, London: Quiller Press, revised edn, 2000.

Ricoeur, Paul, *Freud and Philosophy: An Essay in Interpretation*, New Haven, CT, and London: Yale University Press, 1970.

Rieff, David, *Swimming in a Sea of Death: A Son's Memoir*, New York, NY: Simon & Schuster, 2008.

Robinson, Victor, *Victory over Pain: A History of Anesthesia*, New York, NY: Henry Shulman, 1946.

Rodman, F. R., ed., *The Spontaneous Gesture: Selected Letters of D. W. Winnicott*, Cambridge, MA, 1987.

Rohr, Deborah, *The Careers of British Musicians, 1750–1850: A Profession of Artisans*, Cambridge: Cambridge University Press, 2001.

Roth, Philip, *Patrimony: A True Story*, Vintage Edition, 1991.

Sacks, Oliver, *A Leg to Stand On*, London: Picador, 1991.

Salith, Sara, '*Camilla* and *The Wanderer*', in Peter Sabor, ed., *The Cambridge Companion to Frances Burney*, Cambridge: Cambridge University Press, 2007, pp. 39–53.

Sampson, John, ed., *The Poetical Works of William Blake*, Oxford, [1913].

Shuttleton, David, *Smallpox and the Literary Imagination 1660–1820*, Cambridge: Cambridge University Press, 2007.

Sichel, Walter, *Sheridan, from New and Original Material, Including a Manuscript Diary by Georgiana Duchess of Devonshire*, 2 vols, Boston, MA, and New York, NY: Houghton Mifflin, 1909.

Smith, J. R., *The Speckled Monster, Smallpox in England, 1670–1970*, Chelmsford: Essex Record Office, 1987.

Solnit, Rebecca, *The Faraway Nearby*, New York, NY: Viking, 2013.

Spenser, Jane, 'Evelina and Cecilia', in Peter Sabor, ed., *The Cambridge Companion to Frances Burney*, Cambridge: Cambridge University Press, 2007, pp. 23–37.

Stinson, Robert W. and Stinson, Peggy, *The Long Dying of Baby Andrew*, Boston, MA, and Toronto: Little, Brown, 1983.

Styron, William, *Darkness Visible: A Memoir of Madness*, New York, NY: Vintage Books, 1992.

Stuart, Grace, *A Private World of Pain*, London: George Allen and Unwin, 1953.

Sutton, Daniel, *The Inoculator, or Suttonian System of Innoculation, Fully Set Forth in a Plain and Familiar Manner*, London, 1796.

Syme, Rodney, *A Good Death: An Argument for Voluntary Euthanasia*, Melbourne: Melbourne University Press, 2008.

Tallis, Raymond, *Hippocratic Oaths: Medicine and Its Discontents*, London: Atlantic Books, 2004.

Thaddeus, Janice Farrar, *Frances Burney: A Literary Life*, London and New York, NY: Macmillan, 2000.

Tolstoy, Leo, *War and Peace*, trans. Richard Pevear and Larissa Volokhonsky, London: Vintage, 2009.

Tolstoy, Leo, trans. Antony Briggs, *The Death of Ivan Ilyich*, Penguin Classic, 2016.

Tomalin, Clare, *The Life and Death of Mary Wollstonecraft*, Penguin, 1977.

Trench, Charles C., *The Royal Malady*, London: Longmans, 1964.

Trotter, Thomas, *A View of the Nervous Temperament*, London: Longman, Hurst, Rees and Orme, 1807.

Wadler, Joyce, *My Breast*, London: Women's Press, 1994.

Walsh, Denton, *A Voice through a Cloud*, London: John Lehman, 1950.

Ward, B. R., ed., *A Week at Waterloo:Lady De Lancey's Narrative*, London: John Murray, 1906.

Wearing, Deborah, *Forever Today, A Memoir of Love and Amnesia*, Doubleday: 2005.

Welling, D. R., Burris, D. G. and Rich, N. M., 'The Influence of Dominique-Jean Larrey on the Art and Science of Amputations', *Journal of Vascular Surgery*, 2:3, September 2010, 790–793.

Wetherall Dickson, Leigh, ed., *Depression and Melancholy, 1660–1800, Vol. 3*, London: Pickering and Chatto, 2012.

Williams, Bill, *Bleed*, Victoria: Wildman Press, 2015.

Williams, Gareth, *Angel of Death: The Story of Smallpox*, London: Palgrave Macmillan, 2010.

Wiltshire, John, 'The Patient Writes Back: Bioethics and the Illness Narrative', in Richard Freadman, Jane Adamson, and David Parker, eds, *Renegotiating Ethics in Literature, Theory, Philosophy*, Cambridge: Cambridge University Press, 1998, pp. 181–198.

Wiltshire, John, '"Gay Sam, Agreeable Sam": The Johnson of Frances Burney', in *The Making of Dr Johnson*, Hastings: Helm Information, 2009, pp. 129–144.

Index

Since this book mentions Frances Burney, aka Madame d'Arblay, on almost every page, references to her under both names are omitted in this index. Works published in her lifetime are listed under their titles; works completed but unpublished in her lifetime are also listed.